The Passion According to Luke

Theological Inquiries

Studies in Contemporary Biblical and Theological Problems

General Editor
Lawrence Boadt, C. S. P.

PAULIST PRESS
New York • Ramsey • Toronto

The Passion According to Luke

A Redaction Study of Luke's Soteriology

Jerome Neyrey, S.J.

PAULIST PRESS
New York • Mahwah

Two articles in this book appeared earlier. They are reprinted in expanded and revised form with permission of their respective publishers:

"The Absence of Jesus' Emotions—the Lukan Redaction of Lk. 22,39–46," *Biblica* 61 (1980) 153–171.

"Jesus' Address to the Women of Jerusalem (Lk. 23.27–31)—A Prophetic Judgment Oracle," *New Testament Studies* 29 (1983) 74–86 (published by Cambridge University Press).

Library of Congress
Catalog Card Number: 84-62566

ISBN: 0-8091-2688-5

Published by Paulist Press
997 Macarthur Boulevard
Mahwah, New Jersey 07430

Printed and bound in the United States of America

CONTENTS

IN MEMORIAM

Olga
2·5·84

Henry
9·7·84

INTRODUCTION

The project of this book is timely in the development of scholarship on the Third Gospel. Although there has been much written on the passion and death of Jesus in Luke's Gospel, the approach taken in past studies has tended to concern itself with questions of Luke's sources and issues of historicity. A new focus has emerged in Lukan studies, redaction criticism, which asks different questions and begins from new starting points. This book pursues a redaction-critical investigation of the passion narrative in the Third Gospel. Since redaction criticism is not the only method of approaching a text, it will be used in conjunction with other standard scholarly approaches to the New Testament. But it is a fresh, useful, and timely perspective.

Along with the other evangelists, Luke is now considered as a genuine author who edited and revised older traditions as well as composed fresh narratives about Jesus of Nazareth. The four evangelists not only introduced distinctive motifs and themes into their accounts, but shaped the narrative story in literary ways for calculated effect. Since Conzelmann's groundbreaking work,[1] Luke the theologian,[2] historian,[3] and literateur[4] has been the focus of many studies, but studies which seemed to sidestep the passion narrative. The passion narrative, of course, is the most sacred part of the Gospels. And while Luke's creative activity is readily recognized and appreciated in other parts of the Gospel narrative, our reverence for the sacredness of Jesus' passion and death has tended to block a thorough investigation of these episodes from a redaction-critical perspective. It is not out of disregard for the important traditions of Jesus' passion or out of a spirit of iconoclasm that this book takes up the issue of Luke's redaction of the passion narrative. I hope that by pursuing a redaction-critical approach with vigor, fresh light can be shed on the text and its rich and distinctive theology made available for lovers of the Third Gospel.

In this study, Luke will be considered as a learned and creative author with an eye for the large canvas of Church development and salvation history. He is presumed to be a master of literary styles and forms typical of Jewish and Hellenistic authors, and an historian in the Graeco-Roman mode.[5]

The second distinctive feature of this book is the place and function of Acts of the Apostles for interpreting the Lukan Gospel. It is now a commonplace in Lukan studies that Luke authored a two-volume work, Luke and Acts of the Apostles. In fact, the New Testament guild regularly speaks now of Luke-Acts as a single entity.[6] The precise relationship of Acts to the Gospel, however, is still an emerging question. It is generally recognized that there is extensive parallelism between the Lukan Gospel and Acts. The works of C.H. Talbert[7] and A.J. Mattill[8] have exposed more and more of the structural and thematic parallels between Luke and Acts. W.C. van Unnik once wrote of Acts as "the confirmation" of the Gospel apropos of a bridge between the saving activity of Jesus and a people living at a distance.[9]

I am building on these studies, adding from this study of the passion narrative my own contribution to the growing catalogue of parallels between the Gospel and Acts. In addition to this, I will make several fresh suggestions on the value and function of Acts for interpreting the Gospel. In many places and on many topics, it would seem that Acts is the goal and completion of Luke's theology and literary redaction. Acts does not merely echo or rehash Lukan themes. Rather, in many ways concern for the way the story turns out in Acts prompts changes in the redaction of the Gospel and controls the way Gospel stories are shaped. Since in some way Luke knows the shape of the Church represented in Acts, and since he appreciates the Christological and soteriological statements which he made in Acts, he purposefully edited the Gospel to point to the full articulation of these new themes and issues in that more discursive work, Acts.

There are certain natural controls on the Gospel: its focus is Jesus as he is known through the tradition; it is a narrative of events; it purports to recount the career of the historical Jesus, not the exalted Lord. Despite our understanding of redaction criticism, the Gospel is still governed by the tradition of the Church and the reports of eyewitnesses. Not so Acts of the Apostles. While based on historical data, the history of the emerging Church in Acts allows its author considerable scope to select, shape, articulate, and create a rich narrative. The speeches in Acts, for example, are now generally attributed to Luke's own creativity; they constitute a formidable witness to the genius of the author and his creativity. It is with the editorial explicitness of Acts in mind that Luke made many of his redactional changes in the Gospel. Small but important changes in the Gospel await their articulation and development in Acts. Like silhouettes and shadows, the narrowest opening and the smallest angle of a cutout cast large and rich shadows on the wall.

Assumed in redaction-critical studies is the axiom that the evangelist writes for a specific Church. A distinctive Church experience means a distinctive Gospel. In the case of Matthew, Mark, and John, we must read between the lines to get a sense of the experience and history of those Churches. Not so with Luke, for Acts reflects Luke's understanding of his Church both as an ideal and as an historical reality. We have ready access to Luke's Church in Acts. It is with this Church in mind that Luke redacted the Gospel and even parts of the passion narrative. Acts, then, not only confirms the Gospel and is parallel to it, but it also controls the way parts of the Gospel story are told and matures the literary and theological seeds planted there. Acts is the *telos,* completion and goal, of the Gospel.

This monograph is written for the biblically literate, but not overly so. I have intentionally limited the use of Greek to make the volume as reader-friendly as possible. In keeping with this focus, the documentation is admittedly limited. These six chapters may ultimately lack a certain unity, except for the fact that they all focus on Jesus' passion narrative in Luke's Gospel. This cannot be helped, since the nature of the project is to listen to Luke. And if Luke is not as unified or systematic as we would like, so be it.

Chapter One

JESUS' FAREWELL SPEECH
(LK 22:14–38)

Many questions have been asked of Lk 22:1–38. What was Luke's source? Why the strange account of the two cups in 22:17 and 20? Inasmuch as there are two textual traditions about the Eucharist in 22:19–20, which is the authentic tradition, the longer or the shorter version? These questions have been dealt with extensively in previous studies of the Lukan passion narrative. The focus of this study is not primarily about questions of source[1] or text. Rather, I am taking a fresh approach and asking different questions.

Standing within the growing body of redaction criticism scholarship on Luke-Acts, I will seek to determine the editorial activity of the evangelist and to assess the purpose and theology of Lk 22:14–38. From this perspective, questions of source may partially be answered by a redaction-critical perspective: Luke composed *this,* put *that* here, edited *these* sayings into this pattern. In past times, when the evangelist's editorial activity was deemed limited and suspect, scholars sought out the evangelist's sources. But now, when the evangelist's editorial activity is judged to be extensive and valuable, he may be given greater credit for shaping a passage and giving it a definite editorial focus. The need to find the evangelist's sources correspondingly diminishes.

Besides treating Lk 22:14–38 from the perspective of redaction criticism, I will inquire about the form of a farewell speech and its relationship to Lk 22:14–38. Several recent studies of Lk 22:14–38 have suggested this type of investigation,[2] and my own exposition builds on these, even as I seek to expand and correct some of the earlier suggestions. What I bring to this discussion is a serious and thorough attempt to read the passage from a strictly Lukan perspective. This will entail a formal comparison of it with the other Lukan farewell speech, viz., that of Paul in Acts 20. The changes which Luke makes in his Gospel materials may seem indeed small and insignificant, but when viewed in terms of both Luke and Acts, these changes take on greater importance. Acts, then, may confirm the editorial intention and activity of Luke, and indicate the author's purpose more clearly.

I.
THE FAREWELL SPEECH

The casual reader of Lk 22:14–38 immediately notes that Jesus has considerably more to say at the Last Supper in Luke's account than is found in his Markan source (Mk 14:17–26). The immediate explanation for this is Luke's use of the convention of the farewell speech in 22:14–38, a convention found extensively in the New Testament. We find farewell speeches ascribed to *Jesus* (Jn 13–17; Mk 13; Lk 22:14–38),[3] to *Paul* (the Pastorals; Acts 20:17–35), and to *Peter* (2 Peter 1:12–15).[4] This convention, moreover, is rooted in Jewish biblical traditions. The Old Testament contains the farewell speeches of Jacob (Gen 47–50), Joshua (Jos 23–24), and Moses (Dt 31–34). The most notable flowering of this convention is the literary collection entitled The Testament of the Twelve Patriarchs, a work of Jewish provenance from the intertestamental period. In it each of the twelve sons of Jacob gives a farewell speech to his clan. Luke was surely cognizant of this tradition, for his composition of Paul's farewell speech in Acts 20 according to the formal conventions of a farewell speech is a convincing argument that he knows the convention and is using it in structuring Jesus' farewell speech at the Last Supper.

In the expanding scholarly discussion of farewell speeches, several types of this literary convention have been identified. In his work on the covenant formulary, Klaus Baltzer pointed to the intimate association between the making of a covenant and a death, an association which corresponds on the literary level to the connection between covenant formulae and testamentary farewell speeches.[5] Based on the examples of Jos 23–24, Dt 31–34, Jubilees 21 and TXII, Baltzer identified one type of this convention as a covenant farewell speech which stressed exhortation, succession of leadership, and continuity of the group's religious tradition. Anitra Kolenkow, however, has analyzed other texts such as Gen 27:27–29 and 49:1, 1 Enoch, The Life of Adam and Eve, and The Assumption of Moses.[6] She concludes to another type of farewell speech, for her examples stressed the prophetic experience of the dying leader which included prophecies of the future, trips to the heavens to receive esoteric knowledge, and apocalyptic forecasts. Although it is possible to sketch two different types of farewell speeches, it is more profitable for this study of Lk 22:14–38 to note that most New Testament examples of the farewell speech are blends of both types.

Some general features of a typical farewell speech can be identified which will help us begin our investigation of Lk 22:14–38. The following description is by no means exhaustive, as we shall shortly see, but it will assist our initial appreciation of the formal character of Lk 22:14–38 as a farewell speech.

1. *Prediction of Death.* The patriarch or leader of the group is either dying or predicts his imminent death, which constitutes the occasion for the address. In the case of Jesus, see Lk 22:15, 22; Jn 13:1, 11, 36 and 16:16, 19; for Paul, see Acts 20:23, 25; 2 Tim 4:6–8; concerning Peter, see 2 Pet 1:14–15.
2. *Predictions of Attacks on Leader's Disciples.* The patriarch may see imminent danger to his immediate circle of sons or disciples (see Lk 22:31–34; Acts 20:29; Jn 15:2, 18–25; 16:2), or he may predict the future coming of heretics into the group to subvert its distinctive faith (see 2 Pet 3:3; 1 Tim 4:1; 2 Tim 3:1 and Mk 13:5–6, 21–23).
3. *Ideal Behavior Urged.* It is common that farewell speeches contain an exhortation in which are urged ideas of community service (Jn 13:3–10, 12–17; Lk 22:24–27) or generosity (Acts 20:35).
4. *Commission.* The Pastoral Epistles are the clearest example of this feature, for their primary function is to establish an orderly succession of Church leaders from Paul to Timothy and Titus and to their successors. It is precisely in these letters that we find lists of qualifications for bishops and deacons, rules for dealing with elders, and, if we take the instructions to Timothy and Titus at their face value, a description of the duties of the bishop.

As general as these features are, they do provide one important interpretative clue: in farewell speeches the focus of attention tends to be on the disciples addressed rather than on the speaker. So we should not be surprised if Lk 22:14–38 tells us more about Luke's view of the apostles, their commission, and the succession of leaders in the Church than about Jesus.

II.
MEALS, TABLE FELLOWSHIP, AND ETIQUETTE

It will be helpful in appreciating Lk 22:14–38 to situate it in its proper context: a meal, the Last Supper. To do this we address the issue of Luke's concern for meals and table fellowship. Jesus' farewell speech takes place at a meal, the Last Supper, a setting fraught with significance for the evangelist. It is not accidental that references to meals and eating occur in most of the sections of the speech:

(1) In 22:15–18 Jesus insists on his great desire to eat *this meal* with the disciples.

(2) 22:19–20 describes the *cultic meal* of the group, the Eucharist.

(3) In 22:21 we are told that "the hand of the betrayer is with me *on the table*," implying horror at finding treachery among table companions.

(4) In vv. 26–27 the ideal style of leadership is described as *diakonia*, serving table.

(5) In v. 30 the great reward of the disciples is to "eat and drink *at my table* in my kingdom."

Not only does concern with meals, table fellowship, and etiquette stitch the farewell speech together, it has considerable thematic importance as well. In Luke's Gospel there are nineteen or so mentions of meals, thirteen of which are distinctive to Luke's editorial hand. I have surveyed this material and suggest the following thematic thrust to this data.

A. Meals in Luke's Gospel are *inclusive events*. 1. *Jews eat with Gentiles* (e.g., Elijah and the widow of Zarephath, 4:25–26). In accord with this, Lk 10:7–8 stresses in the missionary discourse that missionaries should "eat and drink what they (the hosts) provide," be it kosher or non-kosher food; the missionary is to "eat what is set before you" without regard for dietary restrictions, instructions which are not found in Matthew's more Jewish version of the same mission instructions (see Mt 10:5–6). 2. *Saints eat with sinners.* In a slight change of the Markan text, Luke stresses that the Pharisees are shocked that Jesus' disciples eat with tax collectors and sinners and so ask them (not Jesus), "Why do you all eat and drink with sinners and tax collectors?'' (5:30). This same complaint becomes the setting and introduction to the three parables in ch 15: the Pharisees and scribes murmured at seeing Jesus eating with tax collectors and sinners (15:1–2). In the same vein, we remember the crowd's horror at Jesus' eating with Zacchaeus (19:5–7). Although the Emmaus disciples are not exactly apostate sinners, they had lost hope and left the group; nevertheless, Jesus eats with them (24:29–35). Inclusiveness, then, is the hallmark of Jesus' table in Luke-Acts. 3. *Clean eat with unclean.* One does not invite familiars, relatives, and friends, but strangers, even the poor, maimed and blind (14:12–13).

B. In Luke's Gospel, Jesus gives elaborate instructions concerning Christian *table etiquette.* In general, instead of concern for table purity rules (see Mk 7:2 and Lk 11:38), *diakonia* characterizes Christian tables in Luke. Besides the praise given to the women who minister to Jesus (4:39; 8:3; 10:40), special commendation is given to the leaders in the Lukan Church who serve and minister (Acts 6:1–6; see John 13:12–17). The prime qualification of the group's leader is service at table (Lk 22:26–27). More specifically, we find instructions on where to sit at table (14:7–11) and whom to invite (14:12–14). In fact, Lk 14 serves as an extended exhortation on table etiquette for the Lukan church. Alternately, the Pharisee who invited Jesus to dinner is reproached for his lack of etiquette (7:44–46).

C. Meals are a prime symbol of *election, forgiveness, and eschatological blessing* for Luke. Diligent servants will be rewarded by eating at the master's table (12:35–37); those who are saved will ''come from north, south, east and west and sit at table in the kingdom of God'' (13:29). Belonging to God's kingdom is described in the parable in 14:15–24 as an invitation to a banquet. The sign of Zacchaeus' conversion is his eating with Jesus (19:5–7). And reconciliation for the Emmaus disciples is the meal shared with Jesus (24:30–35).

D. Meals in Luke stress *reversal of roles,* how the lowly are raised up and the proud are put down. The Pharisee's dinner with Jesus in 7:36–52 serves as the occasion to raise up the sinful and sorrowful woman and to criticize the inhospitable host. In another example of reversal, faithful servants will find themselves seated at the master's own table, with the master himself waiting on them (12:35–37). Those who take the places of honor at table are shamed while the lowly are invited higher (14:7–11). None of the invited guests ''shall ever taste of my banquet''; they are replaced by a conscription of motley people found on the road (14:16–24).

And so we see that meals serve a very important function in Luke. Jesus came "eating and drinking" (7:33–34); he ate with Pharisees (7:36; 11:37) as well as with tax collectors and sinners (15:1–2). In fact, Jesus' inclusive table fellowship mirrors the inclusive character of the Lukan Church: Gentiles, prostitutes, tax collectors, sinners, as well as the blind, lame, maimed, and the poor are welcome at his table and in his covenant. Besides inclusiveness, the prized community table virtues are hospitality, service and charity to the poor.

In the light of this survey of the significance of meals in Luke, let us look at 22:14–38 once more. The *inclusive* character of Jesus' table fellowship is replicated. Sinners are surely present and welcome: first in v. 21 ("the hand of the traitor is with me"), then in the report of a dispute in v. 24, and finally in the prediction of Peter's denial in v. 34. It is reported that the apostles will need "strengthening" (v. 32), implying that they are weak and frail. They seem, moreover, to misunderstand Jesus' missionary instructions in vv. 35–38. Jesus' table, then, includes Judas, his betrayer, Peter, who denied him, and the squabbling and obtuse apostles. Jesus eats with sinners, even at the Last Supper.

Meals, moreover, are symbols of *eschatological blessing.* For example, Jesus signals that meals will be celebrated "in the kingdom of God" (vv. 16–18), when Jesus himself is vindicated and raised up by God. Likewise the persevering apostles will find a special place in the new kingdom of Jesus where they will "eat and drink at my table in my kingdom" (v. 30).

Reversal of roles, likewise, takes place at the Last Supper. At Jesus' table the greatest becomes the youngest, and the leader as one who serves (v. 26). The master Jesus is their servant (v. 27); the greatest one (Jesus) is among them as one who serves.

Picking up on the motif of the reversal of roles, a point of *Christian etiquette* is noted by Luke. The master is a servant and also a model for the disciples, indicating an ideal behavior which will characterize the followers of Jesus.

Granted that Luke uses meals as occasions to stress important Christian covenant values, do meals have anything to do with farewell speeches? W. Kurz[7] in a forthcoming study has drawn attention to Graeco-Roman symposia as events at which meals were shared and serious discussion, usually of a sectarian or in-group nature, was held. Meals and teaching were joined in Plato's *Symposium*, Xenophon's *Symposium*, etc. Food for the body is naturally linked with food for the soul.

A recent anthropological study of the Christian Eucharist offers further suggestions on the linking of food and teaching. The anthropologist's eye of Gillian Feeley-Harnik surveyed Old Testament literature on God's feeding and teaching of the covenant people. She concluded to a number of thematic statements which are pertinent to this study.

1. The power and authority of the Lord is manifested in his ability to control food: to feed is to bless.[8]
2. Acceptance or rejection of the authority of the Lord is symbolized by acceptance or rejection of his food.[9]
3. God's food is God's word.[10]
4. Eating joins people with the Lord or separates them.[11]

These statements rest on the basic principle: as God gives food to the covenant people, so God gives Torah-instruction to them. Bread/food are a clear and unmistakable symbol of Torah-instruction. All students of the Johannine bread of life discourse[12] are familiar with this material: how wisdom sets a banquet (Prv 9:5), offers bread and wine which will satisfy (Sir 24:21). The link between food and instruction is quite explicit: "She will nourish him with the bread of understanding and give him the water of learning to drink" (Sir 15:3).

From an anthropological perspective, then, Lk 22:14–38 is both a meal and a teaching. These reinforcing factors suggest the following: (1) The meal is for *group members* only, that is, for those who have fellowship with Jesus. (2) Jesus' gift of Eucharistic bread is a food which is specifically Christian and so serves to reinforce specific *group identity*. (3) Jesus' teaching is likewise *group specific* to the covenant around him. In eating the distinguishing Christian food and holding to the distinguishing teaching of Jesus, the covenant gathered in his name is *constituted as a distinctive group*. Each time it meets to eat Jesus' food and hear his instruction, it reinforces its identity as a distinctive group. (4) Food and instruction are *interchangeable* symbols, *replicating* each other. In other words, a meal is a perfect setting for teaching, as Wisdom in the Old Testament or symposia in Greek literature indicate.

III.
EXEGESIS OF LK 22:14–38

A. Lk 22:14

The passover meal which contains Jesus' farewell speech begins with the simple note that "when the hour came," Jesus sat at table with his apostles. The term, "the hour," has definite theological connotations in John's account of Jesus' passion (see Jn 13:1; also 12:23, 27; 17:1).[13] And in Lk 22:53 Jesus' arrest and death are said to be attributed to "your hour and the power of darkness." In these two instances, "the hour" identifies a highly significant moment: in Lk 22:53, Jesus' nadir and in Jn 13, his triumphant entrance into glory. But no climactic importance is attached to "the hour" in Lk 22:14, for the Last Supper and its farewell speech are hardly Jesus' nadir or his triumph.

Luke indicates that Jesus sits at table with his apostles (Mk 14:16 says "disciples"). This slight change indicates that the farewell speech in 22:14–38 is not a general address to Jesus' followers (see Sermon on the Plain, Lk 6:20–49). Rather, it is addressed to "the apostles," and it will have something specific to say about each of the individual apostles: (a) about Judas (22:21), (b) about Peter (22:31–34), and (c) about all of them (22:24–27, 28–30, 35–38). Inasmuch as a farewell speech typically deals with leadership succession, the specific address to the apostles helps to focus this scene on them as figures authorized for leadership by the departing Lord.

B. Lk 22:15–18

Jesus' first words in the farewell speech are frought with emotion: "With desire I desire to eat this Passover with you" (22:15a).[14] The reason for this heightened emotion is the prediction of Jesus' imminent death, ". . . before I suffer" (v. 15b). The initial item in Jesus' speech, then, is the prediction of his death, a formal characteristic of farewell speeches.

The prediction of Jesus' death, however, is not confined to the initial remark in the farewell speech. An explanation is given immediately in 22:16–18 about this present meal as the final one in a certain order. 22:16–

18 tell us two basic ideas: (a) in one sense, this is Jesus' last meal, for he will not eat or drink again, yet (b) future eating and drinking are predicted in God's kingdom. Taking these items separately, we see that vv. 16a and 18a reinforce the prediction of Jesus' death in v. 15 by insisting on some form of radical transition in Jesus' career. The Last Supper is the terminus of one phase of that career; he will not eat or drink again until a transition occurs in that career. 22:15, 16, and 18, then, serve the purpose of identifying this meal and its accompanying speech as Jesus' final one.

But 22:16 and 18 say more. As well as they contain a prediction of Jesus' death, they likewise predict a future triumph. One aspect of his career may be terminated by his death, but Jesus' career is not thereby terminated. 22:16 and 18 say that Jesus will not resume eating and drinking "until it is fulfilled in the kingdom of God." But what is this "kingdom of God" in regard to Jesus: the parousia (see Mk 14:62)? his resurrection? According to Luke, Jesus' experience of the kingdom of God is his vindicating resurrection and his establishment as Lord and Christ on David's throne (see Acts 2:36). Lk 22:16 and 18, then, should be seen as predictions of Jesus' vindicating resurrection, balancing the predictions of his death.

The eschatology of Luke-Acts is by no means uncomplicated.[15] The kingdom of God, for example, is described as present (Lk 8:20; 17:21), but also as future (21:31). Yet we can ask if God's kingdom in regard to Jesus is not a special act of God toward him; or, to phrase it differently, what might the relationship be of God's kingdom in Jesus' regard and the establishment of Jesus' predicted reign? It is solemnly predicted by a heavenly messenger in Lk 1:32–33 that God will give Jesus the throne of his father David and that he will reign forever. When was this prediction fulfilled in Luke's scheme of things? Jesus was acclaimed as king in his entry into Jerusalem (19:38), in his trial (23:2–3), and on the cross (23:37–38); but his reign was not yet. When the good thief asked to be remembered by Jesus "when you come into your kingdom" (23:42), he is assured that "today" he will be with Jesus in paradise. Jesus' assumption of a royal role is imminent. Yet in Luke's perspective, Jesus' reigning is not a remote future event, realized only at the parousia as in Mt 25:31–46. Jesus is recorded as saying in Lk 22:29 that God *has given* him a kingdom, which serves as the basis for his transference of authority to the apostles. We are encouraged, then, to think of Jesus' passion, death and resurrection as the context of Jesus' coming into his kingdom.

In Luke's heightened sense of time and duration, we can even tell "when" Jesus assumed his reign. Lk 23:43 indicates "today," a proximate but general time which is made clearer in Acts. Although "kingdom" and "king" do not occur formally in the terminology of Acts 2:36, the sense is surely there. In God's raising up of the crucified Jesus, he is seated on a throne beside God and made "Lord and Christ." He reigns; he has been given David's throne. One might argue that the parable in Lk 19:11–27 contains allusions to the passion in the rejection of the nobleman by his fellow citizens (v. 14), his departure to a far country to receive kingly power (vv. 12, 15), and the subsequent exercise of that power (vv. 15, 27).[16] Thus, rejection and the reception of kingly power are closely linked. And so God's kingdom in regard to Jesus can be said to come when God raised him from the dead and established him on David's throne.

Luke, however, describes the kingdom of God for Jesus in terms of eating and drinking. Our previous discussion of the importance of meals in Luke-Acts may help us here. 22:16 predicts that Jesus will not eat "until it is fulfilled in the kingdom of God"; but how are we to interpret "fulfilled"? It is an ambiguous term, for it could mean:

(a) until the *Passover* is fulfilled (antitype-type);[17]
(b) until the *eschatological banquet* is celebrated;
(c) until *God fulfills his promises* concerning Jesus.

Although Paul rushes to celebrate Pentecost in Jerusalem according to Acts 20:16, there is no reference in Acts to a Christian celebration of a new or authentic version of Jewish feasts.[18] Like other New Testament writers, Luke knows of the eschatological future as a banquet.[19] But as we shall see in regard to 22:29–30, the apostles' eating and drinking with Jesus at his table in his kingdom does *not* refer to a heavenly messianic banquet. Luke tells us repeatedly of Jesus' eating with the apostles and close associates *after* the resurrection and *before* the parousia. But perhaps the concern for "which meal?" is to be eaten in the kingdom is the wrong question. I suggest that the emphasis in 22:16–18 lies in a prediction of death and vindication. The focus is on the imminent sense of the kingdom of God, although it is couched in terms of the Lukan theme of meals.

The main points of 22:15–18 may be summarized: (a) a prediction of Jesus' death is made in v. 15 and implied again in vv. 16a and 18a; (b) this prediction of death is a formal characteristic of farewell speeches, necessarily setting the scene for the leader's last words; (c) yet balancing this prediction of Jesus' death is a prediction of future eating and drinking when God's kingdom comes (vv. 16b, 18b), which in Luke's perspective is a prediction of Jesus' resurrection and his establishment on David's throne. (d) The reader is alerted to the recurrence of the theme of ''meals'' in Luke's farewell speech as well as to the presence of predictions of the future, which will continue to be common and typical elements of this farewell speech.

C. Lk 22:19–20

The most important interpretative clue for understanding Lk 22:19–20 is to remember that these verses are situated in the context of Jesus' farewell speech. This formal observation leads us to see elements in the narrative in a fresh light. Inasmuch as 22:19–20 speak of the bread as the ''body given for you'' and the blood as ''poured out for you,'' some reference is made to Jesus' imminent death, a point emphasized in 22:15–18. Independent of the special soteriological meaning attached to these phrases, they clearly intensify the prediction of Jesus' death begun in 22:15–18, which, of course, is one of the formal characteristics of a farewell speech.

In many farewell speeches, moreover, it is typical of the dying leader to leave some legacy or blessing to his sons and daughters. As his farewell boon to Joseph, the dying Jacob adopts Joseph's two sons, Ephraim and Manasseh, giving them a special patriarchal blessing (Gen 48). Moses likewise left a blessing (Dt 33). Joshua is recorded as willing the land of Canaan to the tribes of Israel: ''Behold I have allotted to you as an inheritance for your tribes those nations that remain, along with all the nations that I have already cut off'' (Jos 23:4). In the New Testament, Peter leaves to the Church a legacy of the correct interpretation of its eschatological tradition for all times (2 Pet 1:12–15).[20] In the Pastoral Epistles,

Paul leaves as his legacy letters of authorization to Timothy, Titus, and their successors. In Lk 22:19–20, Jesus leaves the Eucharist as his legacy[21] to his covenant group.

Second, Eucharistic meals in Lk 24 and Acts seem to have a distinctive character which may shed light on the Lukan viewpoint in 22:19–20. We noted above how important meals were for the Lukan presentation of Jesus' ministry. This importance is not confined to Lk 5–19, for as Jesus' command in 22:19b indicates, the Eucharistic meals of the community will continue that tradition in the life of the Church. In Lk 24:30–35, the first meal after the Last Supper is recorded. Although Jesus is invited as a guest to that meal, he assumes a leadership role there and "blesses, breaks, and gives" the bread to the disciples. They in turn are enlightened and enthused by this meal shared with the risen Lord and return to Jerusalem and the apostolic community as a result of their fellowship with Jesus at that meal. After all, meals symbolize covenant fellowship. A strong case can be made that Luke's redaction of the Emmaus meal contains Eucharistic allusions.[22] Jesus, then, continues his saving ministry in the Eucharistic meal at Emmaus; he acts to gather, serve, and save his followers.

According to the ideal portrait of the Church in Acts, the new group met regularly for "fellowship, breaking of bread, and prayers" (Acts 2:42). Those who so met were the newly baptized, the ones who "saved themselves from this crooked generation" (2:40). But the formation of this new covenant group is due to Jesus, for he himself kept rounding up converts, "adding to their number those who were being saved" (2:47). If we may consider these breakings of bread as distinctive Christian meals, i.e., as Eucharists, they symbolize the continued ministry of Jesus, for those who eat together are those whom Jesus saves and brings into the fold (see Acts 20:7–11).

J. Wanke's careful study of the Eucharist[23] in Lk 24 and Acts led him to the following summary conclusions, which have a bearing on this discussion. (1) Luke highlights at those meals the presence of the Kyrios, the exalted Lord, (2) who is envisioned as mystically present to the Church; (3) the risen Lord is not distant from the Church, returning only as an occasional visitor; rather he is continuously immanent to it; (4) at these meals the risen Jesus acts as the majestic leader of the scene; (5) he is *Soter* to the disciples, the giver and confirmer of salvation.

This material on the Lukan meaning of the Eucharist in Lk 24 and Acts should affect our reading of Lk 22:19–20. The stress in Luke's understanding of Eucharist is not on the death of Jesus or the representation of the Crucified One; nor is it concerned with the sacrificial character of his death as a saving event. The Eucharist for Luke is basically a meal, and as such is an occasion of group solidarity when the risen Lord acts once more to gather and confirm his followers as covenant members of a new group. Group specific food is shared by a specific   roup. Group identity and boundaries are maintained all around.

Third, no one doubts that Luke is reflecting the long and sacred tradition about the Eucharist when he records the interpretative words over the bread and wine. Although his emphasis is not on the meaning of this interpretation, it will help us grasp the richness of the tradition if we note how these interpretative words explain the significance of Jesus' death. Three types of sacrifice are alluded to. 1. The Eucharist is a *passover,* in which Jesus' blood protects the gathered covenant as it passes from slavery to freedom. 2. It is a *covenant* sacrifice, a communion of life. The blood which is sprinkled on the people consecrates them as God's chosen and holy people (see Ex 24:8). 3. It is an *atonement* sacrifice, for the blood is "poured out for you." When the focus is on the blood of Jesus in the Eucharist, the emphasis is clearly sacrificial. But while Luke records these traditional words, his emphasis is on the Eucharist as meal, not sacrifice.

D. Lk 22:21–23

A consideration of the Lukan editing of 22:21–23 offers fresh insights into the meaning of the text.[24] Whereas Mark began the Last Supper with the prediction of Judas' betrayal, Luke began it with predictions of Jesus' own death (22:15) and with his legacy to the apostles (22:19–20), both characteristic elements of a farewell speech. Luke locates the prediction of Judas' betrayal in a new place, the significance of which is grasped by appreciating that new context. It is juxtaposed to two blocks of material, offering a sharp contrast to their message. First, in 22:19–20, Jesus was benevolently concerned for the apostles, leaving them the Eucharist and insisting that his flesh and blood were "for them." To this is juxtaposed Judas' hostile presence at Jesus' table in 22:21. He is hardly "for Jesus," since he is a traitor. He no longer belongs to Jesus' group; but he is a servant of Satan (22:3) and an ally of Jesus' enemies (22:4–6). Second, 22:21–23 are juxtaposed to 22:24–27. After a betrayer (surely the "least" of the apostles) is predicted, the group intently questions about him (v. 23). Yet they immediately stop this questioning about the "least" and start asking about who is the "greatest" (v. 24). The two questionings (vv. 23, 24) rub against each other in sharp dramatic contrast.

Besides locating this incident in a new place, Luke has introduced into the prediction of the betrayer some of his characteristic vocabulary. For example, Luke notes that the "Son of Man goes *as it has been determined*" (22:22). It is characteristic of Luke to speak of the passion as God's ordained plan for Jesus.[25] In Acts 2:23, Peter preaches concerning ". . . this Jesus, delivered up according to the definite plan and foreknowledge of God." And in Acts 4:28, the assembled community confessed of Jesus that his enemies acted "to do whatever thy hand and thy plan had predestined to take place." An apologetic point, therefore, is made of which we should not lose sight. Whatever Jesus' enemies do to him, either the Jewish leaders, Herod, Pilate or Judas, the real power, the genuine plan, and the true meaning of Jesus' death are *not* found in the assassination plot. Rather Jesus' passion is totally under God's providence: it is fore-known and fore-ordained by God. Jesus' death was not an act of God's vengeance on a sinner, but an act of providence.

Inasmuch as Luke has situated the prediction of the betrayer as part of Jesus' farewell speech, we should look at it more closely under that rubric. (1) In one sense, it intensifies the prediction of Jesus' death which begins the farewell speech, a theme linking it with vv. 15–20. (2) And it is characteristic of many farewell speeches to predict hard times coming upon the speaker's sons or disciples, viz., either future heretics, wolves, or deceivers menacing the group. Here in Luke, the traditional prediction of the betrayer functions in the same way.[26] (3) Prophecies of the future are another characteristic of farewell speeches, a point which is very important to Luke's presentation of Jesus in the passion narrative.[27] According to Luke, Jesus makes innumerable predictions in chs. 22–23: Jesus predicts (a) his own death (22:15, 22), (b) his betrayer (22:21), (c) the ultimate beatitude of his disciples (22:28–30) as well as their proximate problems (22:31–32), (d) Peter's denial (22:34), (e) the future vindication of the Son of Man (22:69), (f) the fall of Jerusalem (23:28–31), and (g) the salvation of the good thief (23:43). Patriarchs who prophesied during their farewell speeches are thereby credited with prophetic stature by this activity. Luke's notice of Jesus' prophecies fit his presentation of Jesus as a holy prophet of God. Jesus' prophetic identity rests on two phenomena: his work and his words. We are accustomed to recall how Jesus was a prophet "attested to you by signs and wonders" (Acts 2:22); but he is a prophet also in virtue of his words: "Jesus of Nazareth, a prophet mighty in deed and word before God and all the people" (Lk 24:19). This also serves an apologetic function in Luke's narrative, for true prophets are surely God's men, anointed by God, and duly sent by God. They are not sinners or criminals. (4) We noted earlier that farewell speeches tended to focus on the disciples or sons of the leader rather than on the leader himself. With 22:21–23, this emphasis begins to emerge. The focus of the farewell speech in Lk 22 is squarely on the covenant followers of Jesus.

In regard to Luke's passion narrative, we note that Luke is distinctive among the evangelists for telling the most complete story of Judas' involvement in Jesus' death. Individual items are found in Matthew and John, but Luke's account is by far the fullest.

1. He notes in 22:3 that Satan entered Judas, a point found also in John 6:70; 13:2, 27.
2. The use of Judas' betrayal money to buy a "field of blood" (Lk 22:5 and Acts 1:18–19) is found also in Mt 27:3–10, although in a slightly different form.
3. Judas' involvement in the plot against Jesus, and his kiss of Jesus at his arrest (Lk 22:4–6, 47–48), is found also in Luke's source, Mk 14:10–11 and 43–45.
4. Judas' death (Acts 1:18) is likewise recorded in Mt 27:5.
5. Even intimations of Judas' avarice, so strong in John 12:4–6, are echoed in the priests' offer of money in Lk 22:5, for it serves to secure Judas' services in the plot.

Luke, then, tells the fullest account of Judas. But why this interest? Is it merely an historian's gathering up of pieces of information or does it have some thematic importance?

Aside from the inclusion of Judas and his story as part of the general tradition about Jesus' betrayal, the figure of Judas seems to have symbolic significance in Luke-Acts. As the Lukan version unfolds, Judas is contrasted with Peter and it is in this vein that we sense his importance in the narrative. (1) Both Judas and Peter are said to be associated with Satan during the passion narrative. Satan entered Judas (22:3), suggesting Satan's success with him, especially since the text implies that as a result of this "entering" Judas went to Jesus' enemies to help them in their plot (22:4–6). Satan asked to sift Simon and the remaining ten disciples (22:31), but his success in regard to Peter is offset by Jesus' prayer (22:32). Satan succeeded with Judas, but not with Peter. (2) Judas functions as a leader in the passion narrative, albeit a leader of Jesus' enemies. Unlike Mark, Luke describes Judas as "leading" (*proērcheto,* 22:47) the arresting party, a point confirmed in Acts 1:16 where Judas is spoken of as "guide to those who arrested Jesus." Peter likewise is leader of Jesus' apostles: Jesus commissions him to "strengthen the brethren" (22:32). But how different are the two leaderships! (3) Judas' wickedness is cursed (22:22), which implies that his strange death in Acts 1:18 was an appropriate punishment. Peter's denial of Jesus is a terrible act, but his end is radically different from that of Judas. Jesus prays for him (22:32), turns and looks at him (22:61), and appears to him first of all on Easter (24:34). No curse here! In short, Judas is depicted as a thoroughly evil, hypocritical assassin who got his just deserts; conversely, Peter is portrayed as a weak, boastful, but remorseful disciple who nevertheless remained faithful to Jesus and became leader of Jesus' followers. The contrast may have significance in that it contrasts Jesus' covenant followers with unbelieving and hostile Jews, a pattern which is developed extensively in Acts.

Despite some recent suggestions,[28] it is difficult to see that Judas is a type of treacherous apostate in the Lukan Church. His treachery is unique. Other enemies of Jesus are given a second chance in Acts, for it is argued that they acted in ignorance. Not so Judas! Nor does Judas have any counterparts in Acts; no apostates are recorded there who betray their fellow Christians. The story of Judas serves several functions: (a) as agent of Satan (22:3), Judas indicates that the forces of evil rose up against God's Holy One, indirectly attesting to Jesus' closeness to God and his innocent suffering; (b) his role is the fulfillment of Scripture (Acts 1:16); thus his treachery is not outside God's knowledge or control; (c) Judas functions as a foil to Peter and to the faithful followers of Jesus. As we shall see, Luke consistently tells of a schism in God's people between believers and unbelievers, between the true covenant members and "this crooked generation."

E. Lk 22:24–27

The next item in the farewell speech is carefully stitched to 22:21–23. As regards its rhetorical form, the opening question, "which of them" (*to tis autōn*, 22:24), picks up both the questioning which concluded 22:21–23 as well as its formal expression, "which of them" (*to tis . . . ex autōn*, 22:23). Whereas in 22:21–23 the issue is "who is the worst or least apostle," i.e., the traitor, the theme of 22:24–27 is "who is the greatest?" The context of this material is also a clue to its interpretation. Mark located it on Jesus' journey to Jerusalem (Mk 10:41–45), whereas Luke put it in the context of Jesus' farewell speech. This new context will determine how we understand Jesus' words.

Not only is the new location due to Luke, but there are other significant editorial changes and additions to the text which shed light on its meaning and function in the Lukan passion narrative. Unlike Mk 10:35, not just James and John, but *all of the apostles* join in the dispute in 22:24. The issue is not as it was in Mark a question of "whoever wants to be" at Jesus' right hand; in Luke it is presupposed that these twelve men are in fact the official apostles and witnesses of Jesus. The issue is not whether leadership should exist or how close the twelve are to be to Jesus; the question is rather how that leadership is to be exercised. The ambivalence about apostolic leadership found in Mt 23:8–12 is completely absent from Luke.

Luke tightened the Markan story, compressing the discussion and thereby heightening the advice. He has modified Mk 10:43–44 to emphasize the contrast of leader/servant and to underscore the point of the new exhortation.

MARK 10:43	LUKE 22:26
Whoever wishes to be *great* among you,	Let the *greatest* among you
he will be your *servant*.	become as the *youngest*
Whoever wishes to be *first* among you	and the *leader*
he will be *slave* of all.	as the *servant*.

Greatest/youngest, leader/servant—the meaning is traditional in regard to Christian exhortations on leadership in the Church. But perhaps this advice echoes the Lukan axiom which was first seen in the Magnificat where the proud and mighty are brought low and the lowly are exalted (Lk 1:51–53). And in Lk 14:11 and 18:14, Luke insists that whoever humbles himself will be exalted but those who exalt themselves will be humbled.

The Lukan redaction of 22:24–27 is climaxed by the addition of v. 27 to the Markan text. In form it resembles the initial question raised in v. 24:

22:24 "which of them was . . . the greatest?"
22:27 "which is the greatest . . .?"

And so the passage is framed in an *inclusio*,[29] or bracketing technique. Like Mk 10:45, it constitutes the basis for the advice given in the passage, for an appeal is made to the example of Jesus as model. The precise phrasing of 22:27 highlights meals and Christian table etiquette, a Lukan theme we commented on earlier in this chapter. "Who is the greater, the one who sits at table or the one who serves?" Naturally the person seated at table is the higher ranking person,[30] but here the Lukan paradox is inserted: "But I am among you as one who serves." The text is quite cryptic here, and no explanation is given about Jesus' service at the Last Supper. John, who includes a comparable exhortation by Jesus in his farewell speech, has Jesus act the role of the servant by getting up from the table and washing the feet of the disciples (Jn 13:12–17). But this is not found in Luke, for Jesus remains seated with them.

It has long been noted that Luke omits at this point in the exhortation the Markan verse which specifies Jesus' service as soteriological, as "giving his life as ransom for many" (Mk 10:45). Inasmuch as the focus of the farewell speech is on the apostles, their fidelity, leadership, and service, the absence of the Christological focus is quite in keeping with the exhortatory character of the final words of Jesus to the apostles. The emphasis in Luke's farewell speech has not been soteriological but pastoral; the focus is less on the speaker than on the apostles.

An examination of 22:24–27 in the light of typical farewell speeches further aids our appreciation of these verses. In 22:24–27, something is proscribed (vv. 25–26) and something prescribed (v. 27). The tone and function of 22:24–27 are clearly exhortatory. In many farewell speeches we find a comparable exhortatory strain, often with specific vices proscribed and virtues prescribed. In most general terms, the sons of the twelve patriarchs in TXII are told to obey the commands of God (T. Reuben 1:5; T. Levi 1:1; 10:1; 13; T. Zebulun 5:1; T. Benjamin 3:1).[31] But in these same verses we find exhortations about specific virtues and vices. Judah specifically inveighs against lust (T. Judah 13:2–8; 14:3; 15:1–3), drunkenness (14:1; 16:1), and avarice (17:1; 19:1–4). Reuben attacks fornication (T. Reuben 1:6–10; 3:4–6:4). Alternately, specific virtues are urged: Issachar praises singleness of heart (T. Issachar 3–5); Zebulun urges compassion of heart (T. Zebulun 5:1–3; 7:1–2; 8:1); Joseph speaks in favor of chastity and purity (T. Joseph 3–9; 10:2). More common is the pattern whereby a specific vice is proscribed and its corresponding virtue prescribed. Dan proscribes anger (T. Dan 2:1–5; 3:1–4:7) and lying (5:1; 6:8), while prescribing love (5:3), truth and long-suffering (6:8). Gad speaks against hatred (T. Gad 1:9; 2-5) and for love (6:1); Asher attacks hypocrisy, while urging singleness of heart (T. Asher 5:4; 6:1).

New Testament examples of farewell speeches often contain a comparable exhortatory thrust. 1 Tim and Titus contain general exhortations, especially codes of household duties and in particular the duties of bishops, deacons, and elders. In Jesus' farewell speech in John 13–17, specific virtues are urged upon the disciples: (a) service of one another (Jn 13:12–17), (b) love (13:34–35; 15:12–13), (c) abiding in the vine (15:4–10), and (d) unity (17:20–23). And in Paul's farewell speech to the elders of Ephesus in Acts 20, he specifically calls the elders to generous service of the weak, basing his exhortation on the word of the Lord that it is better to give than to receive (Acts 20:34–35). It is precisely in this interpretative context that we should view 22:24–27 as Jesus' solemn exhortation to the apostles. In his farewell speech, Jesus proscribes self-important leadership and prescribes *diakonia* or service.

F. 22:28–30

These verses provide an excellent example of Luke's editorial perspective. As regards source, standing behind these remarks is an early tradition from the Q source (see Mt 19:25). But Luke has both relocated this material in a new context and greatly expanded it to bear a new meaning.

First, the context of these remarks in Luke is distinctive. Matthew (and Q) situates the promise of the apostles' sitting on thrones and judging the twelve tribes of Israel in the context of their leaving all to follow Jesus.[32] Luke puts it in Jesus' farewell speech, juxtaposing it to other remarks about the apostles:

1. a prediction of apostolic treachery (22:21–23),
2. an exhortation to selfless apostolic leadership (22:24–27),
3. an apostolic commissioning (22:32),
4. and a prediction of apostolic weakness (22:31, 33–34).

The Lukan context links 22:28–30 with other statements about Jesus' apostles, but not one entirely favorable to them as was the case in Matthew. According to Luke, Jesus' promise in 22:28–30 transcends the apostles' sinfulness and weakness, rather than merely rewarding virtue.

Second, the substance of Luke's remarks is quite different from Matthew, as the following synopsis indicates:

MATTHEW 19:28	LUKE 22:28–30
1. You who have followed me	1. You are those who have continued with me in my trials.
2. _____	2. As my Father appointed a kingdom for me, so do I appoint (a kingdom) for you,
3. _____	3. that you may eat and drink at my table in my kingdom
4. in the new world, when the Son of Man shall sit on his glorious throne,	4. _____
5. you will sit on twelve thrones, judging the twelve tribes of Israel.	5. and sit on thrones, judging the twelve tribes of Israel.

Interpreting the synopsis we find: (1) Luke has changed Matthew's general "following of Jesus" to a more specific statement that the apostles have shown fidelity to Jesus in a host of trials. (2) Luke modified the time when Jesus' promise would be in effect. In Matthew, the fulfillment is unmistakably "in the new world" (_paliggenesia_), at the parousia; but in Luke, Jesus says: "I (now) appoint you," which indicates that the promise is fulfilled in a more proximate time. (3) In 22:29, Luke records a solemn and sweeping conferral of authority, ("I appoint a kingdom for you"), a point not found in Matthew.[33] (4) The faithful apostles will experience the full extent of their fellowship with Jesus by continued sharing of his table, a point important to Luke's viewpoint but not found in Matthew. (5) In Matthew, a parallel is drawn between the apostles' sitting on twelve thrones and the sitting of the Son of Man on his throne at the parousia. But in Luke the focus is less on Jesus (his enthronement is omitted) and more on the apostles as valid leaders, duly authorized.

The position and function of 22:28–30 is clearly different in Luke's narrative from its place in Matthew's account. In Matthew the remark about the apostles' enthronement is seen as a supreme reward, not for perseverance or in prospect of apostlic service of the Church, but for leaving all to follow Jesus. In Luke, however, the context is Jesus' farewell speech in which great and continuous stress is put on apostolic leadership, especially the issue of leadership succession. The drift of these redactional changes points to a special Lukan description of the apostles as: (a) ultimately faithful to Jesus, (b) destined to share Jesus' table, and (c) commissioned to judge Jesus' followers.

Third, the Lukan editing of 22:28–30 is such that it is carefully linked with other parts of the farewell speech. (1) The "meal" motif (see 22:15, 16–18, 19–20, 27) is repeated in 22:30. Table fellowship with Jesus signals shared faith and true membership in the circle of Jesus' followers. (2) The mention of "kingdom" in 22:29–30 links this passage with 22:16–18 where Jesus also spoke about eating in the "kingdom of God." (3) We noted above how apostolic leadership is a dominant theme in 22:24–32, especially in vv. 29–30. Meals, kingdom, and leadership are the three themes which stitch Luke's redaction of these traditional passages into a unified address.

The Lukan redaction takes on further significance when it is seen in the context of the convention of farewell speeches. A persistent element in most farewell speeches is the concern of the dying leader for his successor. T. Levi and T. Judah predict the coming of new leaders in the remote future as the way of insuring valid succession. The Pastoral Epistles are unmistakably concerned with: (a) the authorization of Timothy and Titus, (b) the establishment of qualifications for and job descriptions of bishops and deacons, and (c) the validation of their successors.[34] John's farewell speech not only is concerned with the special quality of leadership (Jn 13), but contains a commissioning as well: "As you have sent me into the world, so I have sent them into the world'' (17:18; see Jn 15:16; 20:21). And most convincingly, Luke's version of Paul's farewell speech in Acts records the confirmation of the leadership of Paul's successors in the Churches of Asia Minor: ''Take heed to yourselves and to all the flock in which the Holy Spirit has made you guardians'' (Acts 20:28). In Lk 22:28–30 and Acts 20:28, then, Luke insists in the context of a farewell speech that the Church is adequately provided with clear and authorized leaders to carry on its mission. This, then, is the proper background in which to situate Lk 22:28–30. Commissioning of followers to exercise leadership after the death of the master is a common feature of many farewell speeches, including Luke's.

Even the phraseology of 22:29 supports this, for we find in Josephus a statement remarkably similar to Lk 22:29 which clearly points to testamentary transfer of authority. When the Hasmonean king died, even though he had two sons to succeed him, he ''bequeathed the royal power to Alexandra,'' the same phrase which is found in Lk 22:29.

Josephus: *Ant.* XIII.407   ''he bequeathed (*dietheto*) . . . the kingdom''
Luke 22:29   ''I appoint (*diatithemai*) a kingdom''

A host of exegetical questions remain to be resolved. Jesus' ''trials'' (v. 28) are to be thought of in rather general terms as trials which include Satanic assaults (22:3, 31), as well as assorted tribulations, plots, and forensic hearings. The general character of ''trials'' is brought out most clearly in Paul's farewell speech in Acts where he testifies to his fidelity to Jesus through ''the trials which befell me through the plots of the Jews'' (Acts 20:19). In Acts, Jesus is said to insist that the persecution of his apostles is persecution of himself (9:5; 22:8; 26:15), and so it may be said that Jesus' ''trials'' continue in the trials of his apostles. The phrase ''continued with me in my trials'' (v. 28), then, should be interpreted as including the full range of Satanic assaults,[35] Jewish plots, persecutions, imprisonments, and forensic trials of the apostles in Acts. According to Acts, the apostolic leadership remained faithful through all of that.

The remark in 22:28 about the apostles' ''continuing'' refers to their faithfulness. It probably has much the same sense as Paul's exhortation to the churches in Asia Minor when he exorted them ''to continue in the faith . . . through many tribulations we enter the kingdom of God'' (Acts 14:22; see 11:23). Since ''continuing'' has a spatial connotation, it is possible to see Judas' "turning aside, going to his own place" (Acts 1:25) as the opposite of it; for Judas did not continue with the Eleven or with Jesus. And it can probably be linked with Peter's "strengthening of faith" among the apostles (Lk 22:32).

The faithful apostles are commissioned to "eat and drink at my table in my kingdom" (22:30a). Although there is a New Testament tradition of future eschatological life with Jesus as a messianic banquet, this is not the sense of the Lukan text here. Luke relates that Jesus continued to eat and drink with his apostles and close associates after his resurrection (Lk 24:30–35, 41–43; Acts 1:3–4). Beyond Lukan concern for meals in general and even Eucharistic meals, we find in Luke-Acts two examples of meals which are linked exclusively with the Twelve, at which meal leadership and ministry are the dominant themes. As we read in Lk 22:30, Jesus predicts future meals with the apostles, which prediction seems to be realized in Acts 10:41–42. (1) This passage refers to *exclusive meetings* between Jesus and the apostles: "Not to all the people, but to us who were chosen by God as witnesses" (10:41a). (2) The meetings referred to were *meals:* "Who ate and drank with him after he rose from the dead" (10:41b; see 1:3–4). (3) The topic is *leadership:* "And he commanded us to preach to the people and to testify that he is the one ordained by God to be judge of the living and the dead" (10:42). Luke 22:14–38 and Acts 10:41–42, then, unmistakably speak of exclusive meals between Jesus and the apostles whose chief topic was apostolic commissioning and leadership. Far from reflecting the perspective of Mt 19:28 that the apostles' enthronement is an event of the parousia, Luke sees their "enthronement" and their eating with the risen Jesus in terms of their present exercise of leadership in the early Church.

Although in Matthew the apostles' "judgment of the twelve tribes of Israel" is a forensic act associated with Jesus' own judgment at the parousia,[36] this is not the case in Lk 22:30. The context of 22:30 is Luke's treatment of the present exercise of leadership by the apostles; the Twelve are to be servant-leaders of the flock of Jesus (22:24–27), and Peter is to "strengthen the brethren" (22:31–32). This context of present leadership encourages us to see in 22:29–30 a formal commissioning of the apostles for immediate ministry in the early Church, not for parousial judgment as in Mt 19:28. By giving the apostles "a kingdom" *now,* Luke suggests that it is to be exercised in the present time. And Luke has given us in Acts a vivid picture of apostolic governance and leadership, a picture which gives immediate realization to the commission in 22:29–30. For example, (1) the first act of the apostles in Acts is to replace Judas, thus signaling that the group's membership must be complete, a completeness which is irrelevant unless Luke sees it as a fulfillment of Jesus' remark that there should be *twelve* judges of the twelve tribes of Israel. (2) On behalf of the new covenant group, members of the Twelve are then deputized as spokesmen to the Jewish crowds (Acts 2–3), to the Sanhedrin (Acts 4–5), and to the deliberating church (Acts 11:2–18). (3) The apostle Peter functions as a forensic judge in the case of Ananias and Sapphira (Acts 5) and in dealing with Simon the Magician (Acts 8:20–23). (4) As regards halachic matters, Peter is instrumental in declaring all foods clean (Acts 11:5–9) and in receiving unclean Gentiles into the Church (Acts 10–11). (5) His testimony at the Jerusalem council forms the basis for the disciplinary decision not to make Jews of Gentile converts (15:7–11, 14). And so, according to the Lukan perspective Peter and the other apostles are shown exercising leadership and governance in the early Church. Their "kingdom" extends from "ministry of the word" (Acts 6:4) to radical halachic rulings for the new group. They determine who is to be included and who excluded. All of this activity, I suggest, is based on the commission to govern which was given the Twelve by Jesus according to Lk 22:29–30.

G. Lk 22:31–34

It is generally helpful for appreciating Luke's distinctive presentation of an event to compare and contrast his version with that found in his sources. In regard to 22:31–34, while Luke shows dependence on Mk 14:27–31 and seems to share other traditions found only in John's account,[37] yet he has still other materials peculiar to his account. Let us briefly identify the contents of the traditions which Luke reflects and see how he has orchestrated them.

1. Mk 14:27–31, the most obvious source for Lk 22:31–34, contains Jesus' prediction of the scandal of the apostles and the denial by Peter:

    a.   You will all fall away (14:27a)

    b.   . . . and the sheep will be scattered (14:27b)

    c.   After I am raised up, I will go before you (14:28)

    d.   Peter: "Even though they all fall away, I will not" (14:29)

e. Jesus: "You will deny me three times" (14:30a)

f. Peter: "If I must die with you, I will never deny you" (14:30b)
The highlighted elements are: the apostles' loss of faith and their scattering (a & b), Jesus' own shepherding of the scattered sheep (c), and Peter's protest that he will die with Jesus and never deny him (d & f).

2. In John's farewell speech, we find a number of items which parallel Luke 22:31–34:

a. Peter: "I will lay down my life for you" (13:37).

b. Jesus: "The cock will not crow before you have denied me three times" (13:38).

c.   "   "You will all be scattered, every man to his home and leave me alone" (16:32).

d.   "   "I pray . . . that you should keep them from the evil one" (17:15).

e.   "   "I will come to you" (14:18; 16:16).

As in Mark's account, Peter is willing to die for Jesus (a); the scattering of the apostles is indicated (c); and Jesus is the future consoler of the scattered flock (e). Unlike Mark, Jesus prays for the disciples to protect them from the evil one (d).

3. Luke's version of this tradition reflects elements found in both Mark and John, as well as distinctive Lukan editorial work:

a. Satan demanded to sift you like wheat (22:31a).

b. I have prayed for you that your faith not fail (22:31b).

c. When you have turned, strengthen your brethren (22:32).

d. Peter: "I am ready to go to prison and to death with you" (22:33).

e. Jesus: "The cock will not crow until you three times deny that you know me" (22:34).

Like Jn 17:15, Luke records Jesus praying to protect at least Peter from Satan; and like Mark, Peter protests his readiness to die with Jesus. Unlike John or Mark, however, Luke does *not* predict that the apostles will lose faith and be scattered. Whereas John and Mark record that Jesus will himself shepherd the scattered flock and come to them, in Luke, Peter is effectively given that task and role when he is told to "strengthen your brethren." These two changes in Luke's account are very important as we shall presently see. The following synopsis indicates six points of contact between Luke's text and other versions of this tradition:

LUKE	MARK	JOHN
1. *Satan active:* "Satan demanded . . ." (22:31a).	1. _____	1. "I pray that you keep them from the evil one" (17:15b).
2. *Scandal of disciples:* ". . . to sift you like wheat" (22:31b).	2. "You will all fall away, for it is written: 'I will strike the shepherd and the sheep will be scattered' " (14:27).	2. "You will all be scattered, every one to his home and leave me alone" (16:32).
3. *Prayer of fidelity:* "But I have prayed for you . . ." (22:32a).	3. "Simon . . . watch and pray that you not enter into temptation" (14:38).	3. "I do not pray that thou shouldst take them out of the world, but that thou shouldst keep them from the evil one" (17:15).
4. *Shepherding:* "And when you have turned, strengthen your brethren" (22:32b).	4. "I will go before you . . . (14:28).	4. "I will come to you" (14:18).
5. *Peter's loyalty:* "Lord, I am ready to go with you to prison and to death" (22:33).	5. "Even though they all fall away, I will not" (14:30a).	5. "I will lay down my life for you" (13:37).
6. *Peter's denial:* "The cock will not crow until you three times deny that you know me" (22:34).	6. "This very night, before the cock crows twice, you will deny me three times" (14:30b).	6. "The cock will not crow before you have denied me three times" (13:38).

4. Yet there is still another tradition which Luke reflects in 22:32, the special commissioning of Peter. Mark records a commissioning of Peter in the context of his leaving all to follow Jesus (Mk 1:17); Matthew records a Petrine commissioning after Peter's bold confession of Jesus (Mt 16:17–19); John, on the other hand, records Peter's commissioning in a scene which boldly acknowledges his triple denial (Jn 21:15–17) yet which makes him shepherd of Jesus' flock. In Lk 22:32, Peter's admitted

failure ("when you have turned") is juxtaposed to Jesus' commission that he shepherd the flock ("strengthen your brethren"). And so Luke's narrative blends a variety of traditions, not only about the apostles' faith (or lack of it) and Peter's denial, but especially about Peter's special commission.

We turn from comparing Luke with his sources to a study of certain key Lukan themes in 22:30–34. Of particular interest here is Luke's concern over Satan (22:31) and his presentation of Peter's commissioning (22:32). The remark about Satan in Lk 22:31 should, of course, be seen in the light of Lk 4:13, 22:3 and 22:53. The figure of Satan is a familiar one in Luke-Acts, and we can grasp its importance in Lk 22:31 by seeing this remark in the context of Luke's surprisingly extensive discussion of Satan. We can summarize the Lukan presentation of Satan in six points:

1. In Luke's narrative, Satan appears at the beginning of Jesus' ministry to attack him (4:1–13), and he returns at the end, attacking Jesus' disciples (22:3, 31) and even Jesus himself once more (22:53). The Lukan narrative, then, is framed by reference to Satanic attacks on God's Christ and his followers.
2. Within the narrative, Satan is described as the enemy of faith. When a seed of the word of God is sown, Satan takes away the word from the hearers' heart "that they may not believe and be saved" (8:12). Acts 13:8–10 confirms this when Elymas, "the son of the devil," seeks to turn away the consul Sergius Paulus from the faith. And so Satan's attacks, first on Jesus himself, then on Judas (22:3), Peter and the other disciples (22:31), fit into this pattern.[38]
3. This antagonistic role of Satan is dramatized more fully in Luke's presentation of two kingdoms at war, God's and Satan's. Satan's kingdom includes demoniacs and sick people bound by him (Lk 13:16). Yet Jesus' role is to despoil Satan's kingdom and rescue its prisoners (Lk 11:22; Acts 10:38). Jesus' warning to Peter about Satan's attack fits into this role.
4. There is no doubt, however, about the outcome of the warring kingdoms. Jesus himself showed mastery over Satan (Lk 4:1–13), proving that he is God's Son and agent of God's kingdom (Lk 11:20). This is confirmed when Peter speaks about "how God anointed Jesus with the Holy Spirit and with power and how he healed all that were oppressed by the devil, for God was with him" (Acts 10:38).

5. Jesus even proclaimed the ruin of Satan when he exclaimed: "I saw Satan fall like lightning" (Lk 10:18).
6. Jesus' mission was to rescue those under Satan's power (e.g., the bent woman in Lk 13:16), as it was Paul's mission to preach to the Gentiles "that they may turn from darkness to light, from the power of Satan to God" (Acts 26:18).

The upshot of this overview is to confirm that Luke has an extensive and thematic treatment of Satan in Luke-Acts. The conflict between Satan and Jesus, the apostles, and the Church is of major thematic importance for Christians, for it stresses the cosmic significance and the radical importance of Jesus' work.

    With this background, let us examine more closely the remarks about Satan and Peter in 22:31. "Satan demanded (*exēitēsato*) to have you" constitutes a demand for total dominance.[39] This is confirmed by other uses of the verb "demand," one of which occurs in a farewell speech. In T. Benjamin 3:3, the dying patriarch tells his sons: "Even though the spirits of Beliar demand to have you (*exaitesontai*), yet they shall not have dominion over you."[40] The context indicates that Beliar's demanding (*exaiteō*) is a warlike challenge aimed at total domination ("have dominion over you") (*katakyrieusei*). Plutarch, in describing certain savage rites, indicates that these rites are intended to appease evil spirits; as Heracles laid siege to Oechalia, "powerful and impetuous divinities demand (*exaitoumenoi*) a human body" (*Def. Orac.* 417D), obviously to possess and dominate it.

    The demand for surrender is further clarified by examining the metaphorical implications of "to sift you like wheat" (22:31). Luke's Gospel is full of vivid similes describing important events, among whose number we should include "sift like wheat." As a metaphorical expression, "sifting" refers to some sort of threshing, some sort of separation of wheat from chaff.[41] Although in early Christian literature there is a tradition of the devil devouring Christians (see 1 Pet 5:8), the connotation of "sifting" in Luke suggests some form of separation from the group or some form of scandal of faith.[42] Recall that Satan in Luke-Acts is the prime enemy of faith.

    Other Gospel traditions of this event in the passion narrative speak of a prediction by Jesus that "you will all fall away" (*skandalisthēsesthe*, Mk 14:27), which means a "scattering" (*diaskorpisthēsontai*, Mk

14:27b), that is, a separation from the true flock. John likewise speaks of the disciples' scattering (*skorpisthēte*, 16:32). Basically, then, the tradition speaks of the apostles' flight from Jesus and their loss of faith. They are proved to be worthless like chaff and are separated from the wheat and the barn. Using these parallel texts in Mark and John as clues, we note that "sift like wheat" would seem to be Luke's version of "scandalized" and "scattered." Luke, moreover, has frequently spoken of Satan as the enemy of faith. And so Lk 22:31 does not seem to envision a Job-like[43] testing of the disciples so much as a warlike attack on them which would separate them from faith in Jesus and from God's kingdom by putting them under Satan's power.

We turn to the second Lukan theme, the commissioning of Peter. If 22:31 may be said to be Luke's version of the tradition of the apostles' scandal and scattering, is there a tradition behind Lk 22:32, Jesus' prayer for Peter? John 17:15 records Jesus praying for *all* the apostles to be kept from Satan: "I pray . . . that thou shouldst keep them from the evil one." Mark 14:38 records Jesus telling Peter to do his own praying to escape temptation: "Watch and pray that you may not enter into temptation." Luke is distinctive, then, in that he records Jesus praying for *Peter* and for a *specific thing*: "I have prayed for you (Peter) that your faith may not fail" (22:32). This statement is all the more striking when we consider that traditionally Peter is the acknowledged denier of Jesus. Yet ironically Jesus' prayer is for Peter's faithfulness. It must be admitted that Peter's "faith" is to be understood as fidelity,[44] faithfulness in trial (see Acts 14:22). Jesus prays, moreover, that Peter's faithfulness not utterly vanish, which would make him the equivalent of Judas. Luke, then, seems to be radically revising the traditions about Peter in making him the object of Jesus' prayer and by ironically calling attention to his faithfulness[45] in spite of his known denials.

In 22:32, Luke introduced a statement by Jesus which has no parallel in any of the other passion narratives. Consequent to the prayer for Peter's faithfulness, Jesus commands him: "And when you have turned, strengthen your brethren" (22:32b). The phrase "when you have turned" implies some degree of failure on Peter's part, for "turn" (*epistrephō*) has to do with conversion and forgiveness[46] of sins. In Acts, for example, after charging the crowd with complicity in Jesus' death, even their denial of Jesus (*hymeis ērnēsasthe*, 3:14), Peter exhorts them to "repent and turn (*epistrepsate*) that your sins may be blotted out" (Acts 3:19). And

Paul explains that it is his mission to persuade the Gentiles to "turn (*epistrepsai*) from darkness to light and from the power of Satan to God that they may receive forgiveness of sins" (Acts 26:18). "Turn," then, clearly has to do with sin, repentance and forgiveness *even after denial of Jesus*.

Yet despite Peter's sin and failure, Jesus commands him to "strengthen your brethren" (22:32b). I suggest that this verse contains a solemn commissioning of Peter comparable to Mt 16:17–19 and Jn 21:15–17. "Strengthening" is an act of ministerial leadership in Acts 18:23, when Paul "went from place to place . . . strengthening all the disciples" (see Rom 1:11 and 1 Thess 3:2). The "brethren," moreover, are not simply the Twelve; in Acts the common soubriquet for Church members is "brethren."[47] I suggested earlier that Luke reflects in 22:32b a tradition comparable to that found in Jn 21:15–17. In both John and Luke we find the following parallel features:

1. Peter's denial is fully acknowledged,
2. Yet despite his denial of Jesus, he is commissioned as premier leader,
3. And his commission is to shepherd the flock of Christ.

Luke, moreover, frequently speaks of the commissioning of the Church's leaders in the context of their sinfulness. In Lk 5:1–11, Peter confesses: "I am a sinful man" (v. 8) to which Jesus replied: "You will be catching men" (v. 10). Three times in Acts Paul acknowledges his persecution of Jesus and the Church in the context of his commission (9:1–18; 22:4–8; 26:9–15).[48]

Peter's specific commissioning to "strengthen your brethren" comes on the heels of a general commissioning of the Twelve in Lk 22:29–30. So the idea of commissioning is not foreign to Luke's farewell speech. In fact, the concern for succession of leaders after the death of a patriarch is a common feature of farewell speeches.

The strange sense of the "you" who are addressed in 22:31 may be clarified in the light of Peter's new commissioning. 22:31–32 are addressed to Peter exclusively: "Simon, Simon . . ."; yet Jesus announces that "all of you" (*hymas*) are demanded by Satan, not just Peter.[49] Commentators have always found difficulty with the fact that Peter alone is addressed while Jesus states that "all of you" are demanded. There is no difficulty if it is remembered that Peter is given concern for "your breth-

ren," which concern begins with Jesus' notification to Peter of the imminent assault on these very brethren.

When and how does Peter fulfill Jesus' commission in 22:32? As
regards his "turning," there can be no doubt that the Lukan additions to
the scene of Peter's denial are intended to have bearing on the first part
of 22:32, "And when you have turned . . ." At the moment of denial,
Jesus looks at Peter, which glance leads Peter to remember Jesus' prediction of his denial and then to "bitter" weeping (22:61–62). When next
we hear of Peter, he is with the brethren in the upper room on Easter
night, a recipient of a personal vision of the risen Jesus which he has
already shared with them (24:34). The "turning" appears to be accomplished, and the "strengthening" already begun. Peter's "strengthening" is connected not only with his eyewitness announcement that he has
seen the Lord (24:34), but especially with the vigorous role which Peter
takes in Acts 1–11,[50] activity which we have repeatedly noted in this
chapter.

Luke's redaction of the prediction of Peter's denial contains one
more point. Both Mark and John record Peter boasting that, if he must,
he will either die *with* Jesus (Mk 14:31) or die *for* him (Jn 13:37). Luke's
version is broadened, for Peter announces that he is prepared not just to
die with Jesus but "to go to prison with him" (22:33). The addition of
"prison" is ironical in that Luke thrice records in Acts that Peter was in
fact incarcerated as a spokesman for Jesus (4:1–3; 5:17–21; 12:3–11).
Whereas Jn 21:18–19 knows of Peter's death (especially a death like Jesus', i.e., giving glory to God), Luke never mentions Peter's death. The
imprisonment, then, stands out all the more sharply.

Does the material in Lk 22:31–34 have any formal place in a farewell
speech? In the TXII we find a number of similarities between the farewell
speeches of the patriarchs and Lk 22:31–34, precisely in terms of predictions of Satan's attacks on the patriarch's followers and predictions of
their eventual victory over the devil.

1. Predictions abound of Satan's future attacks on the sons and descendants of the patriarch. T. Reuben tells us: "Now hear from me, my
   children, what I saw concerning the seven spirits of deceit . . . seven
   spirits are appointed against man by Beliar" (2:1–2).[51] Concerning
   his descendants, Dan claims to have found a prediction "in the book
   of Enoch" about Satanic rule over them: "Your ruler is Satan and all

the spirits of fornication and pride will conspire to attend to the sons of Levi to cause them to sin before the Lord'' (5:6). As we noted above, Benjamin also speaks of ''the spirits of Beliar demanding you to afflict you'' (3:3). Finally Issachar predicts that ''in the last times your sons will forsake the commandments of the Lord and cleave to Beliar'' (6:1).

2. The TXII contains a dualistic perspective of the world: one belongs either to God's kingdom or to Satan's, thus implying that all wickedness comes from and places one under Satan's rule. Levi tells his sons: ''Choose, therefore, for yourselves either the light or the darkness, either the law of the Lord or the works of Beliar'' (19:1; see Acts 26:18). This dualism is perhaps best expressed in Gad's remark: ''The spirit of hatred works together with Satan through hastiness of spirit in all things to men's death; but the spirit of love works with the law of God in long-suffering unto the salvation of men'' (4:7; see also T. Naph. 2:6).

3. Finally, as Satan's attacks on the patriarch's sons are predicted, so also we find predictions of Satan's defeat. Levi predicts a great victory over Satan by a future descendant: ''And Beliar shall be bound by him and he shall give power to his children to tread on evil spirits'' (18:12; see Lk 10:18–19). Issachar also predicts a victory: ''Do these things and every spirit of Beliar will flee from you and no deed of wicked men shall rule over you'' (7:7). The prime example of the prediction of victory is found in Dan's prophecy of a savior from the tribes of Judah and Levi: ''And he shall make war on Beliar and the captivity he shall take from Beliar, the souls of the saints, and turn disobedient hearts to the Lord'' (5:10–12).

In farewell speeches in both TXII and Lk 22:31–34, then, we find predictions not only of Satan's attacks on disciples and descendants, but also of their victory over Satan. While one should be hesitant to say that such predictions are regular features of all farewell speeches, Luke and TXII show that they are not foreign to that convention either.

The drift of Luke's editorial changes in 22:31–34 should be seen in light of the context of 22:31–34 within a typical farewell speech. As regards the mention of Satan (22:31), it is probably a formal variant of the forecasts of future crises. As regards transfer of authority, as the Twelve were commissioned in 22:29–30, so Peter is specially authorized in

22:31–32. As regards predictions of future hard times, Jesus foretells that the Eleven, including Peter, will be the objects of Satan's assault (22:31). As regards an exhortation to special behavior, Jesus prays for Peter's faithfulness and for his generous service in strengthening his brethren (22:32). 22:31–34, then, are carefully edited to reinforce the prime concerns of typical farewell speeches.

The thrust of the Lukan redaction of 22:31–34 may be briefly summarized: (1) In place of the explicit mention of the apostles' scandal of faith and their scattering, Luke speaks of them as only threatened with a "sifting like wheat." (2) In place of prayer for all of them or even their own prayer for escape from the evil one, Jesus prays specifically for Peter that he remain faithful, despite his predicted denial. (3) The focus of Luke's redaction is clearly on the commissioning of Peter, from the announcement of the apostles' crisis to Peter in v. 31, to Jesus' prayer for him and his commissioning of him in v. 32. (4) Whereas in Mark and John, Jesus prophesied his own future role as shepherd of the scattered sheep, this task is transferred to Peter in Luke's account.

H. Lk 22:35–38

The investigation of this final part of Luke's farewell speech has been facilitated by Joan Frances Gormley. In her 1974 dissertation, Gormley worked through the exegetical problems in 22:35–38 and offered a persuasive, enlightening assessment of these troublesome verses.[52] I will telescope her findings, leaving the reader to consult her work for the full argumentation.

1. Although in some way stemming from Q-source material (see Mt 10:9–10/Lk 10:4 and Mt 10:34/Lk 12:51), Lk 22:35–38 are a Lukan composition. Luke's editorial hand is especially evident in the new location of this material at the end of the farewell speech.[53]

2. As regards 22:35–36, Gormley argues that Jesus' vocabulary deals with "preparation for a journey": purse, knapsack, and sandals (v. 35).[54]

3. Assessing v. 36 as an antithetical statement, she translates it as follows:

Let the one who has a purse,
     take it up and likewise a knapsack;

and let the one who does not have a purse,
    sell his cloak and buy a sword.[55]

Gormley based this reading on comparison with antithetical statements
in Luke (12:47–48 and 17:33) and in the Bible (Prv 12:1; 15:20; Ez 7:15;
Jer 21:9). The antithesis in Luke's statement suggests that (a) two exclusive groups are contrasted ("the one who has . . . the one who does not
have"), (b) two exclusive fates are contrasted, and (c) yet *all* are to take
some specific action determined by the circumstances. She paraphrases
v. 36 in a way which incorporates her findings:

Let the one who has resources for a journey,
    take them up;
and let the one who does not possess resources,
    provide himself with a sword.[56]

4. Lk 22:37 is a classical Lukan example of prophecy-fulfillment.
Based on Is 53:12, it predicts Jesus' imminent arrest and passion, the
fulfillment of which "is so imminent as to be spoken of as present."[57]
The "reckoning" of Jesus is ironical, for it refers to what Jesus' enemies
reckon, not God or his followers.[58] On the contrary, 22:37 functions as
a topic statement for the subsequent story, stressing Jesus' being "reckoned" with Satan (22:52–53), Barabbas (23:18–25), and the two crucified thieves (23:39–43). Since 22:37 is ironical, it introduces Jesus'
"innocence" of any sin or crime in the subsequent proceedings against
him.[59]

5. 22:38 records the disciples' misunderstanding of the remark of
Jesus about a "sword" (v. 37), as well as Jesus' own comment which
formally ends the conversation (see Dt 3:26).[60]

6. Gormley compares Lk 22:35–38 with previous instructions to the
disciples in Lk 10. She notes that the sending in Lk 10 occurs in the
context of Jesus' own decision to go to Jerusalem (see 9:51). The disciples
there are fully-authorized preachers who represent Jesus. They announce
the kingdom (10:9) and share in Jesus' power over Satan (10:19). Yet
they are "defenseless and vulnerable," for they may not carry purse,
knapsack, or sandals (10:4). These elements of the commissioning in Lk
10 have bearing on how one reads 22:35–36. Now Jesus' journey reaches
its climax in Jerusalem in his death; the apostles are again fully author-

ized, not just as preachers but as leaders of Jesus' group (22:29–30, 31–32); they not only preach, but are bequeathed "a kingdom" (22:29); and despite the disciples' former victory over Satan (10:17–19), they will face him again (22:31–32).[61]

7. Gormley insists that 22:35–38 be understood as a passion prediction. She compares this passage with other passion predictions, such as 9:44–45 and 18:31–34, and she notes the following formal similarities:[62]

(a) a *prediction* is made:
  9:44 The Son of Man is to be delivered into the hands of men.
  18:32 He will be delivered to the Gentiles, mocked, shamefully treated, and spit upon . . .
  22:37 What is written about me has its fulfillment.
(b) the passion is the *fulfillment* of scriptural *prophecies:*
  18:31 Everything that is written of the Son of Man by the prophets will be accomplished.
  22:37 I tell you that this scripture must be fulfilled in me: "And he was reckoned with transgressors."
(c) the disciples *fail to understand* Jesus:
  9:45 But they did not understand this saying, and it was concealed from them.
  18:34 But they understood none of these things; this saying was hid from them, and they did not grasp what was said.
  22:38 Look, Lord, here are two swords.

8. Gormley insists on the "journey" quality of 22:35–38, linking Jesus' journey to Jerusalem with the missionary journey of the apostles.[63]

9. She calls attention to the Lukan context of 22:35–38. It is immediately located in the meal at the Last Supper;[64] it follows references to a covenant, and authority over that covenant;[65] and it builds on Jesus' remarks about a conflict with Satan.[66]

Joan Gormley's study solved many of the traditional exegetical problems in a satisfactory way. Yet her study remains incomplete, for she did not assess the passage as the final remarks in Jesus' farewell speech, nor did she attempt to see how the Lukan material in 22:35–38 is played out fully in the rest of the passion narrative or in Acts. Yet her remarks are solid and can be built on.

Several of the formal elements of a farewell speech are found in Lk 22:35–38. (1) Inasmuch as Jesus is once more predicting his arrest, we have one final prediction by the departing leader of his death (22:37). (2) There are hard times predicted for the leader's followers, which require immediate preparation (22:35–36). (3) Implied in the journey motif for which the apostles must prepare is a renewed sense of their commissioning as Jesus' official witnesses and leaders of his group. (4) An exhortation is given as Jesus prescribes immediate, decisive action to be taken. Lk 22:35–38, then, formally reflects the conventions of a farewell speech.

The exegetical crux of these verses, however, was not satisfactorily addressed in Gormley's study. What is the meaning of "buy a sword" (v. 36)? She claimed that two types of disciples are contrasted in 22:35–36—"those who have and those who do not have." The former are those who are prepared with provisions for the coming journey; the latter represent those who have no provisions for a journey.[67] Somehow Gormley sees the mention of a sword in 22:36 as referring to a real object. The narrative indicates that some interpreted Jesus' word literally, for they produced two swords (v. 38). But was that the meaning of Jesus' remark?

To get at this issue, it will be helpful to consider three things: (a) the meaning of "sword" in Luke's source, (b) the use of swords in 22:49–50, and (c) the use of swords in Acts.

A. According to the source for Luke's remark in Mt 10:34/Lk 12:51, Jesus sends the apostles not to proclaim peace but "the sword," i.e., division among families resulting from the Gospel. The meaning of "sword" in Mt 10:34 is metaphorical; it means that the apostles will cause a schism by their preaching. This could mean that in Lk 22:36 Jesus predicts a mission less successful than the earlier tour in Lk 10; the new ministry will be less successful in that it will cause separation of the disciples from Jews (i.e., the "journey" motif) and hostility from them (i.e., the "sword").

B. If Jesus literally recommended having swords in 22:36, even for defensive purposes, one would expect some reflection of this viewpoint in the use of swords on the occasion of Jesus' arrest in 22:47–53. This subsequent event would seem to be the logical place for a comment on swords. One of the striking things about Luke's version of Jesus' arrest is the way he has upgraded what appears in Mark as the impetuous act of one man into a policy decision by all the apostles to wield swords. This is clearly brought out in the following synopsis of the episode.

MARK 14:47	LK 22:49–50
1. But *one* of those who stood near by	1. When *those* who were about him saw what would follow
2. _____	2. *they* said: "Lord, shall *we* strike with the sword?"
3. struck the slave of the high priest and cut off his ear.	3. And one of them struck the slave of the high priest and cut off his right ear.

Although only one of them struck with the sword (v. 50), *all of them* are implicated in their readiness to wield swords (v. 49), a readiness which seems to be attributed to them already in 22:38. Luke, then, presented the body of the apostles as ready to use actual swords in 22:38 and 49–50. But is this approved or censured?

The Lukan editorial reaction to the use of swords in 22:49–51 is relevant to this discussion. Although Mark's account of the use of swords goes without comment (Mk 14:47), the other evangelists all record some response by Jesus to the unexpected and violent attack on the arresting party. Mt 26:52 categorically condemns the use of swords: "All who take the sword, perish by the sword." Armed resistance, moreover, is not needed; for Jesus' Father would gladly supply him with "twelve legions of angels," if that were possible here (26:53). In John, Jesus commands the apostle to sheathe his sword and rebukes him with a word about obedience to God: "Shall I not drink of the cup which the Father has given me?" (18:11). In Luke, Jesus' remark is a curt and simple "No more of this!" (22:51). The negative thrust of Jesus' words is backed up by his undoing of the harm caused by the use of the sword. Only Luke records that Jesus "touched his ear and healed him" (22:51b). Jesus' words and actions are fully in accord with his advice in the Sermon on the Plain (6:22–23, 27–31).

C. It is significant that Luke records no use of swords by the apostles and missionaries in Acts. They are twice compared with violent revolutionaries (see Acts 5:34–39 and 21:38), but these comparisons are cited by Luke only to show how false they are. On the contrary, the church in

Acts is the object of violence, which was predicted by Jesus in 22:28 and now in 22:35–38. Trials, imprisonments, persecutions, and death await the apostolic mission in Acts. It seems evident, then, that "buying a sword" is a symbolic statement, referring to general times of crisis coming upon the *ecclesia pressa* of Luke-Acts.

Another interpretative detail is not fully treated by Gormley's study. To whom does the *anomoi* ("'reckoned with 'the lawless,' '' 22:37) refer? Readers of Luke-Acts might expect this to refer to the tax collectors and sinners with whom Jesus associated (see 7:39; 15:1–2; 19:7–10) or the criminals with whom he was crucified (23:39–43). But in the context of these final remarks in Jesus' farewell speech, those references seem quite remote and distant. Yet the context of Luke's remarks provides many clues: (a) the remarks are addressed to the apostles, and (b) they are the final remarks of the farewell speech. With Paul Minear,[68] I suggest that the referent of *anomoi* ("lawless") is the apostles. After all, they already have two swords on hand, an indication that they are not fully in accord with Jesus' directions.

It is not unusual in Luke-Acts to find the apostles presented in a negative light at crucial moments in the narrative. For example, Peter, the head apostle, admits in his vocation story that Jesus should leave him for he is "a sinful man" (Lk 5:8). And on the occasion of Jesus' ascension, when he gave a final commission to the apostles, they misunderstood his words about the kingdom of God (see Acts 1:3, 6). The sinfulness of the apostles and their constant misunderstanding of Jesus' words are regular themes in Luke-Acts.

Such material, moreover, is appropriate in a farewell speech, which is the formal context of 22:35–38. We pointed out in regard to 22:28 that it is characteristic of farewell speeches to contain forecasts of difficult times coming upon one's followers. And 22:35–38 seems to reflect just that sort of prediction. In regard to 22:21, 24–27, 33–34, we noted that it was likewise characteristic of farewell speeches to identify and predict the sins and even failures of one's sons and descendants. The formal context of 22:35–38 suggests that the apostles are the objects of all the remarks in those verses:

(a) commissioning (22:35–36);
(b) prediction of future crises (22:36).

The passage, therefore, reflects the formal characteristics of farewell speeches and the Lukan motif of mentioning the apostles' weakness and misunderstanding. It is the apostles who are "the lawless" with whom Jesus is reckoned; they misunderstand Jesus' final words and produce actual swords when Jesus had forecast future difficulties.

I. Acts 20:17–35

In our investigation of Lk 22:14–38, we have insisted on viewing it formally as a farewell speech. There is a second Lukan farewell speech, Acts 20:17–35, which may have some bearing on our reading of Lk 22:14–38.[69] Luke does things in twos, both within the Gospel itself and in Acts; two farewell speeches would fit into this editorial pattern. Furthermore, a main thrust in contemporary Lukan studies is the investigation of the structural and thematic relationships between the Third Gospel and Acts, one aspect of which has been a study of the parallelism between the passion of Jesus and that of Paul.[70] Building on these approaches, we ask now what relationship might exist between the farewell addresses of Jesus and Paul? What might an investigation of Acts 20:17–35 tell us about Lk 22:14–38? It is hoped that by comparison of the two Lukan farewell addresses, we might gain a firmer sense of the Lukan editorial process, which may lead to fresh interpretative clues and possibly to confirmation of many points of our previous analysis of Lk 22:14–38. Let us compare the farewell addresses in Luke and Acts in terms of their context, content, and function.[71]

1. As regards their respective *contexts,* Jesus has already journeyed to Jerusalem, the city of his passion, while Paul is still on route there (Acts 20:16). Both Jesus and Paul speak of this journey to Jerusalem as one guided by the divine will (see *dei,* Lk 9:22; 17:25; 18:31; Acts 19:21). Jesus is already a victim of Jewish plots (Lk 22:3–6), whereas such plotting awaits Paul (Acts 21:27–36; 23:12–15; 25:2–3). Both Jesus and Paul deliver their respective farewell speeches to their favorite disciples and associates. The farewell speeches of both Jesus and Paul, then, occur in the same context in the narrative of each figure. On the eve of their respective passions at the hands of the Jews, both take leave of their disciples and confirm their succession after the passing of the patriarchal leader.

2. As regards *content,* both addresses may be viewed formally as farewell speeches.[72]

A. *Prediction of Death.* Comparable to the many notices of Jesus' death in Lk 22:14–38 is the prediction of Paul:

> Behold, I am going to Jerusalem . . . not knowing what will befall me there, except that the Holy Spirit testifies to me in every city that imprisonment and afflictions await me. But I do not account my life of any value or precious to myself, if only I can accomplish my course (Acts 20:22–24).

B. *Predictions of Attacks on the Disciples.* Jesus predicted such in Lk 22:31–32, 35–38. Paul likewise foretells hard times for his disciples:

> I know that after my departure fierce wolves will come in among you, not sparing the flock; and from among your own selves will arise men speaking perverse things, to draw away the disciples after them (Acts 20:29–30).

C. *Ideal Behavior Urged.* Jesus proscribed self-important leadership and prescribed *diakonia* (Lk 22:24–27); he urged watchfulness and fidelity (22:31–32). Paul exhorts the elders at Ephesus to generous service:

> In all things I have shown you that by so toiling one must help the weak, remembering the words of the Lord Jesus, how he said, "It is more blessed to give than to receive" (Acts 20:35).

Paul urged watchfulness as well: "Be alert, remembering that for three years I did not cease night and day to admonish everyone with tears" (Acts 20:31).

D. *Succession of Leadership.* Jesus commissioned Peter as leader of his followers (22:31–32) and established the Twelve as "judges" of Israel (22:29–30). Paul confirms the Ephesian elders as his successors in that Church:

> Take heed to yourselves and to all the flock in which the Holy Spirit has made you overseers, to care for the church of God (Acts 20:28).

To this list of formal characteristics of farewell speeches we can add a fifth item, protestations of innocence. Jesus ironically declares his innocence in the citation from Is 53:12 in Lk 22:37 ("and he was reckoned with transgressors"). Luke already affirmed that innocence by his notice that Jesus' death is the result of a diabolical plot (22:21) or is according to the Scriptures (22:22). Paul openly declares his innocence throughout the farewell speech (20:18–27), but especially in his solemn testimony:

> I testify to you this day that I am innocent of the blood of all of you, for I did not shrink from declaring to you the whole counsel of God (Acts 20:26–27).

There are perhaps a number of other close links between the two farewell speeches which are verbal and thematic as well as formal.

1. Jesus' blood in Lk 22:19–20 is sacrificial, covenant blood which constitutes his followers as God's people. In Acts 20:28, Jesus' blood is again the instrument of God's obtaining a new people: "Care for the church of God which he obtained with the blood of his own Son."
2. Jesus speaks of his death as an "end" (*telos*) and of his fulfillment of the Scriptures as an "ending" (*telesthēnai*, Lk 22:37). Paul speaks of his death as the "ending" (*teleōsai*) of his course: ". . . if only I may end my course and the ministry which I received" (Acts 20:24).
3. Jesus announced that the Church's leader was to be "the servant" (*ho diakonōn*, 22:26), and that he himself was among them as "one who served" (*ho diakonōn*, 22:27). Paul speaks of his apostolic labors as "service" (*diakonia*, Acts 20:24).
4. Jesus announced that the Eleven remained faithful to him through all his "trials" (*peirasmois*, 22:28); Paul spoke of his own faithful service of the Lord through many "trials" (*peirasmōn*, Acts 20:19) from the Jews.
5. Jesus was deeply concerned with Peter's "faith" (*pistis*, 22:32) and his "turning" (*epistrephas*, 22:32b). Paul's preaching was a constant offer of repentance and "faith" (*metanoian kai pistin*, Acts 20:21).
6. Jesus looked forward to eating with the apostles in the "kingdom" of God (*basileia*, 22:16–18, 30), which "kingdom" Paul preached (*basileia*, Acts 20:25).

Both farewell speeches, then, are formally structured according to the typical conventions of such speeches. By these conventions both focus on the transition of leadership which occurs at the passing of the patriarchal leader. And so they both thematically touch upon critical topics such as ministry of service, fidelity to task, and shepherding of the flock.

3. As regards *function,* both farewell speeches are similar. In the literature on Acts 20, two basic functions are given for Paul's speech: (a) concern over orthodoxy and heresy,[73] and (b) concern over leadership, succession and office.[74] The two functions are closely related, for the proper succession of leaders serves to protect orthodoxy and to prevent heresy. I suggest, however, that Luke is more concerned with proper succession of authorized leaders in the Church than with heresy. This is based on the notice of Luke's insistence on cataloguing in Acts the rise of spokesmen, preachers, and leaders in the Church. One need only look at the frequent and dramatic raising up of such leaders in Acts to see that this is a major Lukan concern.

Leadership in Acts

1. The complement of the Twelve is filled out immediately in Acts with Matthias' election (1:15–25).
2. Deacons are picked out to assist the Twelve (6:1–6).
3. Philip the deacon evangelizes Samaria (8:5–8) and the eunuch of Candice (8:24–40).
4. Paul, the great apostle of the synagogue and the Gentiles, begins his preaching in ch. 9.
5. After James' death, another James replaces him as head of the Jerusalem Church (12:1–2, 17; 15).
6. Prophets and teachers (Barnabas, Symeon, Lucius, Manaen, and Saul) are at work in Antioch (13:1).
7. And from their midst, Barnabas and Saul are selected for a special mission (13:2–3).
8. We hear of a succession of preachers: John Mark (15:36–39), Silas (15:40), and Timothy (16:1–5).
9. Apollos converts and sets off for a mission at Corinth (18:24–19:1).
10. All through Acts we hear of prophets rising up (11:27–28; 13:1; 15:32; 21:10–11).

11. Likewise elders appear in Jerusalem alongside the apostles (11:30; 15:2–6, 22–23; 21:18), and are appointed in the new churches as Paul leaves them (14:23; 20:17, 28).

Acts reflects a seemingly uncomplicated process whereby new and varied leaders, prophets, elders, evangelists, etc., arise in an unending stream. Acts, moreover, speaks of Jesus' continual involvement, not only with the apostles' ministry, but with the leaders who come after them. Paul is personally called (9:3–6), directed in his mission in a unique way (16:9), warned (22:18, 21), and consoled when attacked (18:19; 23:11).

Furthermore, Luke knows of attacks on the Church's leaders. Acts tells of imprisonment of Peter (5:17–20; 12:3–11) and of Paul (16:24–26; 21–28). There is notice of assaults on Church leaders (12:1–2; 14:19; 16:22–23), of plots against them (9:23–25; 17:5, 13; 20:3; 21:11; 23:12–15; 25:3), and of persecution of them (8:1; 9:14). Finally Acts tells of the forensic trials of Peter (4–5), Stephen (6–7), and Paul (16:19–39; 18:12–17; 22–26). Acts, then, is concerned with the future leadership of the new Church, and with the difficult times in which this leadership will be exercised, just the points which seemed so important in Jesus' farewell speech (Lk 22:21, 28–30, 31–32, 35–36).

The function of each farewell speech, then, has to do with the clear appointment of the leaders after the death of the patriarch and with warnings of assaults on them. Whether Luke is consciously attempting to describe the origin and evolution of specific Church offices is a point beyond the scope of the present discussion.

Differences, of course, exist between Lk 22 and Acts 20. Paul is not Jesus! The Twelve are not Paul! Whereas the treachery, weakness, and sin of the apostles is recorded in Lk 22, Paul insists on his innocence (20:26, 33). Jesus himself appoints the Twelve; Paul serves only as a confirmation of the Spirit's appointment of the Ephesian elders (20:28). Nor is there any mention of a future meeting between Paul and the elders, as there is predicted for Jesus and the Twelve (Lk 22:30); on the contrary, Paul's departure is permanent (20:38). The differences are accounted for in terms of the basic narrative differences between Jesus' career in the Gospel and that of the Church in Acts. But these differences should not blind us to the genuine, extensive parallels between the two Lukan farewell speeches and their respective speakers.

In summary, the comparison of the two farewell speeches yields the following suggestions: (a) Lk 22 and Acts 20 are formally similar as farewell speeches; (b) as such they occur in the same context in their respective narratives; (c) as regards content, they both focus on the disciples addressed, confirming their leadership and predicting hard times which await them; (d) as regards function, both optimistically see the future leadership of the group secured after the departure of the leader. There is no doubt that Acts 20 is in very close relationship to Lk 22:14–38, and this fact tends to confirm the earlier discussion of Luke's redaction of Jesus' farewell speech.

RESUME

We have surveyed Luke's presentation of Jesus' farewell speech according to the perspective of redaction criticism. Comparison with other farewell speeches sensitized us to many of the characteristic features of such literary forms, and these served as fresh and enlightening clues to the structure of Luke's redaction. The following chart summarizes this material:

CHARACTERISTIC FEATURES OF FAREWELL SPEECHES:	LUKE'S FAREWELL SPEECH:
1. predictions of death:	1. Lk 22:15b, 16a, 18a, 19–20
2. predictions of the future:	2. Lk 22:16, 18
3. forecasts of future crises:	3. Lk 22:21, 31–32, 35–36
4. legacy:	4. Lk 22:19–20
5. exhortation about virtue and vice:	5. Lk 22:24–27 22:31–32, 35–36
6. succession confirmed:	6. Lk 22:28–30, 32, 35–36.

Luke's farewell speech, moreover, is held together by several recurring motifs. The context is a meal, and mention of meals and sitting at table recurs regularly throughout the speech. The focus of farewell speeches, we noted, was on the speaker's sons or descendants; such is the case here as well. And in this light, Luke continually noted the crises and even failings of the apostles with a certain regularity. The thrust of Jesus' remarks read like a table of contents for Acts of the Apostles, for it is there that Luke sees the fulfillment of Jesus' prophecies to the apostles and the realization of their commissioning.

Chapter Two

JESUS IN THE GARDEN
(LK 22:39–46)

Luke's version of the prayer of Jesus in the garden raises many questions. It is strikingly different from Mark's account, which is presumably Luke's immediate source, so different that many commentators have suggested a special source for this material. Another explanation of the Lukan distinctiveness is possible, viz., Luke's own redaction of the Markan material. And it is from this perspective that I will explore Lk 22:39–46 in this chapter.

With the advent of redaction criticism, attention is now properly being paid to all the changes, omissions and additions between Luke's passage and his source. As regards omissions from the garden scene, Luke dropped the charge to "Watch!" (Mk 14:34) and the mention of "the hour" (14:37, 41). According to Luke, Peter, James, and John are *not* separated from the rest of the disciples to share Jesus' special experience (Mk 14:33); nor does Jesus pray three times (Mk 14:39–40). The most curious omission, however, is the absence of the Markan statement about Jesus' emotions: "My soul is grieved (*perilypos*) even unto death" (Mk 14:34). This omission is highlighted by the corresponding addition by Luke that the disciples were "grieved": "He found them sleeping for grief" (*apo tēs lypēs*, Lk 22:45). The strengthening angel, the *agonia*, and the sweat-like blood are also Lukan additions to Mark's text.[1]

Our attention is attracted to one major redactional change, the omission of the mention of Jesus' emotion ("My soul is grieved unto death") and the corresponding attribution of emotion to the disciples ("asleep for grief").[2] I suspect that the omission of "grief" from Jesus is a significant thematic statement by Luke, and I propose to investigate the background of that term and other related items in the passage. Previous attempts to explain Luke's garden episode never satisfactorily accounted for his many redactional changes because it was assumed that Luke, with minor variations, was basically reproducing Mark's portrait of Jesus.[3] This is not the case. And it is my hope that a fresh inquiry into the redactional changes and the background of these materials[4] will help us to appreciate Luke's distinctive interpretation of this passage.

I.
THE BACKGROUND OF "GRIEF"

The phrase which Luke omitted from Mark ("My soul is grieved") itself resembles the cry of the psalmist in distress:

Mk 14:34   My soul is exceedingly grieved unto death.
Ps 41:6, 12   Why are you exceedingly grieved, O my soul?
   42:5

Although it should have been attractive to Luke to retain one more instance from the Scriptures foretelling that the Christ must suffer, he did not keep it.[5] Why? What is wrong with "grief"?

According to Stoic philosophy, there are four general classes of passions or emotions: grief, fear, desire, and pleasure.[6] By definition, these passions are "movements of the soul disobedient to reason,"[7] hence they are diseases or disorders of the soul. Plutarch goes so far as to say that every passion is a sin and everyone who grieves or fears or lusts commits a sin.[8]

Our concern is with "grief," which is commonly defined as "the idea of a serious present evil."[9] When "grief" takes hold of one's mind, it produces shrinking in that person,[10] a contraction in the face of pain, suffering or death. "Grief," moreover, is a genus of passions whose subspecies explain the extent of the evil inherent in it:

Heaviness or vexation is "grief," which weighs us down, annoyance which coops us up and straitens us for want of room; distress, a pain brought on by anxious thought that lasts and increases; anguish, painful grief; distraction, irrational grief, rasping and hindering us from viewing the situation as a whole.[11]

Cicero vividly described the devastating effects of "grief" (*aegritudo*) as follows: "It means decay, torture, agony, hideousness; it rends and corrodes the soul and brings it to absolute ruin."[12] And "grief" inevitably leads to another of the four infamous passions, fear, and thence to dejection, depression, and finally to a feeling of subjection and defeat.[13] On one level, therefore, it could seem highly improper that Jesus be presented as afflicted by "grief," for this would imply that he was subject to evil passions, irrational, out of control, and defeated.

In Hellenistic Jewish circles, both the LXX and Philo associate "grief" with sin and punishment. In Gen 3:16–17LXX, the punishments for the first sin include the massive burden of "grief." God said to Eve, "I will multiply your griefs" (Gen 3:16), and to Adam, "In griefs will you eat all your days" (3:17). Cain, whose sacrifice was not acceptable to God, was "deeply grieved" (Gen 4:5LXX). When God asked "Why are you deeply grieved?" (4:6), the LXX implies that Cain's offering was unacceptable because of guilt on his part, implicating "grief" as a cause.[14] In Is 1:5LXX, "grief" is seen as part of the punishment for the sinful nation: "Every head for pain, every heart from grief." Consignment to grief is part of God's sentence on sinners: "In grief you will be put to sleep" (Is 50:11LXX). On the occasion of Israel's sin of miscegenation with foreign nations, Ezra grieved for their wickedness, "I sat anxious and grieved" (8:68); "grief" again is the child of sin: "Because of my lawlessness, I sat grieved" (8:69). In 1 Mac 6, the effects of Antiochus' defeat bring numerous griefs to him which he recognizes as punishment for sacking Jerusalem and its temple. His collapse is due to "grief": "He fell into sickness because of grief" (6:8); he is then permanently immobilized by "grief": "A great grief consumed him" (6:9); and he acknowledges his crimes as he suffers the punishment of grief for his sins: "See, I am destroyed by a great grief" (6:13).

Sirach repeatedly tells the wise person to eschew "grief," for it is a destructive force, even unto death:

Sir 30:21   Do not give your soul over to grief.
      30:23   Remove grief far from you
              for grief has destroyed many.
      38:18   For death results from grief
              and grief saps strength of heart.

Biblical traditions prior to the first century, then, associate "grief" with sin, punishment, and death. It has a decidedly negative connotation.

Philo knows Hellenistic philosophy as well as Jewish scriptural traditions. On the one hand he knows that "grief" is one of the infamous four passions (*Op.* 79; *Leg. All.* ii.113; iii.250; *Det.* 110; *Conf.* 90; *Mig.* 60; *Congr.* 172; *Mut.* 72; *Abr.* 236, 238; *Jos.* 79; *Spec. Leg.* ii.30, 157; *Praem.* 71; *Quod Omn. Prob.* 18, 159; *Vit. Cont.* 2; *Decal.* 142–145). He knows that "grief" contracts and shrinks its victim (*Quis Her.* 270; *Mos.* i.139; *Quod Omn. Prob.* 159), depresses and causes loss of power (*Quis Her.* 270), even paralysis (*Virt.* 88) and speechlessness (*Jos.* 214). Philo also knows the LXX traditions that "grief" is a punishment for Eve's sin (*Op.* 167; *Leg. All.* iii.200; *Det.* 119; *Virt.* 200; *Praem.* 71). And he explicitly relates LXX comments on Adam and Eve's punishment to the Stoic doctrine on the passions.

Philo, moreover, notes that Cain's punishment includes the evil passion, "grief." Unlike the MT of Gen 4:12, which reads, "You shall be a fugitive and a wanderer on earth," the LXX reads, "You shall be groaning and trembling on the earth." When Philo describes this punishment of Cain, he cites the LXX: "He is found 'groaning and trembling' on the earth." But he interprets "groaning and trembling" to mean that as a result of his sin, Cain is subject to two of the cardinal vices, viz., grief and fear: "He (Cain) is found 'groaning and trembling' upon the earth, that is to say, a victim to grief and fear" (*Det.* 119).

The association of evil persons with vices may be a purely formal association on Philo's part (see *Det.* 140), but it may also have a linguistic basis as well. "Groaning" (*stenōn*) may be a play on "to make narrow" (*stenoō*). Now one of the chief effects of "grief" is that it causes shrinking and contraction, and thus leads to narrowness. In Diogenes Laertius, one of the species of "grief" is "trouble" which "coops us up (*stenochōrousan*) and straitens us for want of room."[15] The punishment of Cain, nevertheless, was not death but "grief" (*Praem.* 71), which is a perpetual dying, "a constant succession of griefs and fears, carrying with them full apprehension of the miseries of his most evil plight" (*Virt.* 200). Philo, then, both from Hellenistic philosophy as well as from LXX and scriptural traditions, views "grief" both as a cardinal vice and as the result and punishment for sin.

This survey of the normal use of "grief" indicates that it is (1) one of the four cardinal passions, (2) a typical form of punishment for sin, and (3) an indication of guilt. While the relationship of Luke to these traditions remains to be examined, it is clear that moral judgments would certainly be implied in descriptions of Jesus as "grieved" and of his disciples as sleeping "because of grief."

II.
JESUS' EMOTIONAL STATE IN THE GARDEN

Was Luke aware of the negative implications of "grief" and was this influential in his omission of the Markan reference that Jesus was "grieving unto death"? I suggest that this was the case. Evidence for this comes from several avenues.

First, "grief" results in shrinking and contraction. Overcome by grief, Antiochus fell into sickness (1 Mac 6:8), and, according to Mark, Jesus fell to the ground (Mk 14:35) when overcome by grief. But Luke describes Jesus as kneeling.[16] The uncontracted posture of Jesus is consistent with the mood of Jesus as *not* being subject to "grief." Luke adds another detail concerning Jesus, "rising because of prayer," which, as I will explain below, suggests that as regards posture, Jesus never shrinks or collapses.

Other Lukan redactional changes support the hypothesis that Jesus is unaffected by "grief." (1) The distraught emotional state of Jesus is dramatized in Mark by Jesus' thrice coming to the disciples for support and by his reproaching them for not "watching with him." But Luke has categorically omitted these and other hints of Jesus' distraction or grief in the garden. (2) In Mark, moreover, Jesus' prayer complicatedly consists of: (a) two indirect-discourse petitions that the "hour" and the "cup" be removed from him (Mk 14:35–36), and (b) a report about the Father's will (14:36). Luke compressed the prayer by omitting the first petition about the "hour" passing. And he firmed up the focus of the second petition by a small but significant change:

Mk 14:36   Father, *all things are possible to you* . . .
                 not as I will, but as you will
Lk 22:42   Father, *if you will* . . .
                 not my will but thine be done.

Greater attention is given in the Lukan version to God's will.[17] (3) Jesus' triple prayer in Mark is consolidated into one prayer in Luke. The drift of these redactional changes indicates that Luke omitted Markan details which might suggest Jesus as distraught or lacking in moral control.

Positively, there are indications in Luke which suggest that Jesus exemplifies the cardinal virtue of "courage" (*andreia*), which is the antithesis of the passion "grief."[18] The substance of "courage" lies in the correct perception of what is to be endured or faced with fortitude.[19] In accord with tradition, for example, Philo defined "courage" as "the knowledge of things that we ought to endure and not endure, and of things that fall under neither head" (*Leg. All.* i.68). And it is precisely this aspect of obedience ("what must be endured") that stands out in the literature on this virtue.[20] Cicero called courage "obedience to the highest law."[21]

By reducing the triple Markan prayer into one prayer, Luke gives the impression that Jesus quickly knew what was to be endured and what was the will of God to which he would be obedient. And Jesus is not distracted from this in Luke, as he was in the Markan report that he repeatedly went to Peter and others for support ("Could you not watch one hour with me?" 14:37, 40).

Mark's presentation of Jesus' "grief," his seeking for support, and his need to pray three times is edited in Luke to present Jesus' greater courage and obedience, and his arrival at this virtuous state much sooner than the Markan text suggests.

The Lukan redaction of Mk 14:36 may likewise have some bearing on this topic. Cicero says that it belongs to the wise man to have *voluntatem* (*boulēsis*), which is defined as a correct rational longing (irrational passion is a vice).[22] When Luke changes Mark's "if you are able" to "if you will (*boulei*)," he focuses on God's will and Jesus' obedience. And by changing Mark's "not what I will but what you will" to "not my will (*thelēma*) but thine be done,"[23] Luke makes God's will the center of Jesus' prayer. Like the wise man, Jesus actively seeks the correct *voluntatem*, the will of God concerning what he must endure and to which he will be obedient.

Although the term "courage" does not occur in Luke's text, Jesus is shown to be dramatizing the practice of that virtue and would have been perceived as such, a suggestion which gains plausibility when it is linked with Luke's omission of "grief" from Jesus.

III.
THE AUTHENTICITY OF LK 22:43–44

The issue of the authenticity of Lk 22:43–44 is of central importance for the rest of this chapter. A recent article, which has comprehensively surveyed the evidence and the debate on this text, can serve as a point of departure.[24] Following traditional text-critical procedure, Ehrman and Plunkett suggest arguments for and against the authenticity of Lk 22:43–44:

1. *External Evidence*. Lk 22:43–44 is either an interpolation into Luke's text or an omission from it. The tradition of the assisting angel and the sweat like blood is known in the second century by Justin[25] and Irenaeus.[26] If Lk 22:43–44 is an interpolation, it was added to the text before 160, when Justin used it; if an omission, it was deleted from the text at the beginning of the third century. The ambiguity of this situation invites conjectural arguments based on a sense of probability.

2. *Reasons for Interpolation or Omission*. This issue is ancient, for as early as Epiphanius, the text was seen as a potent argument used by Irenaeus against the gnostics. Other ancients were said to omit the text "out of fear," because they did not understand it.[27] If an interpolation, Lk 22:43–44 would tend to emphasize Jesus' humanity against its detractors. On the other side, modern commentators allege three reasons why it might have been omitted for dogmatic reasons:

> (1) Jesus' being strengthened could imply his subordination to the angel; (2) Jesus' being in agony and sweating great drops like blood could sound Arian; (3) Jesus' agony over his approaching fate could discredit the view that he laid down his life freely and willingly.[28]

3. *Internal Evidence*. Arguments arise from a study of the vocabulary and themes in the passage, whether they are characteristically Lukan or not. The argumentation of Ehrman and Plunkett's article is more important than their conclusions, for on many points I think that they have omitted or misconstrued key Lukan evidence.

As regards external evidence, the text is known and used in the second century; its absence is documented to the beginning of the third century. Although this is itself a datum which needs to be evaluated, it suggests a certain presumption in favor of authenticity. Our earliest sources attest to its authenticity.

As regards reasons for a possible interpolation or omission, Ehrman and Plunkett indicate a certain bias when they suggest that the controlling question for them is "There is really only one pressing question to be answered: 'Which reading is more readily explained as originating in the theological climate of the second century?' "[29] The issue of its appositeness in the first century is somehow excluded, as they adopt a hermeneutic of suspicion. They point out how important for second-century apologists was the issue of Jesus' humanity, as though that were the substance of the verses—a point with which this chapter would take issue. As far as their "argument from plausibility" goes in regard to the second century, it is not illogical or unhelpful. But it begs the question of the meaning and utility of Lk 22:43–44 for Luke and the first century.

As regards Lukan vocabulary in the passage, Ehrman and Plunkett have underplayed the extent of Lukan vocabulary and themes. For example, the simile comparing Jesus' sweat with drops of blood should be seen alongside other vivid similes in Luke-Acts, a point which will be noted shortly. Ehrman and Plunkett reject the Lukan flavor of "more earnestly" (v. 44) because it is common in LXX; yet contemporary studies of Luke-Acts underscore Luke's use and imitation of septuagintal style. They find difficulty with a "silent angel," ignoring that Luke's possible source (Mk 1:13) does not record angelic speech to Jesus either (see also Lk 4:10–11). Arguments about what is Lukan and what is not Lukan can be very difficult to establish; and so it is regrettable to find Ehrman and Plunkett making so strong a case against Lukan authorship or ignoring evident data.

Ehrman and Plunkett claim that "there is no compelling reason to think that Luke needed to make an addition to his Mount of Olives scene to accomplish his redactional purpose."[30] This is an inadequate and unfortunate claim, for their article is hardly a thorough redactional study of the passage. Too many important critical issues are simply ignored here. No mention is made of Lk 4:13 which predicts a return of Satan for further attacks on Jesus. Yet according to redaction-critical perspectives, Luke made a most serious redactional change in 4:13 that permits and even requires a fulfillment of that remark. It is not enough to assert—which they do not even do—that Satan's return occurs in the assaults on Judas

(22:3) and Peter (22:31), for Luke said that Satan would return to attack Jesus, not his disciples. As this chapter will argue in a moment, the continuation of *peirasmos* of 4:13 is found in Jesus' *agonia* in 22:43–44.

Nor did Ehrman and Plunkett suggest what the thematic structure of the Gethsemane scene is for Luke. In Chapter Six I will go into great detail to show that Luke has a definite model of soteriology operative in the passion narrative which sees an Adam-Jesus comparison. In that perspective, Lk 22:43–44 is the plausible and necessary complement to Lk 4:1–13.

Ehrman and Plunkett concede that Luke's redaction of the Gethsemane scene is done with a view to the presentation of Jesus as "emotionally restrained." In this regard they are following my earlier article,[31] but they are uncritically picking only the surface elements of that study and ignoring the explanations why Jesus is presented as "emotionally restrained." As we have seen in this chapter, the reason for this redactional focus of Luke is his presentation of Jesus as virtuous, victorious, and obedient. Lk 22:43–44 do not clash with this perspective at all, but indicate how Jesus strives as a virtuous person to maintain his virtue even when it is under attack. On the contrary, 22:43–44 *confirm* Jesus as one not subject to passion. For the issue is not our modern "emotions," but the ancient view of "passions."

In summary, their arguments and my own are in many ways fragile and subjective. But for the following reasons, I consider Lk 22:43–44 to be part of Luke's original text. The external evidence, while not entirely probative, is persuasive for me: the tradition of the strengthening angel and the sweat like blood was known to exist *before* it disappeared. From my redactional study of Lk 22:39–46, I judge vv. 43–44 to be very much in accord with Lukan vocabulary and motifs. In assessing Luke's large redactional purpose, 22:43–44 is demanded as the completion of the remark in 4:13. The meaning of 22:43–44 does not lie in an abstract affirmation of Jesus' humanity, especially in an apology to gnostics or docetists; rather, the redactional meaning is found in Luke's soteriology where Jesus is presented as a second Adam. Since the issue cannot be settled on the basis of external witnesses to the text, more play is given to questions of Lukan style, vocabulary, and themes. If this is the best evidence, then I would unquestionably argue for the Lukan authorship of Lk 22:43–44.

IV.
Agonia as Victorious Struggle

Beyond Luke's tidying of the confused Markan portrait of Jesus at prayer, there are further redactional suggestions in the text that Jesus is presented positively combatting "grief" and other assailants. The text continues with the note "being in an agony (*agonia*)." *Agonia* can be interpreted in two radically different ways: (1) an experience of debilitating fear or (2) victorious combat.[32] The lexicons cite "contest, struggle for victory" as the primary meaning, but also list "anguish, agony of mind" as a secondary, derivative meaning.[33] In certain strands of Hellenistic philosophy, *agonia* is one of the subspecies of "fear," itself one of the cardinal passions.[34] In this regard Philo cites it as the vanguard of "fear" (*Decal.* 145).

The meaning of *agonia* which best seems to suit the context in Luke is that which suggests "contest, struggle, gymnastic exercise."[35] The proof of this is twofold; it is improbable that Luke, who omits "grief" from Jesus, would attribute *agonia* (as "fear") to him. Positively, the context of the episode suggests a "victorious struggle." But let us examine the background of the term *agonia* in Philo, where he relates it to the struggle against the vice "grief."

A. Agonia *as Philosophical Combat in Philo*

Philo understands *agonia* as a combat waged by the rational mind against "grief." As we noted earlier, Philo portrays "grief" as the prime enemy of the mind, destroying its strength and power, paralyzing its victim, and finally enslaving it (*Quis Her.* 270; *Virt.* 88). The antidote to the onslaughts of "grief" is to act aggressively as an athlete and wrestle with that passion. Apropos of Gen 3:16, where Eve is punished with increasing "grief," Philo discourses on the contrast between the excellent mind and the foolish mind. The foolish mind is assaulted by the senses, especially by the attacks of "grief." It submits to "griefs" as intolerable mistresses and is powerless to look them in the face (*Leg. All.* iii.200–202). But the man of knowledge is like an athlete "who opposes and withstands and shakes off the blows of grief that are falling on him" (*Leg. All.* iii.201). "Stepping out like an athlete," he meets all grievous things with strength and robust vigor; he counterattacks and so is not wounded by "grief" (*Leg. All.* iii.202).

Again in the case of Abraham on the occasion of Sarah's death, "when grief was stripped and dusted already against his soul," Abraham "as an athlete aggressively rushed upon it." Abraham strengthened the antagonist of passions, his reason, and so prevailed over "grief" in the arena of the soul (*Abr.* 256).

And in a more philosophical vein, Philo describes the truly free person as the one "who has never fallen under the yoke of desire, fear, pleasure, or grief" (*Quod Omn. Prob.* 18). The evil, unfree person is encumbered by passion and has no independent action. In contrast, the good and free person acts independently; he "stands high and is triumphant over desire, fear, cowardice, and grief as an athlete in a contest (*en agoniai*) over those who have been thrown in wrestling" (*Quod. Omn. Prob.* 21). It is clear that for Philo, the virtuous, wise, and free person struggles like an athlete in a combat with the onslaughts of "grief"; acting aggressively and in strength, he prevails over the enslaving, irrational passion of "grief." The antidote to "grief" clearly is the combative exercise of virtue, *agonia*.[36]

B. Agonia *as Combat in Luke*

The text of Luke does not simply mirror the Philonic pattern of reason combatting "grief," for Luke's language and his historical perspective are different from Philo's philosophical allegory. Luke's understanding of *agonia* is in the context of a combat (*peirasmos*); and the combat is as much against Evil as it is against "grief."

Unlike Mark's version, the episode in Luke is framed with Jesus' advice to the disciples: "Pray that you may not enter into temptation" (22:40, 46). While it forms an *inclusio* around the episode, it is not simply a formal decoration, for the text of the passion account indicates that Judas (22:3), Simon, and the other apostles (22:31) are all targeted for combat with Satan, that is, *peirasmos*. Formally, Luke stresses that prayer to escape temptation is Jesus' constant advice to his followers all through the Gospel. In the context of learning to pray, Jesus tells the disciples to escape coming temptation (11:4). And in the eschatological discourse in 21:34–36, Jesus tells the disciples to be sleepless and to pray to escape the coming things (21:36). In the same vein, Jesus now tells the apostles in 22:40, 46 to pray that they not enter into temptation. Despite Jesus' repeated advice to them, the Gospel suggests that combat and temptation will indeed come upon them (see 22:3, 31). In 22:28, Luke goes so far as to say that Jesus himself will endure further "trials" along with his disciples: "You are those who have continued with me n my trials" (*peirasmois*). Luke, then, clearly indicates that Jesus and the disciples will experience combat or trials during the passion.

Jesus' prayer in the garden contains a petition, "Remove this cup from me" (22:42). This petition is formally similar to the advice given to the disciples in 22:40 and 46, for Jesus' prayer *not* to be presented with the "cup"[37] is analogous to their prayer *not* to enter into temptation. Both Jesus and the apostles pray to escape from something.

But Jesus' second prayer is different, for it is not a request to escape anything but to be faithful to God's will. As the story unfolds, Jesus will *not*, in fact, have "the cup removed" nor will he avoid "my temptations" (22:28). He will obediently and faithfully undergo an experience which at first glance he prayed to escape. To pray that second prayer ("Thy will be done") is to pray something quite opposite to the first prayer, for it presupposes that the "will of God" may *not* want to remove the cup or prevent the temptations, which is, in fact, the case with Jesus' passion and death. By virtue of Jesus' second prayer, Luke sees him as not escaping the "cup" but beginning to experience what the "cup" symbolizes. The text continues with the note in 22:44, "being in an *agonia*." I suggest that "being in an *agonia*" is for Jesus what "enter into temptation" is for the disciples. Jesus' *agonia* is a combat.

New light is shed on Jesus' *agonia*-as-combat when the use of this language is compared with the Lukan treatment of Jesus' earlier combat (*peirasmos*) in 4:1–13. That episode, clearly described as a "combat" (*peirasmos*," 4:2, 13), was a contest between Satan and Jesus. If the note in 4:13 is of any importance, the opponent who battled with Jesus in the earlier "combat" threatened to return to continue the assault,[38] which I am suggesting is none other than the *agonia* of 22:44.

At this point I urge the reader to consult the fuller treatment of the relationship of 4:1–13 and 22:39–46 in Chapter Six of this book. For the sake of the present argument, I will summarize the drift of that discussion, for it has considerable bearing on the way Lk 22:43–44 are interpreted. The relationship of 4:1–13 and 22:39–46 rests on an appreciation of

Luke's presentation of Jesus as the new Adam. As the "son of Adam, Son of God," Jesus is tempted by the devil in the wilderness (4:1–13), and the assaults on this new Adam resemble the temptations of the first Adam in Gen 1–3.

1. Adam and Eve were forbidden certain foods (Gen 2:15–17; 3:1–5); but when tempted, they ate, sinned and died. The new Adam, when tempted to eat (4:3), prized obedience to God over food, and so remained the true and faithful Son of God (4:4) by *not* eating.
2. The first Adam was given dominion and rule over the whole world (Gen 1:26–28). Despite this, he was tempted to act aggressively "to be like God" (Gen 3:5). The new Adam did *not* seek personal power or kingdom but remained faithful to God as Lord of all (4:8).
3. Adam and Eve were told by the tempter "you shall not die" (Gen 3:4) if they took a bold risk in eating the forbidden fruit (cf. "The day you eat it, you shall die," Gen 2:17). The new Adam was invited to spurn death by leaping from the temple, but refused to "tempt God" (4:12).

The true Son of God, therefore, did not disobey God nor was he led away from grace. Rather, he was shown to be supremely obedient to God as well as victorious over the tempter. Functionally, 4:1–13 confirms Jesus' identity as "son of Adam, Son of God" by his obedience; and his success in the temptation indicates that the subsequent public ministry is to be seen in the light of that victory.

At the end of the first combat/temptation, Satan "departed from him until an opportune time" (4:13). Inasmuch as this notice of Satan's return at an "opportune time" is not found in Luke's sources, it is judged to be a Lukan redactional addition to the passage. At the beginning of Jesus' passion, Luke signals that the "opportune time" has come; according to 22:3 and 31, Satan's temptations resume with his attacks on Judas, Peter and the apostles. Yet these are not attacks on Jesus, but on his disciples. Jesus' *agonia* in the orchard, rather, should be seen as the "opportune time" when Satan resumes his combat against the Son of God.

Many of the key elements of the first temptation are repeated in the garden scene:

1. Jesus calls God "Father," which suggests that Jesus relates to him as "Son," just the relationship which was threatened in the first temptation.[39]

2. Jesus' obedience to the will of God is clearly the focus of his garden experience, just as obedience and fidelity to God were the qualities of the "Son of God" which were central in the first temptation.

3. Since, as we noted earlier, the punishment for the first sin of the old Adam was "grief," Luke omitted this because he did not want to suggest that Jesus was unfaithful or disobedient like the old Adam— on the contrary.

4. What is new is the sense that, whereas the old Adam died as the punishment for sin and disobedience, the death of the new Adam must ironically be understood as the result of his fidelity and obedience to God. The passion of Jesus, then, is not the result of failure to pray or faithlessness or disobedience. The will of God remains the paramount concern of the new Adam in the garden, as well as in the temptations in the desert. His death, therefore, must have a special meaning.

5. As the first victory over temptation enlightened the rest of Jesus' public ministry, so the implicit victory of the new Adam in the garden casts light on Jesus' passion and death, explaining how Jesus can later tell a repentant sinner that he will share "paradise" with the new Adam when his victory is revealed (23:43). The new Adam clearly did not lose paradise because of sin, nor did he die because of sinfulness.

This line of thinking may clarify several points of Luke's narrative. The *agonia* in the garden is to be understood as a combat. Philo's text suggests a combat against "grief," but Luke's own redactional perspective suggests a link between the first and second temptations of Jesus (4:1–13; 22:39–46), a combat nevertheless. And the terminology of conflict (*agonia*) and temptation (*peirasmos*) further suggests that there is nothing less than an eschatological struggle taking place in the orchard. For, as in Adam all sin and die, so in the Son of God all are faithful and live. The combat, moreover, is victorious, for "paradise" is not lost again (23:43), nor is Jesus in any way subject to passion, sin, or guilt. How inappropriate it would be to attribute "grief" to Jesus at this point, for it would suggest his likeness to the old Adam and imply sinfulness and the burden of punishing "grief."

V.
THE VIVID DETAILS IN LK 22:43–44

The details in 22:43–44 have considerable bearing on the interpretation of Jesus' *agonia*-as-combat. First, Luke's addition of an "angel from heaven" (22:43) probably comes from the Lukan redaction of the earlier scene of the temptation in the desert. Mark 1:13 notes that after that first combat, "angels ministered to him." Luke omitted this detail in his version, but apparently held in reserve this helping angel for the second temptation of Jesus. In Lk 4:10–11, moreover, Ps 91:11 was quoted as indicating that as a man Jesus has guardian angels: "He has given his angels charge of you, to guard you." Mt 26:53 indicates that such angelic assistance was possible even in the passion, but he understood the presence of angels in terms of preventing Jesus' capture, whereas Luke's text precludes this notion and focuses on the angel "strengthening" Jesus, presumably for his contest and not to prevent his capture. While it belongs to angels to fight Satan and evil spirits, in Luke, Jesus is the primary combatant; the angel is there to strengthen him. In keeping with the Adam imagery, whereas angels barred the sinful Adam from paradise (Gen 3:24), the second Adam is in harmony with the angels, indeed guarded by them. The angel, while it is not strictly an "answer" to Jesus' prayer[40] because he had not asked for an angel, is a gesture from the heavenly Father confirming that Jesus is his true "Son," that he is not disobedient or unfaithful, and that God stands beside Jesus in his passion and death. The angel is not a "second" for Jesus in his athletic contest.[41]

Mark stated that "the flesh is weak" and that the sleeping Peter was not able (*ouk ischusas*) to watch, both of which items Luke omits. Luke alternately insists that Jesus certainly was able and strong, for an angel "strengthened"[42] him. Sirach 38:18 notes the deleterious effect which "grief" has on one's strength: "Grief of heart saps one's strength." And in many places, Philo echoes this by indicating how people become weak and powerless under the onslaughts of "grief." For example, he typically states that "grief laid them prostrate through their powerlessness to find any remedy" (*Flac.* 188; cf. *Her.* 279; *Virt.* 88). Part of the reason for the description of the angel precisely as "strengthening" Jesus may lie in Luke's desire to portray Jesus as *not* under the influence of "grief" by showing him in strength, which "grief" characteristically destroys.

The next detail, ". . . and his sweat became as . . . ," dramatizes in Luke's graphic style the reality of the combat. It is often stated that this struggle is imagined as an athletic contest.[43] The sweat is that of an athlete in the arena. There is evidence in Philo of a sweat which accompanies the struggle for virtue (*Leg. All.* iii.251; *Ebr.* 150; *Sp. Leg.* ii.91). In 2 Mac 2:26, a military combat in defense of God's law is accompanied by much sweating. Furthermore, in 4 Mac 7:8, the observant Jew, Eleazar, symbolizes reason steering over the sea of passions (7:1) and reason conquering those passions (6:32–34). He was praised for defending God's law "with his own blood and honorable sweat" unto death. Jewish religion and Hellenistic philosophy both present a vivid image of the struggle to be virtuous and faithful.

The Lukan text adds a note about Jesus' sweat: "His sweat became like great drops of blood falling to the ground." Luke liberally uses similes throughout his work, usually in contexts which make concrete the number of persons or the length of time in an episode. But he also uses similes in metaphorical contexts (Lk 24:11; Acts 2:3; 6:15). Vivid similes, moreover, are part of Luke's style: Satan falls *like lightning* (Lk 10:18); the Pharisees are *like hidden graves* (Lk 11:44); Simon is to be sifted *like wheat* (Lk 22:31); something *like scales* fell from Paul's eyes (Acts 9:18); and something *like a great sheet* descended from heaven to Peter (Acts 10:11; 11:5). Luke, furthermore, tends to be very physical in his descriptions of numinous or wonderful events: at the baptism, the Spirit descends physically "as a dove" (3:22).[44] At Pentecost the Spirit's coming is audibly described "like the rush of a mighty wind" (Acts 2:2); and the Spirit's descent is physically depicted "like tongues of fire" (2:3). Whatever the medical merits of an actual sweat like blood,[45] such a vivid physical description, especially of an important or numinous event, is characteristic of Lukan narrative style.

What is added by comparing Jesus' sweat with "blood falling to the ground"? Luke knows of Abel's blood which called to God (11:51); the blood of prophets, moreover, is not forgotten by God (11:47–51). God, then, is privy to the struggles and deaths of his innocent ones and prophets. But the proper context for interpreting this simile of "sweat like great drops of blood" seems to be the combat situation described above. Blood suggests the gravity of the *agonia,* the intensity of the struggle, and the importance of the event: it is an eschatological combat whose outcome will effect salvation history. So, it seems appropriate to recall at this point

4 Mac 7:8; for the virtuous man defends God's law with "honorable sweat and blood." Or, as Heb 12:4 suggested, "In your struggles against sin you have not yet resisted to the point of shedding your blood." The comparison of sweat which is like blood may also be functional apropos of the Adam imagery which I find in the background of the Lukan narrative. Adam's sweat was a punishment for sin (Gen 3:19); but the sweat of the new Adam is entirely removed from sin, for it belongs to his struggle to avoid disobedience to God and to resist Satan. It belongs to the victory of the new Adam, not to his defeat.

VI.
THE NON-COMBATANTS IN LK 22:45–46

In 22:45, Luke radically edited the Markan text. Instead of Mark's simple remark about Jesus ("And he came and found," 14:37), Luke stated: "And when he arose from prayer, he came . . ." (22:45). The addition of "he arose from prayer" is paralleled by a second editorial change in 22:46 where, instead of Mark's "Watch and pray" (14:38), Luke records Jesus saying "Arise and pray." In this context "arise" does not seem to mean "*stand up* and pray"; the sense lies rather in the direction of moral stance.

According to Luke's redaction, Jesus found the apostles in a deplorable state, "sleeping for grief." This substitutes in Luke's account for a complex of compromising details in Mark's narrative:

Simon, are you asleep?
Could you not watch one hour?
Watch . . .
The Spirit is willing, but the flesh is weak (14:37–39).

"Grief" is Luke's one term for summarizing Mark's longer notice of the apostles' lack of strength ("are you not able . . .?" 14:37) and their weakness ("the flesh is weak," 14:39). This weakness, moreover, contrasts them with Jesus, who is not subject to "grief" but is strong (see "strengthening him," Lk 22:43) and who struggles against "grief" as well as other opponents. We noted earlier how "grief" is defined as fear of imminent conflict—either pain or death. It causes loss of strength and paralysis; it results in shrinking or contracting. The person subject to this passion is a conquered victim. Now in Luke the disciples were warned of impending conflicts (notably 22:40, but also recall 22:22, 28, 31). And Luke's text suggests that in the face of their impending conflict, they were indeed overcome by grief and fear; they became weak, shrank to the ground, and contracted themselves in sleep. Luke presented them as victims of the passion of "grief."

The Lukan change in 22:45 seems slight but is charged with importance. Mark noted that Jesus found the disciples asleep (14:34) because the flesh was weak; again in 14:40 they are asleep because their eyes were heavy; and again in 14:41 they were found asleep a third time. But Luke changed both the word for sleep (not *katheuō*, but *koimaō*) as well as the reason for it (not weak flesh or heavy eyes, but "because of grief"). We have suggested reasons for the insertion of "grief," but what about the new term for sleep (*koimōmenous*)? In Jewish traditions, "not to sleep" is a sign of a faithful servant. Jesus himself prays all night long (6:12) and other holy people do likewise (see Lk 2:37; 18:7; 21:36). The new term for "sleep" (*koimaō*) would seem to be a capricious change except for an example such as Is 50:11LXX where the ones who did not obey the voice of God's servant and did not trust in the name of the Lord were punished with "grief-filled sleep."

> Is 50:11   You shall sleep in grief.
> Lk 22:45   They were asleep for grief.

Luke's text does not suggest that the disciples were punished by trouble-filled sleep; rather, they went to sleep as victims of "grief." But the LXX stands as a suggestive explanation of the Lukan redaction here.

Jesus, on the other hand, tells them: "Arise and pray." The force of "arise" is to be understood in tension with the contrasting effect of "grief." The apostles are told to leave their shrunken state of grief and to struggle against the impending crises by praying, just as Jesus had. To this point, Philo notes that the person who struggles against the passion of grief "stands" defiant and triumphant over a foe as one who threw an opponent in a wrestling contest (*Quod Omn. Prob.* 21). "Arise and pray," therefore, belongs more to moral posture than to physical position.

But concerning Jesus, Luke's text also states: "And when he arose from prayer . . ." (22:45). Does this imply that he was overpowered by "grief" and so was contracted? The critical phrase, *"from prayer,"* may be translated in several ways: (1) it could mean that Jesus finished praying and rose *from (ek)* prayer; (2) but it could also mean *because (hypo, para)* of prayer,[46] implying that Jesus was buoyed *by* prayer. He stands uncontracted *because* of prayer. This is certainly possible when we note how Luke contrasts Jesus with the apostles: they were "sleeping *for* grief," in which context "for" *(apo)* must mean "because of":

Jesus:	"arising	because of *(apo)* prayer"
Apostles:	"sleeping	because of *(apo)* grief"
[1 Mac 6:8	"he fell	because *(apo)* grief."]

Jesus' word in 22:46, then, is intended to free the apostles from the contracting effect of "grief" and to set them to combat the impending crisis.

In Mark, Jesus ultimately tells his disciples: "Sleep on and take your rest. It is enough" (14:41), a remark which Luke entirely suppressed. For in Luke's account, the apostles' sleep is the result of their succumbing to "grief" and Jesus would not have them continue in that state.

CONCLUSION

I return to the starting point of this investigation. My hypothesis concerning the background of "grief" offers a plausible explanation for Luke's omission of this from Jesus. As regards Jesus,

1. He is not said to be "grieving unto death."
2. Nor is he contracted by "grief"; on the contrary, he kneels upright in prayer and is "raised by that prayer."
3. Jesus suffers no diminution of strength because of this passion; rather he is "strengthened" from heaven.
4. He practices "courage," the antithesis of "grief," as he seeks to know the correct will of God, i.e., what is to be endured.
5. He combats "grief" as an athlete or warrior in a successful *agonia*.

Jesus, therefore, is not a victim, out of control, subject to irrational passion. On the contrary, he is portrayed as practicing virtue, singlehandedly searching for God's will and being fully obedient to God.

As regards the apostles, however:

1. They are clearly victims of "grief."
2. They are put to sleep by it.
3. As a result of this, they disobey Jesus' repeated command to "pray that you not enter into temptation."
4. As non-combatants in the struggle against "grief," they contract themselves in grief-filled sleep.

Unlike Jesus, they are mastered by passion, and made weak by it. And because of their disobedience to the correct will of Christ, they are guilty and unfaithful.

This plethora of details about "grief" presupposes knowledge of the LXX and of popular Hellenistic philosophy, much on the order of Philo's knowledge of the two. But the LXX is surely Luke's Bible and a ready source of salvation history. And popular philosophical attitudes about the infamous four passions are just that, popular traditions, found extensively even in Hellenistic Jewish literature (see 4 Mac).

This investigation sheds light on the authenticity of 22:43–44, for these verses are shown to be apposite of Luke's presentation, even required by his scenario. The temptation broken off earlier (4:13) is resumed in the passion narrative, especially in the combat in the garden (see *agonia,* 22:44). The sweat which is like blood is typical of Luke's use of vivid similes. And these verses function as the dramatization of Jesus' great eschatological victory as the true Adam, Son of God.

Chapter Three

THE TRIALS OF JESUS
IN LUKE-ACTS

I.
JESUS' TRIALS IN THE PASSION NARRATIVE

After the account of Jesus' arrest, Luke narrates a series of trials, four to be exact: (a) before the Sanhedrin, (b) before Pilate, (c) before Herod, and (d) before the assembled Jewish crowds. These forensic trials all portray a formal legal process which aims at clarifying the charges against Jesus. As trials, they all contain solemn testimony uttered in the most serious of forums, and they express the national will in regard to God's prophet, Jesus. The four trials, then, deserve to be considered as a unity, "The Trial of Jesus."[1] The bearing they have on Luke's presentation of Jesus' passion can only be discussed after the four scenes are individually examined. After that, we shall turn to Jesus' prediction of the Church's trials in Luke 12 and 21 and then to the fulfillment of that prediction in the trials of Peter (Acts 4–5), Stephen (Acts 6–7), and Paul (Acts 21–26).

A. Lk 22:63–65

In terms of content, context, and function, Luke's account of the maltreatment of Jesus differs from that found in his Markan source. As regards context, the Lukan version of the maltreatment takes place before the Sanhedrin trial, and not after it as in Mk 14:65. Luke presents a scene of gross legal impropriety,[2] comparable to the scene in Acts where Paul is unjustly struck before his trial began (Acts 23:2). As regards content,

Luke's version differs considerably from Mark's account, as the following synopsis shows.

MK 14:65	LK 22:63–65
1. And some began to spit on him	1. Now the men who were holding Jesus mocked him and beat him.
2. and to cover his face and to strike him, saying: "Prophesy!"	2. They also blindfolded him and asked him, "Prophesy! Who is it that struck you."
3. And the guards received him with blows.	3. And they spoke many other words against him, reviling him.

Interpreting this synopsis, we find that, whereas Mark stressed physical spitting and striking, Luke sees the horror of the scene in the mockery: "They mocked him . . . asking him and saying 'Who struck you?' . . . and they spoke many other words against him, reviling him."[3] The significance of Luke's new emphasis may be explained in terms of two themes running through the story. (1) Jesus predicted in 18:32 that the Son of Man would be "mocked," a prophecy fulfilled in 22:62 and 23:11, 36.[4] (2) More importantly, Luke insists at this point in the passion narrative that Jesus is a "prophet." In Mark, Jesus was called a prophet because of his miraculous powers (Mk 6:14–15; 8:28). Luke, however, acclaims Jesus as prophet throughout the Gospel, a title which has far richer meaning than it did in Mark's account. Jesus' inaugural appearance at the Nazareth synagogue contains three key elements of what "prophet" means for Luke: (a) prophets are rejected in their homeland (4:24); (b) prophets minister to Gentiles, as Elisha and Elijah did (4:25–27); (c) prophets are killed by those to whom they are sent (4:28–29).[5] The rejection and maltreatment of prophets, which is heralded at the beginning of the Gospel, is repeated at the end of the story in the account of Jesus' maltreatment in 22:63–65.

As regards function, Luke's account presents Israel's rejection of God's prophet, a central Lukan theme found again and again in the Gospel (Lk 6:22–23; 11:47–51; 13:33–34; 20:10–15) and in Acts (Acts 7:51–53). The presentation of this theme before the beginning of Jesus' trial suggests that Israel will not listen to him, no matter what testimony he might give. Such is the fate of Israel's prophets.

B. Lk 22:66–71

The Lukan account of the Sanhedrin trial of Jesus differs from Mark's in content and function. First, in Luke's version the judicial body assembled to try Jesus is significantly fuller and more representative than in Mark's account. Luke notes that "the *presbyterion* of the people, both chief priests and scribes" gathered and "led Jesus to their council" (22:66). Luke emphasizes that the broadest possible official representation of Israel was present. The purpose for this lies in Luke's view of Israel once more rejecting the prophets whom God sent to it. Comparable to this is Luke's note in 23:13–15 that Jesus is tried once more in front of "the chief priests, rulers and the people."

Second, unlike the Markan account, the procedure in Luke's narrative is legal. The assembly is not meeting at night (see Mk 15:1), nor is the hearing in the private chambers of the high priest (see Mk 14:54); no false witnesses are suborned (Mk 14:57–59). This is not to say that Luke ignores the assassination of character of the Jewish plot; he has already emphasized how spies were sent to catch Jesus' controversial words (20:20) and how Judas agreed to act as a paid traitor (22:4–6). The whole plot is exposed and condemned by the evangelist, but that is not the point here. It serves Luke's purpose to describe a solemn, valid, and formal trial of Jesus by Israel.

Third, Luke omits many items from Mark's version. There are no false witnesses testifying against him, no temple charges, or other accusations made against him (see Mark 14:55–60). Luke has streamlined the narrative to focus on Jesus' testimony before the solemn assembly of Israel. How often, however, we find commentators comparing Jesus' behavior during this trial to that of the Suffering Servant of Isaiah. This comparison is tied to Jesus' alleged silence before his accusers (Mk 14:60–61; 15:4–5). But Luke's version omits all mention of silence and stresses that Jesus bears solemn testimony to this court. Unlike Mk 14:60, it is not just the chief priest who asks Jesus but the whole assembly: "And they said, 'If you are the Christ . . . '" (22:67). Far from being silent, Jesus bears formal testimony to Israel assembled before him.[6]

Fourth, in Mark, only one question concerning Jesus' identity was asked of him, "Are you the Christ, the Son of the Blessed?" (14:61). Luke, however, intensifies the importance of this questioning by recording two such questions asked:

22:67 "If you are the Christ, tell us."

22:70 "So you are the Son of God?"

Whether these titles are synonymous or complementary,[7] Luke has called attention here to the foundational confession of Jesus by his Church. And these important confessional titles are supplemented by a third, the Son of Man (22:69).[8] A comprehensive discussion of the identity of Jesus is presented to the assembled court of Israel.

The importance of Jesus' remarks to the assembly lies in their character as the solemn testimony (*martyrion*) of Luke's Church. This becomes clear when we situate this material in terms of Luke's narrative.

1. In his prediction of the Church's troubled future, Jesus prophesied that his followers would be brought before Jewish and Roman tribunals for trials and hearings. These events would be formal occasions for testimony to the Gospel about Jesus (*eis martyrion,* Lk 21:13).
2. Jesus' own testimony in his trial before the assembly of Israel serves as a model for the testimony of the Church.
3. And Jesus' prophecy in 21:13 is fulfilled by the Church in Acts. First, Peter bears testimony before the same assembly that tried Jesus: "We are witnesses (*martyres*) of these things and so is the Holy Spirit whom God has given us" (Acts 5:32). Paul is likewise divinely appointed as a formal witness to Jesus before the Roman courts, "Take courage, for as you have testified about me at Jerusalem, so you must bear witness (*martyrēsai*) also at Rome" (Acts 23:11).

Trials, then, are the occasion for solemn testimony to the Gospel.

Fifth, in Luke's version, Jesus' response to the formal questioning of the court contains additions not found in Mark's account. When asked to testify about his identity, Jesus replied that the Jews refuse to accept his testimony: "If I tell you, *you will not believe.*" These words are literally fulfilled not only in the trial scene, but throughout the Gospel. The first testimony of Jesus the prophet is rejected by those of his homeland (4:24); and rejection is the fate of the prophet Jesus throughout his career (see 6:7, 11; 7:31–35; 10:13–16; 11:47–51; 13:33–34; 19:14, 17; 20:10–15). Israel, then, "will not believe" the words of Jesus the prophet.

It has long been noted that Jesus' remarks in 22:67–68 resemble the reply of Jeremiah to Israel's king in Jer 45:15LXX. Jeremiah was arrested, brought inside the palace, and solemnly asked about his prophetic word from God. He prefaced his difficult oracle with the words:

If I tell you, you will not certainly put me to death?
And if I give you counsel, you will not listen to me.

To be sure, the king did not believe him or release him. So with Jesus' answer. Like Jeremiah, Jesus is arrested and stands before Israel's rulers. As with Jeremiah, Jesus is asked for his testimony about God's Christ and Son; Israel refuses to accept the testimony when given. And so, Jesus' "You will not believe me" echoes Jeremiah's "You will not listen to me."

A comparable instance of this is found in Paul's testimony to the synagogue at Antioch in Pisidia. In the course of his testimony on Jesus' behalf, Paul says: "Beware, lest there come upon you what is said in the prophets: . . . 'I do a deed in your days, a deed you will never believe, if one declares it to you'" (Acts 13:40–41). This seems to be remarkably similar to Jesus' remark to the Sanhedrin. Like Jesus, Paul testifies to a Jewish assembly; like Jesus, he cites the Jewish Scriptures as prophecy that Israel will not believe God's prophets (Acts 13:40–41 = Hab 1:5); as with Jesus, the prophecy is fulfilled as Israel in fact "does not believe, even if one declares it to you." The word of God's prophets is always rejected by Israel. Such is the fate of the prophets.

Jesus' remarks in 22:67–68 serve a second purpose. Not only is he a formal witness for the Church's preaching about Jesus as Christ, but he is acting as a witness against Israel when he proclaims: "You will not believe me." Jesus' testimony cuts both ways: (a) on behalf of the Christ, and (b) against Israel. This twofold aspect of Christian testimony will soon be shown to be important in Luke's presentation of the trials of the Church in Acts of the Apostles.

Sixth, in Luke, even Jesus' response to the court's questioning is different than in Mark's account:

MK 14:62	LK 22:69
1. You will see	1. _____
2. _____	2. But from now on
3. the Son of Man seated at the right hand of the power,	3. the Son of man will be seated at the right hand of the power of God.
4. and coming with the clouds of heaven.	4. _____

Both Mark and Luke contain Jesus' prediction of his vindication by God. The title "Son of Man" refers here to the one rejected on earth, but vindicated in heaven.[9] Luke, however, changes the time reference for Jesus' vindication. In Mark, Jesus' ultimate vindication is linked with his return at the parousia when the Judged One will become the Judge. But in Luke, the time of Jesus' vindication is radically foreshortened: "But from now on . . ." (22:69a). According to Luke, it is not the parousia but Jesus' resurrection which is his vindication and his session at God's right hand. Peter testifies in the Holy Spirit that Jesus is now seated at God's right hand in virtue of his resurrection:

> *Being exalted at the right hand of God,* and having received from the Father the promise of the Holy Spirit, he has poured out this which you see and hear. For David did not ascend into the heavens, but he himself says, "The Lord said to my Lord, *Sit at my right hand,* till I make your enemies a stool for your feet" (Acts 2:32–34).

Jesus prophesied to the assembly that God would vindicate him. The prophecy is fulfilled in his resurrection,[10] a prophecy which was made not only by Jesus but by the Scriptures as well.

This prophecy of the vindication of the Son of Man serves an important function elsewhere in Luke's work. Not only is Jesus himself the "rejected one," but Jesus' own prophet, Stephen, is also rejected. Like Jesus, Stephen is rejected by the Jewish court (Acts 6:11–14); like him, Stephen testifies to Israel's unbelief in God's prophets (7:51–53); and like him, Stephen knows of the vindication of the rejected prophet. Stephen is granted a vision of the vindicated Son of Man "standing at the right hand of God" (7:55–56). Surely Jesus is already vindicated in his resurrection and has even now become the vindicator of his rejected followers. By foreshortening Mark's scenario from the parousia to the resurrection, Luke sharpened the function of Jesus' reply in 22:69. It is no vague prophecy of future vindication, but a prediction of an immediate vindication in his resurrection. And that prophecy served as a word of encouragement to his followers in Acts who share his fate.

Seventh, the Jewish reaction to Jesus' confession is distinctive in Luke. Mark had the high priest coax the Sanhedrin into its condemnation: "'What is your decision?' They all condemned him as deserving of death" (14:64). Luke, however, portrays the full assembly of Israel spontaneously and with one accord rejecting Jesus' testimony: "They said, 'What further testimony do we need? We have heard it ourselves from his own lips'" (22:71). There is no charge of blasphemy in Luke, no capital sentence. What is dramatized is Israel's solemn rejection of Jesus as God's prophet. Instead of discontinuing the search for *other witnesses* (*martyrōn*, Mk 14:64), Luke describes the assembly rejecting *further witnessing* by Jesus himself (*martyrias*, Lk 22:71), a statement prophetic of the same assembly's reaction to the witnessing of Peter, Stephen, and Paul in Acts. This suggests that in Luke, Jesus is the sole and chief *witness* to God's Christ. And his witnessing, which is solemnly given to Israel's official court, is formally rejected.

In summary, the drift of Luke's redaction of Jesus' trial before the Sanhedrin contains the following thematic points:

1. Jesus is presented as a formal witness before Israel's assembly. He bears testimony to God's prophet as the Christ, Son of God, and Son of Man. As such, he serves as a model for the apostles in their trials in Acts as formal witnesses to Jesus.
2. His testimony is rejected by Israel. In this Jesus is like all of Israel's prophets whose word was always rejected.
3. The trial of Jesus, then, also becomes the trial of Israel. In judging Jesus, Israel judges itself.
4. In keeping with this in 22:69, Jesus predicts his vindication, a prophecy fulfilled in his resurrection. The vindicated Son of Man functions as the vindicator of his prophets whose testimony to Israel continues to be rejected by the same assembly in Acts.

According to Luke, then, Jesus is for the Church a model of an official witness to the Gospel. He embodies also the pattern of rejection on earth and vindication in heaven. The significance of Luke's editing of Jesus' Jewish trial cannot be confined to the passion narrative, for Luke edited the Acts of the Apostles to reflect the importance of the redactional changes in Lk 22:66–71.

C. Lk 23:1–5

In Jesus' first trial before Pilate, Luke made many small but significant changes in the Markan account of the same incident. Whereas Mark narrated that the Sanhedrin sent Jesus to Pilate, Luke has "the whole company" rise up as a body and bring Jesus to Pilate. This suggests that all of Israel is assembled before Pilate, ready to reject their prophet once more. Instead of Jesus' being "handed over," a technical term in Mark's account (see Mk 10:33; 14:18, 42; 15:1), the Jews "brought" Jesus to Pilate, a phrase repeatedly used in Acts for the haling into court of Christian witnesses (see Acts 5:27; 6:12; 25:6, 17, 23).

The trial before Pilate formally begins with three charges leveled against Jesus. No explicit charges were mentioned in Mark, but Luke expands the narrative here, recording the substance of the charges:

1. he perverts the nation;
2. he refuses to pay tribute to Caesar;
3. he claims to be Christ, the King (23:2).

One charge is patently false, for Jesus openly endorsed "rendering to Caesar what is Caesar's" (20:20–25).[11] Ironically, if anyone should be judged as Rome's enemy, it is the Jews who chose Barabbas, a genuine revolutionary (23:19, 25). The only charge which Luke says is worthy of Pilate's notice is Jesus' claim to be Christ the King. And so Pilate conducts his personal *cognitio* of that charge.

Mark also recorded two sets of questions put to Jesus, general accusations to which Jesus remained silent (Mk 15:3–5) and a formal question, "Are you the King of the Jews?" (15:2), to which he responded. It is not clear why Jesus speaks in one instance and is silent in another. This is simplified in Luke where the charges are made and Pilate conducts his personal inquiry. Only one question is asked, "Are you the King of the Jews?" which Jesus readily answers. This question-answer exchange resembles the question-answer pattern before the Jewish assembly in

22:67–70; Christological questions are asked and true witnessing is given. The same pattern recurs here: Jesus, on trial, bears testimony to God's Christ. Again he is a model of Christian witnessing.

The proceedings before Pilate are described by Luke according to traditional Roman trial proceedings.[12] Charges are made (23:2); the magistrate conducts his *cognitio* (23:3), and pronounces a verdict (23:4). Pilate dismisses the charges: "I find no cause in this man," which Luke notes as the first of the governor's three verdicts of Jesus' innocence (see 23:14–15, 22). The trial should end with Pilate's verdict in 23:4, but new charges are urged: "He stirs up the people . . . from Galilee even to this place" (23:5). The reader again remembers Jesus' inaugural visit to Nazareth's synagogue and the ensuing riot (4:16–30). That riot was not Jesus' fault, for the blame lay in Israel's rejection of God's prophet. Ironically, the Jews are guilty of rebellion, not Jesus, a point underscored in their choice of the rebel, Barabbas. The irony is compounded in Acts where Paul is repeatedly charged with and acquitted of the same accusation (Acts 16:20; 17:5; 24:5). The Jews themselves instigate the riots against Paul in Thessalonica (17:5) and at Jerusalem (21:27–30).

In summary, Luke's account of Jesus' first trial before Pilate emphasizes four points: (a) correct and full judicial procedure is noted (charges, *cognitio,* verdict); (b) Jesus' innocence is affirmed; (c) ironically the Jews accuse Jesus of rebellion; (d) Jesus gives another example of witnessing on trial.

D. Lk 23:6–12

The most important issue connected with Jesus' trial before Herod is the question of Luke's source of this material. It is often identified as stemming from a special passion source available only to Luke.[13] Some go so far as to argue for traditions from the followers of Jesus who were members of Herod's household. The wife of Chuza, one of Herod's stewards, was an early supporter of Jesus (Lk 8:3), and Manaen, a member of Herod's court, is listed with three other prophets in the Church at Antioch (Acts 13:1). But it may also be argued that Lk 23:6–12 is a Lukan composition.[14]

Various pieces of the narrative fabric may be successfully accounted for by seeing their parallel in the Lukan Gospel or their presence in Luke's source:

1. Lk 23:8 directly parallels Lk 9:9, the report of an earlier inquiry about Jesus at Herod's court, which is based on Mk 6:14–16. In this episode Herod asked "Who is this about whom I hear such things?" (Lk 9:9), a remark which expresses in direct discourse the narrative statement in Mk 6:14, "King Herod heard of it." To this question Luke added, "And he sought to see him" (Lk 9:9c), a comment *not* found in Mark, but surely added by Luke himself. In Lk 23:8, Herod is described as very glad to see Jesus, for "He had long desired to see him." Having heard about Jesus in the past (9:7, 9), Herod desires to see him "because he had heard about him" (23:8). The two inquiries are formally linked together by Luke.

2. Even the comment that Herod's desire was long-standing (*ex hikanōn chronōn,* 23:8) is a typically Lukan expression (see Lk 8:27; 20:9; Acts 8:11).

3. The details of the narrative lie close to Luke's hand in his Markan source. The Jewish charges and Jesus' silence (23:9–10) directly parallel the Markan account of Jesus and his accusers in Mk 15:3–5. The specific Lukan mention of "high priests and scribes . . . accusing him" to Herod (23:10) resembles Mark's note that "high priests, elders and scribes . . . accuse" Jesus before Pilate (15:1, 4).

4. Herod's "asking" ("He questioned him," 23:9) and Jesus' silence ("But he made no answer," 23:9b) parallel the Markan account of Pilate's "asking" ("He questioned him," 15:4a) and Jesus' silence ("He made no further answer," 15:5).

5. The subsequent treatment of Jesus by Herod and his soldiers (23:11) may likewise be drawn from Markan sources. In Luke, there is no account of Romans mocking Jesus or clothing him in a purple robe. But these elements of mockery and royal investiture are ready to Luke from Mk 15:16–20.

6. Alternately, the treatment of Jesus by the Jewish crowd in Lk 22:63–64 offers a parallel to 23:11. In the former passage, they "mock him" (*enepaizon auto*), even as they "mock" him at Herod's court (*empaixas*). Mockery was a key term in the Lukan passion prediction in Lk 18:32.

7. It is remarked that Herod "treated him with contempt" (*exouthenēsas*), a term used again in Acts 4:11 to describe the treatment of the rejected stone of Ps 118:22 which was "treated with contempt" (*exouthenētheis*).[15]

8. The final comment that Herod and Pilate became friends over this event is often explained by a cross-reference to Acts 4:25–27 which cites Ps 2:1–2 to the effect that "The kings of the earth . . . and the rulers were gathered together against the Lord and against his anointed." Luke noted in Acts 4:27 that both "Herod and Pontius Pilate, with the Gentiles and the people of Israel, were gathered together against thy holy servant, Jesus."[16]

In short, all of the materials in Lk 23:6–12 may be found either in the Markan source to the passion narrative (15:3–5, 16–20), in Lukan redactional additions to Mark's text (Lk 9:9 to Mk 6:14–16), or in scriptural prophecies which are fulfilled (Acts 4:25–27). There is no need to demand a special source for 23:6–12. Yet however the sources are assessed, it remains for us to evaluate the content and function of the trial of Jesus before Herod.

Luke intends the meeting of Jesus and Herod to be another formal trial, the third of Jesus' trials. Luke pays close attention to forensic issues. First, the question of legal jurisdiction[17] is noted: ". . . when Pilate learned that he belonged to Herod's jurisdiction" (*ek tēs exousias*, 23:7). Charges are brought against Jesus: "The chief priests and the scribes stood by, vehemently accusing him" (23:10). The verdict is unexpressed in 23:6–12, although in 23:14–15 Pilate indicates that Herod rendered a verdict of innocence.

As regards the function of 23:6–12, we are best advised to begin with 23:14–15. Luke insists that Herod and Pilate agree on Jesus' innocence. According to Jewish law, two competent witnesses—a king and a governor—are unwittingly brought forward in defense of Jesus. Yet the Lukan narrative suggests concern for other issues. The Church in Acts was violently attacked by this same Herod who killed James (Acts 12:1–2) and arrested Peter (12:3–5). After all, this is the same Herod who sought to kill Jesus (Lk 13:33), an action which he oddly did not carry out in 23:6–12. The parallel treatment of Jesus and his Church is made thematically intelligible by an appeal to a most important text. In Lk 21:12, Jesus predicts that his followers would be "brought before kings and governors for my name's sake." James was brought before a king, viz., Herod (Acts 12:1–2); Peter would have been, except for his miraculous escape; and Paul was tried before King Agrippa (Acts 25–26) and was brought to Rome to appear before Caesar (Acts 26:32). Inasmuch as the trials and passions of Peter and Paul are paralleled to that of Jesus, there is a strong Lukan argument for a parallel to the appearance of the apostles before kings in Jesus' own appearance before Herod. Jesus, the model of a good confession (see 1 Tim 6:13), led the way, and was haled before governors (Pilate) and kings (Herod) to bear witness to the Gospel. As Jesus, so his Church.

In discussing the parallels between Acts 4:25–27 and Lk 23:12,[18] we should note that in the passion narrative both Pilate and Herod agree, not against Jesus but in support of his innocence. Herod, however, was said to want to kill Jesus (Lk 13:33). Nevertheless, the full Lukan perspective hardly sees Herod as in any way favorably disposed to Jesus (see "He treated him with contempt . . . he mocked him," 23:11). Herod's basic hostility is replicated in his treatment of Jesus' followers throughout Luke-Acts:

(a) he imprisons Christians and their sympathizers
    (Lk 3:19–20; Acts 12:3–5);
(b) he tortures them, and seeks to kill them
    (Lk 9:7; 13:31; Acts 12:1–2, 19);
(c) he shows general hostility to them
    (Acts 4:27).

John the Baptizer, Jesus, James, and Peter are all threatened by him.

In summary, 23:6–12 seem to have a complex function in Luke's narrative. It is a third formal trial of Jesus, from which another protestation of Jesus' innocence emerges. In it Jesus models for the Church how to act when brought before kings and governors. Inasmuch as "the chief priests and scribes . . . vehemently accused him" (23:10), Luke presents one more instance of Israel rejecting God's prophet.

E. Lk 23:13–25

The fourth trial of Jesus opens with Luke narrating how Pilate summoned a solemn assembly of Israel to himself, "the chief priests, the rulers, and the people" (23:13).[19] This should be seen in continuity with Luke's other presentations of the Jewish composition of Jesus' various trials.

A. Jewish Trial (22:66)

"The *presbyterion* of the people, chief priests and scribes . . . led him to the Sanhedrin."

B. Pilate's First Trial (23:1)

"The whole company of them rose up and took him to Pilate."

C. Herod's Trial (23:6–12)

"The chief priests and the scribes stood there, vehemently accusing him."

D. Pilate's Second Trial (23:13–25)

"Pilate summoned the chief priests and the rulers and the people."

In each case, Luke has suggested the broadest possible Jewish representation of the Jews in keeping with his interest in presenting Israel's formal rejection of God's prophet.

This Lukan episode, more so than the Markan source, presents a formal trial scene and recapitulates in a more complete way typical forensic proceedings.[20] The following breakdown of 23:14–15 illustrates the fullness of the judicial procedure:

1. Arrest	"You brought me a man" (23:14a).
2. Charges	". . . as one who was perverting the people" (23:14b).
3. *Cognitio*	"and after examining him before you" (23:14c).
4. Verdict	"I did not find this man guilty of any of your charges against him"(23:14d).
5. Supporting verdict	". . . neither did Herod, for he sent him back to us" (23:15a).
6. Acquittal	"Nothing deserving of death has been done by him" (23:15b).
7. Judicial warning	"I will therefore chastise him and release him" (23:15c).

Other forensic aspects of the trials before Pilate are highlighted by Luke, including the full range of charges made (23:2, 5), the concern for proper jurisdiction (23:6), three distinct verdicts of acquittal (23:4, 14–15, 23), and a final sentence ("He gave sentence . . ." 23:24). Luke has taken considerable pains to present Jesus' hearings before Pilate as forensic trials, legally correct in all aspects, and readily recognizable as such.

Although Luke seems to be following Mark's account in 23:18–25, he has significantly changed the narrative to make several thematic points. First, Mark notes the so-called custom of releasing a prisoner and describes how a gradual movement developed in the crowd in memory of that custom, which climaxed with the request for Barabbas (Mk 15:6–11). Luke abruptly[21] narrates: "All cried out together 'Away with this man! Release to us Barabbas'" (23:18). The abruptness of the cry and the fact that it comes from *all of the Jews* assembled before Pilate again points to Luke's interest in presenting a solemn choice by Israel. Second, Mark identified Barabbas as a man arrested for murder during an insurrection (15:7), basic information repeated in Luke except for two new details: (a) Luke identified Barabbas' revolt as taking place "in the city" (23:19); (b) Luke twice notes in full the crimes of Barabbas, "murder and rebellion" (23:19, 25). Luke clearly portrays the Jews as favoring rebellion in choosing a murderous rebel to Jesus. The narrative, moreover, suggests that Barabbas' rebellion was quite recent and well known ("in the city"), and that it met with considerable sympathy among the Jews.

This conscious move by Luke should be seen in connection with several other developments in Luke-Acts. We noted earlier that certain of the Jewish charges against Jesus have an ironic twist to them. The Jews claim that Jesus refuses tribute to Caesar (23:2) and that he stirred up the people to revolt (23:5). Ironically in the great war of 70 A.D. it was the Jews who had recently rejected Caesar's rule and stirred their nation to rebellion. The theme of Jewish responsibility for that war and the accompanying destruction of Jerusalem will be extensively treated in the next chapter. In presenting the Jews as formally choosing a murderous rebel over God's prophet, Luke insinuates that this choice is an act of apostasy. Luke's works, moreover, are curiously filled with reports of Jewish rebellions which reports contrast Jesus and his followers with genuine rebels. Gamaliel cannot distinguish Jesus and his early followers from the rebels Theudas and Judas the Galilean (Acts 5:35–39), and so he urges a hands-off policy toward them. The tribune who arrested Paul in the temple confused him with "the Egyptian who recently stirred up a revolt and led the 4,000 men of the assassins out into the wilderness" (Acts 21:38). Luke's intention in these three episodes points to Christian innocence of rebellion, assassination, and revolt, even as it underscores how the Jews repeatedly revolted, assassinated, and plotted revolution. No doubt a strong political apology is being made through this for Jesus and the early Church, especially in light of the Roman-Jewish war so recently concluded.

Third, Luke's most important thematic change occurs in the way the Jewish crowd is portrayed. We noted earlier the representative character of the crowd assembled before Pilate. Luke draws special attention to them as *choosing:*

1. They choose Barabbas and reject Jesus (23:18).
2. Their shouting prevails, *choosing (aitoumenoi)* Jesus to be crucified (23:23).
3. Pilate gave sentence that their *choice (aitēma)* be granted (23:24).
4. He released Barabbas, whom they *chose (ētounto, 23:25a).*
5. And he handed Jesus over *to their will (to thelēmati autōn, 23:25b).*

Each of these five notices of Jewish choosing is distinctive to Luke[22] and is not found in his source. Luke's intention to portray a national choice is confirmed in Peter's speech in Acts 3:14–15, where he chides the assembled Jews: ''You denied the Holy and Righteous One and *chose (ētēsasthe)* a murderer to be granted to you.'' The Jews' choosing should be interpreted in the same vein as Mt 27:25 and Jn 19:15 where Israel's solemn rejection of God's prophet is similarly dramatized.

The trial of Jesus before Pilate is so full of irony that it invites us to look carefully at it in another light. Who is judge here? Who is witness? The same actors play a variety of roles depending on what trial one sees being conducted. There are two trials going on in 23:1–25. On the surface 23:1–25 presents a *trial of Jesus:* (a) he is arrested; (b) witnesses testify against him; (c) Herod and Pilate judge him, (d) declaring him innocent and acquitting him. But 23:1–25 present a second trial, the *trial of Israel:* (a) witnesses testify to the assembly of Israel about Jesus' innocence; (b) Israel rejects this testimony and condemns an innocent man to death. The roles of witness and judge can be reversed. Although Pilate is Jesus' judge, he testifies as a witness to Jesus' innocence to the Jews. Although the Jews are present as witnesses against Jesus (23:1–5), they act as judges condemning him. *The trial of Jesus becomes the trial of Israel,*[23] for in unjustly condemning Jesus they bring down God's judgment on themselves. The unjustness of their judgment is shown not only in their rejection of Jesus' innocence but also in their preference of a murderous rebel over an innocent prophet. A man who ought not to see the light of freedom is released by them and the declared Innocent One is sentenced to death. They acquit the guilty and condemn the innocent. This twofold character of Christian trial will be continued in Acts of the Apostles.

In summary, then, the Lukan redaction of the trial of Jesus before Pilate emphasizes the legality of the proceedings against Jesus. There is a triple verdict of innocence and guiltlessness from two solid witnesses. Alternately, the representative character of the assembled Jews and their fivefold *choosing* against Jesus underscore Luke's perception of the trials as Israel's rejection of God's prophet. Their hypocritical accusations that Jesus is a rebel are ironically presented by Luke as a judgment against them instead.

II.
PROPHECY—FULFILLMENT

The simplest, quantitative analysis of Luke-Acts reveals that forensic trials constitute a significant block of material in Luke's works: (a) Jesus' four trials, (b) Jesus' double prediction of future trials for the Church (Lk 12:8–12; 21:12–15), and (c) the trials of Peter, Stephen, and Paul. Lest we underestimate the sheer volume of Acts of the Apostles which is devoted to forensic trials[24] of the early Church, let us briefly list that material:

Text of Acts	Person	Place
4:3–23	Peter *et al.*	Jerusalem
5:17–40	Peter *et al.*	Jerusalem
6:9–7:60	Stephen	Jerusalem
16:19–39	Paul and Silas	Philippi
17:5–9	Paul *et al.*	Thessalonica
18:12–17	Paul	Corinth
21:27–22:30	Paul	Jerusalem
22:30–23:10	Paul	Caesarea
24:1–26	Paul	Caesarea
25:5–12	Paul	Caesarea
25:24–26:32	Paul	Caesarea
28	Paul	Rome

Besides the formal accounts of trials and judicial investigations, we find the same materials discussed in the letter of Claudius Lysias to Felix (23:28–35) and in the meeting between Festus and Agrippa (25:13–22). Forensic trials in Acts have an incredible scope: (a) *all of the major figures* of Acts (Peter, Stephen, and Paul) are tried, (b) in *all of the significant places* where the Gospel was preached (Judea and Jerusalem, Achaia, and Rome); (c) the trials take place *before Jewish courts as well as Roman tribunals.* The legal proceedings, moreover, are never simple or quick; for the Jewish trials of Peter kept recurring without a final verdict, as did the trials of Paul before Felix (Acts 21–24) and Festus (Acts 25–26). The sheer bulk of the forensic materials in Luke-Acts demands that we take it seriously. But what is its importance? And what relation does it have to Jesus' trial in the passion narrative?

The evident link between Jesus' trial and the trials of the apostles in Acts is the double prediction in Lk 12:8–12 and 21:12–15 about the future of the Church. The first prophecy in Lk 12:8–12[25] is basically drawn from the Q source with its parallel in Mt 10. The passage in Luke contains three ideas: (a) fearlessness in the face of physical abuse is urged (12:4–7); (b) the Son of Man will confess or deny those who confess or deny him (12:8–10); (c) forensic trials are predicted and Spirit-supported testimony is promised (12:11–12). The brief mention of forensic procedure in 12:8–12 is subordinated in its context here to the overall exhortation for fidelity.

As regards Lk 21:12–15, Luke is drawing on an established source, but he has greatly revised it to accommodate his own story and perspective, as the following list of redactional changes indicates:

1. Whereas Mark indicates that the arrest and trial of the Church will happen only after a long catalogue of eschatological woes (Mk 13:7–9), Luke reverses this timetable. He declares that the Church's arrest and trial will happen *first*: "But before all this . . ." (21:12), a statement verified by Peter's and Paul's trials in Acts.

2. Luke's description of the hostile process against the Church is considerably fuller than Mark's:

MARK 13:9	LUKE 21:12
1. _____	1. They will seize you and prosecute you
2. You will be delivered up to councils;	2. delivering you up to synagogues and to prisons;

3. you will stand before governors and kings for my sake	3. you will be brought before governors and kings for my name's sake.

Interpreting this synopsis, we learn that Luke adds to the Markan text the following important material: (a) Jesus' followers will be "arrested and prosecuted"; (b) they will be delivered to synagogues "and to prisons" (see Acts 5:17–19; 12:4–5; 21–25). Luke, moreover, takes quite literally the remark that the apostles are "brought before kings": Peter and James were brought before Herod, and Paul before Agrippa and Caesar.

3. The purpose of this hostility is more clearly developed in Luke. Mark expressed the purpose in a mere prepositional phrase, "for testimony to them" (13:13). Luke replaced this with a full clause: "This will be a time for you for testimony" (21:13). As we shall shortly see, the apostles' "testimony" on trial is a major feature of their trials in Acts.[26]

4. Luke heightens Mark's account when he commands Christians not to prepare an "apology" for these occasions (*apologēthēnai,* 21:14). We should not readily equate "testimony" with "apology"; for, as we shall see, they suggest two different kinds of replies in the trial speeches in Acts. At least we are alerted in Lk 21:13–14 that they are different.

5. Lk 21:15 edits Mark by insisting that Jesus himself will be the Paraclete:

Mk 13:11 "Say whatever is given you in that hour."

Lk 21:15 "I will give you a mouth and a wisdom . . ."

Besides his prophecy of their trials and his own model of how to act during them, Jesus announces his presence with the disciple on trial when he says: "I will give you a mouth and a wisdom."

6. In addition to the extended sense of the hostile process in Lk 21:12, Luke likewise stresses the invincibility of the Church's "mouth and wisdom" before its enemies: ". . . which none of your adversaries will be able to contradict or to withstand" (21:15). Of Stephen, Luke says: "They could not withstand the wisdom and the Spirit with which he spoke" (Acts 6:10); Peter's healing in Acts 3 is a "notable sign" which the Sanhedrin cannot deny (Acts 4:16). Paul's trial testimony is never refuted; in several instances he would even seem to have persuaded his judges (Acts 24:22–26; 26:28).

7. The Lukan account assures Jesus' protection for the Church: "Not a hair of your head will perish" (21:18). Success is predicted: "By

your endurance you will gain your lives'' (21:19). These are much more concrete promises than Mark's mere "Who endures to the end will be saved'' (13:13).

Luke's version of Jesus' prediction, then, is much fuller than Mark's, as it tells of (a) continuous arrests, prosecutions, and trials, (b) testimony and apology, (c) Jesus' continued presence in the Church, and (d) the apostles' eventual success and escape.[27]

When we turn to Acts, Jesus' prediction is amply fulfilled. It is interesting to note how programmatic Lk 21:12–15 is for the narrative of Acts. For each item and each phrase in Jesus' prophecy is quite literally and amply fulfilled in Acts:

1. "They will lay hands on you (arrest you) . . .''
   see Acts 4:3; 5:18; 12:1; 21:27.
2. ". . . and prosecute you''
   see the prosecution of Peter (Acts 4–5), Stephen (Acts 6–7), and Paul (Acts 21–26), as well as Paul's prosecution of the Church (Acts 9:4–5; 22:4–8 and 26:11–15).
3. ". . . delivering you up''
   see Acts 8:3; 12:4; 21:11; 22:4; 28:17.
4. ". . . to synagogues''
   see Acts 6:9; 9:2; 22:19; 26:11 (if one includes appearances before the Sanhedrin, this prediction is more extensively fulfilled in Acts 4:15; 5:21; 6:12–15; 22:30–23:1; 24:20).
5. ". . . and to prisons''
   see Acts 5:18; 8:3; 12:4; 16:24; 20:23; 23:10, 35; 24:27; 26:10.
6. "You will be brought before kings''
   see Acts 12:1–5; 25:23–26:32; to this one should add the references to "I appeal to Caesar'' in 25:11–12; 26:32; 28:19.
7. ". . . and governors''
   see Acts 16:19–20; 17:6; 18:12; 24:1–23; 25:6–12; 25:23–26:32.
8. ". . . for my name's sake''
   see Acts 4:7, 10, 17–18; 5:27–28, 40–41; 18:15; 26:9.
9. "This will be a time for you to bear testimony''
   see Acts 1:22; 5:32; 22:15; 26:16.
10. "Settle it not to meditate how to give an apology . . .''
    see Acts 22:1; 24:10; 25:8; 26:1–2, 24

11. "For I will give you a mouth and a wisdom . . ."
    see Acts 6:10.
12. ". . . which none of your adversaries will be able to withstand or
    contradict"
    see Acts 4:16; 5:40; 6:10; 16:39; 17:9; 26:27–28.

What binds Jesus' trials with the trials of the Church in Acts is not
just the conscious fulfillment of Jesus' prophecies in Acts. In Luke's Gospel, Jesus himself is the archetype and model of the Church's experience,
and so the essential items of the prediction are dramatized first in Jesus'
own story:

Jesus Himself Fulfills the Prophecy:
1. arrest: Lk 20:19; 22:54
2. prosecution: Lk 11:49; 13:34
3. handing over: Lk 9:44; 18:32; 20:20; 22:4–6, 21–22; 23:25
4. to synagogues: Lk 22:66–71
6. brought before kings: Lk 23:6–12
7. and governors: Lk 20:20; 23:1–5, 13–25
9. for testimony: Lk 22:66–71; 23:3–4

This comparison points to several Lukan themes. (a) Jesus' own process
(Lk 22–23) is seen as an archetypal pattern[28] which his disciples follow
(see Lk 9:23). (b) It is not just in the outline of events (arrest, handing
over to kings and governors, etc.) that Jesus is the pattern, but especially
in his modeling of how to give the Church's testimony when on trial. He
is the prime witness and his moral example is intended to be followed.
(c) It is significant that Jesus predicts the Church's future, a prophecy
which is amply fulfilled in Acts. The many trials and legal proceedings
against Jesus' followers were disquieting and potentially scandalizing.[29]
But the fact that Jesus foretold them apologetically serves to show his
authority and to suggest his control over the events of the lives of his
followers, viz., that he is Lord, enthroned at God's right hand. (d) He is,
moreover, described as assisting at Christian trials, inspiring words of
encouragement and confession. He is even identified with the persecuted
Church: "Saul, Saul, why are you persecuting me?" (Acts 9:4–5; 22:7–
8; 26:14–15). And so, Jesus is linked with the trials in Acts in virtue of
prophecy-fulfillment, the process to be experienced, the moral model of
a witness, and assistance and advocacy. As we shall see, their trials are
in fact his trials.

III.
JESUS' TRIALS IN ACTS

I would advance a new hypothesis at this point. The formal link between Jesus' trials in the Gospel and the trials in Acts lies in Luke's perception of the double character of these trials. As Jesus' trials in the Gospel are also trials of Israel, so the apostles' trials in Acts are likewise trials of Israel. But Luke goes one step further in suggesting that the trials of the apostles in Acts are continuations of the trial of Jesus in the Gospel.

Jesus' trial is continued in Acts in the sense that new witnesses testify on his behalf and new evidence is available in his regard.[30] The earlier verdict of Israel against Jesus was premature and the trial of Jesus should continue. Furthermore, as Israel sat in judgment on Jesus and rejected his testimony, Israel ironically judged itself guilty of false judgment in rejecting God's prophet. In Acts, Israel continues to hear testimony and to judge. In judging Jesus in the passion narrative or the apostles in Acts, Israel is ironically judging itself.

A. Peter's Trials

Let us first examine the trials of Peter and John in Acts 4–5. Their trial in Acts 4:3–22 not only contains a forensic investigation of Peter and John themselves, but equally contains a continuation of the trial of Jesus, and so of the trial of Israel. I will initially develop the first idea, that the trial of the apostles is a continuation of the trial of Jesus. There are, of course, numerous parallels between Jesus' trial and that of Peter and John, which can easily be summarized in the following synopsis.

JESUS' TRIAL	PETER AND JOHN'S TRIAL
1. arrest at night, hearing in the morning: Lk 22:47–52, 66–71	1. arrest at night, hearing in the morning: Acts 4:3, 5
2. solemn assembly of Israel: Lk 22:66; 23:10, 13	2. Sanhedrin: Acts 4:5–6
3. Trial begins with questioning: Lk 22:66, 70	3. Trial begins with questioning: Acts 4:7
4. Same question asked: Lk 20:2	4. Same question asked: Acts 4:7

5. Same answer (Ps 118):   5. Same answer (Ps 118):
   Lk 20:17   Acts 4:11
6. Solemn testimony to Jesus: 6. Solemn testimony to Jesus:
   Lk 22:66–70   Acts 4:8–12

Yet it would be a mistake to conclude from this comparison that Peter and John's trial is merely parallel to that of Jesus. The initial question put to them is a formal inquiry *about Jesus*: "By what power and by what name did you do this?" (4:7). Jesus is again the focal figure in the trial, this time in virtue of the healing miracle performed in his name in Acts 3:1–17. The dramatic climax of this new trial is Peter's testimony in 4:8–12. In substance it proclaims the same kerygmatic summary about Jesus as Peter's Pentecostal testimony in Acts 2:23–36, viz., that God raised the dead Jesus to life, enthroned him, gave him heavenly lordship, and constituted him Savior. This testimony is not in Peter's defense but on behalf of Jesus. Peter continues the Gospel trial of Jesus by introducing to this same court new evidence from a new witness.

The new evidence is the healing miracle of Acts 3. Like Johannine miracles, this healing functions as a sign that Jesus is alive and active, that he has heavenly power, and that he is heavenly ordained as Lord and Christ. Peter's Pentecostal speech articulated the function of miracles as signs when he told the assembled Jews about Jesus: "A man attested to you by God with mighty signs and wonders which God did through him in your midst" (2:22). Miracles, then, are God's formal testimony about Jesus. Peter's insistent testimony that the healing of the paralytic was done "in the name of Jesus" (4:10, 12) introduces new evidence to the assembly of Israel about Jesus. Implied in Peter's testimony is a second new piece of evidence on Jesus' behalf, his resurrection. Peter, John, and others were given "many proofs"[31] that Jesus was alive after his passion (Acts 1:3), for they were to give testimony to this new "fact" about Jesus (see Acts 4:10). Likewise Judas' replacement among the Twelve needed special credentials if he was "to testify to the resurrection" (1:22; see 2:32). The healing of the paralytic—itself a powerful sign—rests upon a far greater sign, Jesus' resurrection. New evidence is presented to the Jewish court on Jesus' behalf. The trial of Jesus must continue.

New witnesses appear before this court as well. Evidently Peter and John (and the other ten apostles) are new witnesses on Jesus' behalf. They were not called during his first trial, but they appear on his behalf now.

They do not so much testify to the earthly Jesus (although see Acts 2:22), but rather to the risen Christ: "This Jesus God raised up and *of that we are witnesses*" (Acts 2:32). God, moreover, is a new witness on Jesus' behalf in virtue of his verdict in raising Jesus from the dead. How insistent Peter is in his testimony that God also witnesses to Jesus: "God raised him up" (2:24); "This Jesus God raised up" (2:32). And most solemnly Peter cites God's witness to Jesus when he tells the whole house of Israel:

> Let the whole house of Israel know assuredly
> that God has made him both Lord and Christ,
> this Jesus whom you crucified (2:36).

Again at the healing of the paralytic, Peter cites God's witness: "The God of Abraham, of Isaac and of Jacob, the God of our fathers, glorified his servant Jesus" (3:13). "God raised him from the dead; to this we are witnesses" (3:15). God's testimony, therefore, is appealed to by Peter before the Sanhedrin: "Jesus of Nazareth, whom God raised from the dead" (4:10).

New witnesses appear before the court of Israel with new evidence on Jesus' behalf. Luke indicates that Peter and John are not simply defending themselves but forcing the assembly of Israel to reopen the case of Jesus.

The new trial of Jesus becomes a continuation of the trial of Israel. Israel is indicted for its former rejection of Jesus: "Jesus of Nazareth, whom you crucified" (Acts 4:10). That former crime may possibly be excused; for, as Peter told the crowds in 3:14, "I know that you acted in ignorance, as did also your rulers." Israel is evidently given a second chance to judge justly in virtue of the new witnesses and their new evidence.

According to correct forensic procedure, the court withdraws into its chambers for deliberation (4:14–17). The case is clearly before them. First, the evidence is acknowledged: (a) they saw the healed man, and (b) they conceded that he was indeed "lame from birth" (3:2) and had remained so for forty years (4:22). They admit that this healing sign is incontrovertible: "Seeing the man . . . they had nothing to say in opposition" (4:14) because, as they admit, "A notable sign is manifest to all the inhabitants of Jerusalem, and we cannot deny it" (4:16). *Yet they dismiss the evidence!*

Second, they evaluate the witnesses. Qualities which would make the witnesses credible are noted: (a) they acted with "boldness" (4:13a); (b) they have first-hand evidence: "They recognize that they had been with Jesus" (4:13c). But the court is prejudiced against the testimony of these witnesses, for they consider them "uneducated, common men" (4:13), that is *am ha-aretz*.[32] *They dismiss the witnesses!*

In dismissing the witnesses, the judges are showing partiality in judgment, an act which was proscribed and condemned in the Old Testament. For example, Deuteronomy repeatedly enjoined impartiality in judgment: "You shall not pervert justice; you shall not show partiality" (16:19) and "You shall not be partial in judgment; you shall hear the small and the great alike" (1:17). To dismiss Peter and John on the grounds that they are "common, uneducated men" is an act of partiality in judgment, a perversion. Judging by appearance, they judge unjustly.[33]

The court's judgment is that the apostles should "speak no more in this name" (4:17), and so they give their verdict: "They charged them not to speak or teach at all in the name of Jesus" (4:18). In this judgment they formally reject Jesus again. After ascertaining clearly "by what power and by what name" the miracle had been done (4:7), they reject the evidence and the witnesses, and so continue their rejection of Jesus.

In their continued rejection of Jesus, the court testifies against itself that it is still guilty of rejecting God's prophets. Peter puts the case squarely on their shoulders: *"You must judge*[34] whether it is right for us to listen to you rather than to God" (4:19). The judges are indeed judging themselves by their own actions. And so the trial of Peter and John continues the trial of Jesus by introducing fresh evidence and new witnesses on Jesus' behalf. And as the trial of Jesus continues, so the trial of Israel is resumed.

These same patterns may be observed in Peter's second trial in Acts 5. The arrest is duly noted (5:17–18), as well as the charges (5:28). But the dramatic climax of the trial is Peter's testimony to Jesus in 5:29–32. The material content of this testimony is the same as that in 4:8–12—how God raised Jesus, exalted him as Leader and Savior to give repentance to Israel. Christological testimony is again the central issue at court, and this is what Peter demands that the court solemnly reconsider. No new evidence is produced, but special emphasis is given to the new cast of witnesses to this court. Peter and the other apostles, of course, are "witnesses of these things" (5:32a).[35] But a new witness appears: "And so is the Holy Spirit whom God has given to those who obey him'' (5:32b). Thus God also gives testimony to Jesus through the presence and inspiration of the Advocate, the Holy Spirit, in the bold witnessing of the apostles. Jesus had asserted that when on trial, the disciples were not to fear what to answer or to say, for ''the Holy Spirit will teach you in that very hour what you ought to say'' (Lk 12:11–12). There are, then, new witnesses on Jesus' behalf, witnesses who should be acceptable to this court.

Peter's testimony shifts the focus of the trial off himself: ''We must obey God'' (5:28, 32).[36] The focus is on Jesus: what is the court of Israel going to make of Jesus, God's Christ, whose witnesses boldly testify in his behalf? In accepting Jesus' witnesses, the court would be accepting Jesus himself; in rejecting them, they would continue to reject Jesus. And so, the court fulfills what Jesus had said earlier:

He who hears you hears me,
and he who rejects you rejects me (Lk 10:16).

In rejecting Peter, the court rejects Jesus. The trial of Peter is the trial of Jesus once more.

The forensic proceedings in Acts 5 are also a continuation of the trial of Israel. The judges of Israel sense that they are being formally charged with Jesus' death: ''You intend to bring this man's blood upon us'' (5:28), a charge which Peter restates, ''. . . Jesus, whom you killed by hanging him on a tree'' (5:30). In private council once more, the court is most plainly told by Gamaliel that they are indeed on trial: ''Take care what you do to these men'' (5:35). In rejecting them, they may be guilty of rejecting God: ''You may be found opposing God'' (5:39). Luke cannot express it more clearly that in judging Jesus and his witnesses, the court is judging itself.

This trial ironically ends with the council ''taking his (Gamaliel's) advice'' (5:40), which was ironically *not* to make a judgment at all. Even on this point, the court is far from keeping Gamaliel's counsel, i.e., ''keeping away from these men and leaving them alone'' (5:38). They beat them and charged them not to speak in the name of Jesus (5:40b), thus reconfirming their earlier unjust judgment. In their continued hostility to the name of Jesus, they indicate their continued rejection of God's prophet.

B. Stephen's Trial

We turn to Stephen's trial and speech in Acts 6–7. According to Luke's narrative, Stephen's trial closely resembles that of Jesus. Like Jesus, Stephen is arrested and brought before the Sanhedrin (Acts 6:12; Lk 22:66). "False witnesses testify against him" (6:11, 13), a feature of Jesus' trial in Luke's source, which Luke omitted from the passion narrative and moved here (see Mk 14:56–58). The anti-temple charges against Stephen (6:13) parallel the content of the testimony of the false witnesses against Jesus (Mk 14:58; 15:29), material which Luke relocated here as well. Like Jesus' response to the Sanhedrin, Stephen's speech is prompted by a question from the high priest (7:1; Lk 22:67, 70). Stephen's trial, moreover, literally fulfilled many aspects of Jesus' prophecy of the Church's trials in Lk 12 and 21. Stephen is dragged before synagogue (Acts 6:9//Lk 12:11) and Sanhedrin (6:12//Lk 21:12). Filled with the Holy Spirit, Stephen speaks a powerful word on behalf of Jesus (6:10//Lk 12:11–12 and 21:14–15), a word which cannot be withstood (6:10//Lk 21:15).

The account of Stephen's trial and his speech to the Jewish court is another example of the double character of the Lukan trial motif. As we shall see, Stephen's speech makes two points: (a) against Israel, and (b) on behalf of Jesus. Since according to Luke every trial of the apostles is also a trial of the judges, let us examine Stephen's speech as testimony against Israel.

As Stephen recounts Israel's history, he first remarks that Joseph was sold to Egypt by his brothers out of jealousy (7:9), the same motive for which the high priests and the Sadducees arrested and imprisoned Peter (5:17). Second, Stephen repeatedly notes how Moses, the prophet of God, was rejected by his fellow Israelites (7:25–27, 35, 39).[37] Finally, Stephen concludes this theme with a solemn indictment of Israel past and present for continually rejecting God's prophets: "Which of the prophets did not your fathers persecute?" (7:52a). The present generation is equally guilty of this: "As your fathers did so do you" (7:51). The Israel of old killed those who announced beforehand the coming of the Righteous One, whom the present Israel "has now betrayed and murdered" (7:52b). And so a formal charge is made against Israel, supported by copious data. Stephen's speech functions as testimony against Israel in what must also be called a trial of Israel.

Stephen's testimony against Israel extends beyond Israel's continual rejection of God's prophets. Stephen testifies that Israel has always misunderstood God's oracle that when Israel was led into a new land: "They shall come out and worship me in this place" (Acts 7:7; Ex 3:12). Nils Dahl has convincingly argued that this promise of God should be interpreted in light of the classic Lukan motif of prophecy-fulfillment.[38] According to Luke, the promise of worshiping God "in this place" was not fulfilled in the Jerusalem temple (7:46–50) but in God's Christ, the prophet whom he would raise up (7:37–38). Stephen recounts Israel's history, testifying to its continual error of worshiping the wrong thing in the wrong place; first the golden calf in the desert (7:40–41) and then "the tent of Moloch and the star of the god Rephan" (7:43). Even in regard to the "tent of witness," Israel erred when David and Solomon sought "a habitation for the God of Jacob" (7:45–47). It was plain from the testimony of God's prophet that

> Heaven is my throne,
> and earth my footstool.
> What house will you build for me,
>   says the Lord,
> or what is the place of my rest?
> Did not my hands make all these things?
> (Acts 7:49–50/Is 66:1–2).

Israel disregarded the testimony of its prophets and continued to worship God incorrectly in the Jerusalem temple. Stephen, then, testifies against Israel. It has always worshiped false gods (7:41, 43); it has disobeyed the word of God's prophets in making a temple (7:48–50). Israel has never worshiped God according to God's directive that Israel "worship me in this place" (7:7), for they have rejected Jesus. Stephen testifies against Israel that it has always been guilty of sin before God.

Stephen testifies on Jesus' behalf. First, he implies that the correct worship of God "in this place" (7:7) refers to Jesus, and not to some physical building. The true "house of David" is not some place or building, but as 2 Sam 7:12–16 indicates, an heir of David. Jesus is that heir. Acts 2:34–36 cites Ps 110 to this very point, that Jesus is the Son of David whom God has established on his throne as Israel's Lord and Christ. To worship God correctly "in this place" is to be gathered around Jesus, the

Son of David, as covenant Lord. A second testimony is given on behalf of Jesus when Stephen recounts Moses' prophecy from God: "God will raise up a prophet from your brethren as he raised me up" (7:37; Dt 18:15–16). Luke had earlier stressed this testimony to Jesus in Peter's speech to the crowds of Israel: "Moses said, 'God will raise up for you a prophet as he raised me up'" (3:22). Jesus, then, is the fulfillment of God's prophecies: he is God's new prophet to Israel and he is the Son of David who gathers Israel around himself. Stephen testifies a powerful word on behalf of Jesus and so forces his trial to become a reopening of the trial of Jesus. A new witness has appeared on Jesus' behalf with new testimony. As with Peter's trials in Acts 4–5, Stephen's trial is really Jesus' trial—continued.

Stephen's trial, however, is just that—his trial. In his forensic testimony against Israel and on behalf of Jesus, Stephen substantially responds to the charges made against him in 6:11, 13–14. First, the crowds had charged that Stephen "never ceases to speak words against this holy place" (6:11). In one sense that charge is true, for Stephen argues that "this holy place," Jerusalem's temple, is an erroneous interpretation of God's oracle to worship God "in this place" (7:7). Jesus is "the place," not the temple in Jerusalem. But there is no guilt in Stephen's "speaking words against this holy place," for he stands alongside another of God's prophets in trying to correct Israel's errors in worshiping God (see 7:48–50). Israel is guilty, not Stephen. Second, they charge Stephen with "blasphemy against Moses and God" (6:11) and with trying to "change the customs which Moses delivered to us" (6:14). Ironically, Stephen cites Moses in his defense when he recalls Moses' prophecy that God would raise up a prophet like Moses (7:37), a prophet who would speak a new prophetic word to Israel. If Jesus is truly the promised prophet like Moses, then guilt lies in *not* heeding him. Luke noted this in Peter's remarks about Jesus as the prophet like Moses: "You shall listen to him in whatever he tells you. And it shall be that every soul that does not listen to that prophet shall be destroyed from the people" (3:22–23). Israel is guilty for not heeding this prophet, not Stephen. Israel stands condemned by the very Moses it ironically appeals to (see Jn 5:45–48). By virtue of Stephen's testimony on Jesus' behalf and against Israel, he adequately answers the charges against himself.[39] In showing them to be unfounded, Stephen indicates that he is being judged unjustly. Ironically, the very charges alleged against Stephen are the charges of which Israel is guilty.

Yet Stephen's testifying is not finished, nor is the complicated network of trials over. There is a second part to Stephen's trial (7:55–8:1) where he becomes a formal witness to the risen Jesus and bears new testimony to that new fact, not to complicated arguments from the Scriptures.

Luke narrates that Stephen received a theophany,[40] a vision of heaven which included a vision of Jesus. Full of the Holy Spirit, he looked to the center of heaven and saw "the glory of God." And there was Jesus, established[41] at God's right hand (7:55). The substance of this theophany is God's revelation to Stephen of the risen Jesus. It contains three aspects. (1) Stephen now has divine verification that Jesus is indeed the one whom Moses predicted God would "raise up" (7:37). This experience of Stephen is comparable to the eyewitness experience of Peter and the Eleven in regard to the resurrection of Jesus (see Acts 1:3, 9–11; 10:39–41) and to that of Paul before the Damascus gate (see Acts 9:3–6). (2) In seeing Jesus "at the right hand of God," Stephen knows that David's prophecy that his heir and Lord would "sit at God's right hand" (Ps 110; Acts 2:34–35) is fulfilled in Jesus. Jesus is Israel's Lord and Christ. (3) In seeing Jesus joined with "the glory of God," Stephen is confirmed in acclaiming Jesus as "the place" where Israel should worship (7:7). Stephen's eyewitness experience of Jesus, then, confirms his academic testimony on behalf of Jesus.[42] This vision formally constitutes him as a witness of Jesus' resurrection. This new witness for Jesus has not only arguments from the Scriptures, but new evidence from his own experience. The trial of Jesus continues as Israel must judge this new testimony on Jesus' behalf.

The court's reaction to Stephen's testimony is most unfavorable (7:57–58). Israel judges once more that Jesus is not God's Christ, that he is not the fulfillment of God's many prophecies, and that God did not raise him from the dead. In rejecting this testimony to Jesus, Israel proves that all of Stephen's charges against it are true: (1) they have always rejected God's prophets (Moses, Jesus, and now Stephen); (2) in stoning Stephen (7:58), they verify Stephen's charge that they persecuted and killed all the prophets sent to them (7:52); (3) Stephen spoke "filled with the Holy Spirit" (7:55); in rejecting his testimony, they prove Stephen's charge that they "have always resisted the Holy Spirit" (7:51). Israel, therefore, judges unjustly, and so judges itself once more. In rejecting the word of God's prophets, they stand under the sentence which Moses pronounced: "And it shall be that every soul that does not listen to that prophet *shall be destroyed from the people"* (Acts 3:22; Dt 18:19).

C. Paul's Trials

Like Jesus, Paul stood on trial four times, before governors and kings, before the Jewish council, and Roman tribunals.

JESUS' TRIALS	PAUL'S TRIALS
1. Before the Sanhedrin: Lk 22:66–71	1. Before the assembled Jews: Acts 21:27–22:29
2. Before the governor Pilate: Lk 23:1–5	2. Before the Sanhedrin: Acts 23:1–10
3. Before King Herod: Lk 23:6–12	3. Before the governor Felix: Acts 24:1–21
4. Before the assembled Jews: Lk 23:13–25	4. Before the governor Festus and King Agrippa: Acts 25:23–26:32.

According to the double character of trials in Luke, Paul's trials are also continuations of the trial of Jesus and the trial of Israel.

The first trial of Paul before the Jerusalem crowd (21:27–22:29) contains many aspects of the Lukan pattern we have been observing. The legal proceedings against Paul begin when Asian Jews charge him with "teaching against the law, the people, and this place" (21:28). A tribune arrives who cannot sort out the complicated nature of these charges (21:33–34) and so proposes to take Paul back to the Roman barrracks to conduct his own *cognitio*. One thing the tribune does clarify is that Paul is *not* the Egyptian revolutionary who recently led 4,000 assassins into the desert (21:37–39), a point which bears on a parallel episode in Jesus' trial where the Just One was contrasted with the revolutionary Barabbas. Christians are not linked at any time or in any way with revolutionaries, a point that cannot be made in regard to other Jews (Lk 23:18–19; Acts 5:36–38). Paul responded to the charges in a defense speech to the assembled crowd. Luke's careful attention to all of this technical forensic material suggests that he sees the events and speeches in 21:27–22:29 as a genuine trial.

As with Peter and Stephen, Paul is on trial. And as Jesus enjoined his followers "to make a defense"[43] (*apologēthēnai*, Lk 21:14), Paul tells the crowds to hear his "defense" (*apologia,* Acts 22:1). In response to the charges that Paul is a heterodox Jew (21:28), Paul recounts his orthodox and strict education under Gamaliel (22:3). Besides being "educated according to the strict manner of the law of our fathers," Paul was not deceived about Jesus like the *am ha-aretz* (see Acts 4:13; John 7:45–49). He was an arch-foe of the alleged heterodox Way, "persecuting it to the death" (22:4). He was, moreover, the very agent of "the chief priests and the whole council of the elders," deputized by them to wage war on the Christians, even as far away as Damascus (22:5–6). All of this material defends Paul as an educated, orthodox, zealous person who is not easily deceived. And his testimony can be verified, "as the chief priests and the whole council of elders bear me witness" (22:5a).

According to Luke, this material serves two functions. First, it constitutes the basis for Paul's "defense" against the charges of heterodoxy (21:28). Paul testifies that he was an educated Jew of the strict observance. Second, by this material Paul establishes his credentials as a reliable witness before this court.[44] As A.E. Harvey has shown, in Jewish trials "the all-important question was the character of the witnesses."[45] Unlike Peter and John, who are discredited as witnesses because of their common, uneducated status (4:13), Paul can claim to be trained under one of the leading figures of that time, Gamaliel, and to have been brought up in the strict manner of the law (22:3). And so Paul has laid a foundation for his subsequent testimony about Jesus in 22:6–16.

The next part of Paul's speech testifies to events en route to Damascus (22:6–11). This functions as Paul's solemn testimony on Jesus' behalf. Paul's experience of Jesus is new evidence which he submits to the court, forcing them to rejudge Jesus. Paul can point to an event which he himself experienced, and he can call on supporting testimony as well. The primary fact is that he had immediate experience of the risen Jesus (22:7–8). The Way-persecuting Jews who accompanied Paul can testify to the mysterious light (22:9) as evidence that something heavenly was occurring. Paul's testimony can be corroborated on the word of another witness, Ananias, a witness "acceptable to all the Jews" (22:12). He not only restored Paul's sight, but interpreted Paul's new experience for him. Ananias testified that God himself appointed Paul "to see the Just One and to hear a voice from his mouth" (22:14). The proper meaning of Paul's experience in 22:7–8, then, is God's revelation to Paul that he had vindicated Jesus in his resurrection. And Ananias confirms as well that this experience served to commission Paul as an official witness.[46] A new battery of witnesses, then, are raised up by God on behalf of Jesus; Paul is their spokesman.[47]

Paul's speech, then, has two thrusts. Paul mounts a "defense" to the charges alleged against him. Paul also functions as a witness on Jesus' behalf. He is a valid witness because of (a) his education and background (22:3), (b) his eyewitness experience of the risen Jesus (22:7–8), and (c) his heavenly commission from God (22:14–15). His testimony is to Jesus, alive and active. As Ananias suggested, Paul is witness to God's own testimony that Jesus is the Just One whom God vindicated in the resurrection.

Paul's testimony on Jesus' behalf is just that—he testifies that Jesus is innocent of all charges. When Paul was persecuting the Way, he acted on the judgment that Jesus was an apostate and deceiver who was perverting Israel. He assumed that Jesus was guilty, just as the Jewish court had declared (Lk 22:71). After Paul's experience of Jesus before Damascus, Ananias urges him to revise his judgment: "The God of our fathers appointed you . . . to see the Innocent One" (*ton dikaion,* 22:14). Paul's forensic testimony to Jesus' innocence puts him in the company of numerous other figures in Luke-Acts who also testify to Jesus' innocence:

(a) Pilate: "I did not find this man guilty of any of your charges against him . . ." (Lk 23:14; see also 23:4, 22).
(b) Herod: ". . . neither did Herod" (23:14).
(c) The Good Thief: "This man has done nothing wrong" (Lk 23:41).
(d) Centurion: "Certainly this man is innocent" (Lk 23:47).
(e) Peter: "You denied the Holy and Innocent One" (Acts 3:14).
(f) Stephen: "They announced beforehand the coming of the Innocent One" (Acts 7:52).
(g) Paul: ". . . though they charged him (Jesus) with nothing deserving of death" (Acts 13:28).
(h) Ananias: "The God of our fathers appointed you . . . to see the Innocent One" (Acts 22:14).

The remarks about Jesus' innocence all have a common context in Luke-Acts: they occur in forensic proceedings, and are spoken to Jews who either condemned Jesus or persecuted his apostles. Christian witnesses, then, are telling Jewish judges and courts that their previous judgment of Jesus was unjust, for he is innocent of all charges and sin. Implied in this testimony to Jesus' innocence is the Christian claim on Jesus' behalf that he is a saint.[48]

The assertion that Jesus is "innocent" (*dikaios*, Lk 23:47; Acts 3:14; 7:52; 22:14) should be assessed as forensic testimony on Jesus' behalf.[49] The Jews are now put on the spot, for they must judge Paul's testimony and revise their previous judgment of Jesus. They are forced to make still another judgment about this Jesus of Nazareth.

Paul likewise testifies against Israel in his speech. He testifies to a later vision of Jesus (22:17–21), which contains Jesus' own indictment against Israel. Jesus commanded Paul, "Make haste and get quickly out of Jerusalem, because *they will not accept your testimony about me*" (22:18). Paul relates how he too had belonged to the Israel which did not accept the Church's testimony about Jesus (22:19–20), thus confirming Jesus' remarks. How right Stephen was when he charged Israel, "Which of the prophets did not your fathers persecute?" (7:52). Not only must Israel judge Paul's testimony about Jesus, it must judge the validity of the accusations made against it by God's prophets. The trial of Paul has become the trial of Israel.

What is their judgment? Although the charges against Paul centered around Paul's heterodoxy and his defilement of the temple, Paul has answered the charge of heresy (22:3–5) and the charge of defilement falls to the ground as a false charge (see 21:29). The hearing, then, should end with a complete dismissal of the charges, that is, with an acquittal of Paul. But the Jewish reaction in 22:22–23 indicates that hostility continues, or, rather, that it has found a new basis. In his speech, Paul has testified on Jesus' behalf that he is the Lord of the covenant (22:7–8) and that he is God's Just One (22:14). Paul repeated Jesus' indictment of Israel's unbelief (22:17–18). This is the new impetus to Jewish hostility against Paul, his testimony on Jesus' behalf. Paul forced the Jews to judge his testimony and they did just that, rejecting Paul and Jesus to whom he bore witness. Jesus made it clear that "Who rejects you rejects me" (Lk 10:16). Jesus, then, is persecuted once more when his Church is persecuted, rejected once more when his witnesses are rejected (see Acts 9:4–5; 22:7–8). Israel unjustly judges Jesus, and so brings judgment on itself.

Whereas the first trial of Paul was conducted before diverse Jewish crowds (21:27), Paul's second trial takes place before the formal assembly of Israel, "the chief priests and all the council" (22:30). Luke tells the story of this trial in such a way as to stress only one aspect of the pattern we have seen developing, the trial of Israel.

The trial has two parts: 21:1–5 and 6–10. The first part starts with what appears to be a repeat of Paul's defense of his orthodoxy: "I have lived before God in all good conscience to this day" (23:1; see 22:2). This personal recognizance is immediately rejected by this court in the rebuke authorized by the high priest: "The high priest Ananias commanded those who stood by to strike him on the mouth" (23:2). Paul's subsequent remark highlights Luke's sense that Paul's trial is a trial of Israel: the judges are judging themselves. "God strike you, you white-washed wall! Are you sitting to judge me according to the law, and yet contrary to the law you order me to be struck?" (23:3). In their unjust judgment of Paul, the judges bring down judgment on themselves.

The second part of this trial clearly articulates how this is truly a trial of Israel. Paul demands that the official assembly of Israel make a judgment, not about himself, but about a more important issue: the resurrection of Jesus. Paul refocuses the attention of the court on a matter of supreme importance: "With respect to the hope and the resurrection of the dead I am on trial" (23:6). Depending on the official judgment of this, Israel will testify whether it is "fighting against God" or not (see Acts 5:39; Lk 20:37–39). The assembly's judgment divides. The Pharisees, who admit the doctrine of the resurrection, seem to judge justly. They acquit Paul: "We find nothing wrong in this man" (23:9a). And they give guarded acceptance to Paul's testimony about the events on the way to Damascus (22:6–9). Paul had testified that he heard a heavenly voice (the Jewish *bat qol*), thus claiming that God was the source of his testimony and its guarantor. The Pharisees are said to accept tentatively Paul's *bat qol*: "What if a spirit or an angel spoke to him?" (23:9b). They obviously are not formally accepting Paul's testimony about Jesus, but, like Gamaliel in Peter's trial (5:34–39), they are "not fighting against God." The Sadducees and the high priests, however, judge differently by rejecting the resurrection, even Jesus' resurrection and Paul's testimony to it (23:7, 10). And so they bear testimony against themselves. Paul's second trial, then, forces Israel to judge once more about Jesus and about God. Not only is Jesus being rejudged, but God's power to raise the dead is also judged.

The third of Paul's trials (24:1–21) continues the ironic trial of Israel. Luke is at great pains to detail the forensic proceedings. The governor is seated on his official judgment seat; the plaintiffs, Ananias and some elders, employ a prosecuting attorney, Tertullus. It is formally charged that Paul is an agitator, a ring-leader of the sect, a temple profaner (24:7–8). The judge Felix is invited to conduct a *cognitio* of the charges: "By examining him yourself you will be able to learn from him about everything of which we accuse him" (24:8). Face to face with his accusers, Paul speaks his "defense" (*apologia*, 24:10).

Since Paul is on trial, he addresses the charges one by one and refutes them (24:10–13, 17–20). First, against the charge that he is "an agitator among all the Jews" (24:5), Paul testifies "that they did not find me disputing with anyone or stirring up a crowd, either in the temple or in the synagogues, or in the city" (24:12). Second, he admits that, as charged, he belongs to the sect, but maintains that the sect is orthodox: "According to the Way . . . I worship the God of our fathers, believing everything laid down by the law or written in the prophets" (24:14). Third, against the charge that he "tried to profane the temple" (24:7), Paul testifies that he came to the temple only for works of piety, "to bring to my nation alms and offerings" (24:17). Far from defiling the temple, "as I was doing this, they found me *purified* in the temple, without any crowd or tumult" (24:18). Fourth, Paul calls attention to correct forensic procedure, when he asks where his original accusers are, the Asian Jews who first charged him (24:19; see 21:27–28). A defendant must be charged face to face by his accusers. Their absence here indicates fraudulent legal procedure, or unjust judgment. On the basis of Paul's defense, then, his trial ought to end with the verdict of acquittal because all of the charges are false.

But Luke's account of the trial has another face. The trial of Paul is in fact a trial of Israel. The real issue is not the battery of accusations against Paul but how Israel judges the resurrection. And so Luke directly links this trial with that in Acts 23 by having Paul remark once more: "With respect to the resurrection I am on trial before you today" (24:21; see 23:6). The only judgment worthy of anyone's attention is the judgment about the resurrection. In this regard, Paul claims that some of his accusers already share his position on this when he testifies that he "has a hope in God which they themselves accept, that there will be a resur-

rection of both the just and the unjust" (24:15). This picks up the judgment of the Pharisees in 23:9. At stake is the perennial testimony on Jesus'
behalf which the many witnesses of Acts bring before the court of Israel:
"God raised Jesus and of this we are witnesses." And so, Israel is forced
to react to this testimony once more and judge itself once more. While
Felix suspends the trial without giving his verdict, the court of Israel rejects Paul's testimony, as is seen from the comment about their plot to
kill Paul (25:2–3). And so they indicate their sustained rejection of his
testimony (see 9:23, 29).

The trial of Paul in Acts 26 is often described as the highpoint of
Paul's judicial process. His speech to Festus and Agrippa, however, has
caused no little problem for commentators, for it is a complicated oration
which contains "missionary" elements[50] and "witnessings,"[51] as well
as "apology."[52] Before evaluating its contents and function, we should
see it in its proper forensic context as a trial speech.

Like the trials of Jesus, Paul's various trials are presented as orderly
and legal forensic procedures:

FORENSIC PROCEDURE	PAUL'S TRIALS			
1. arrest	21:27–36	———	———	———
2. court assembled	21:30	22:30	24:1	25:23
3. charges	21:28, 33	———	24:2–9	———
4. previous hearings	———	———	———	25:14–22
5. judge's *cognitio*	21:37–40	———	24:8, 10	25:24–27
6. apology of defendant	22:1–21	23:1, 6	24:10–21	26:2–29
7. verdict	22:22–29	23:9–10	24:22–23	26:31
8. sentence	———	———	———	26:32

The forensic context of Acts 26 becomes clear as we observe Luke's
sense of parallelism[53] between Jesus' trials and those of Paul:

1. As regards the number of trials and participants, both Jesus and Paul
   have four trials, before the same groups, as we noted above.
2. The charges against both are roughly the same: Jesus is accused of
   perverting the nation (Lk 23:2) and stirring up the people (Lk 23:5);

Paul is said to be an opponent of the people (Acts 21:28) and an agitator of the Jews (Acts 24:5).

3. Both Jesus and Paul bear testimony on trial: Jesus affirms the basic Christological confession (Lk 22:67–70; 23:4), while Paul bears testimony to Jesus (Acts 22:6–11; 26:9–18) and affirms the basic kerygma about Jesus (Acts 26:22–23).

4. Both are repeatedly declared innocent: Roman governors individually pronounce them innocent (Lk 23:4, 22; Acts 23:29; 25:25), and governor and king agree on their innocence (Lk 23:14–15; Acts 26:31).

5. Both trials before the Sanhedrin take place in the morning, after an arrest the previous day (Lk 22:66; Acts 22:30–23:1ff).

6. After their trials, the Jewish crowd's reaction to both is "Away with him" (Lk 23:18; Acts 21:36; 22:22).

The importance of this data lies in understanding Luke's presentation of the double character of trials in Luke-Acts. When the apostles are tried, Jesus is again on trial; when judgment is made, the judges are being judged (see Lk 10:16).

According to Luke, Paul's trials are not only similar to Jesus' trials, but also to the trials of Peter (Acts 4–5) and Stephen (Acts 6–7). For example, as Peter, John and Stephen speak as eyewitnesses of the risen Jesus, so does Paul (see 22:6–9; 26:9–18). As they deliver testimony to Jesus, so does Paul (see 26:22–23). As they bear testimony against Israel for rejecting God's prophets and witnesses, so does Paul (see 22:4–5, 18; 26:9–12, 17). From this Luke indicates that the trials of Peter, Stephen and Paul function to reopen the trial of Jesus because new witnesses arise with new testimony and new evidence on Jesus' behalf.

Paul's trial in Acts 25:23–26:32 is hardly new to a Lukan reader, for it closely resembles other trials of Paul in Acts:

1. As regards charges, although the narrative begins and ends with a comment about Paul's "defense" (*apelogeito*, 26:1; *autou apologoumenou*, 26:24), Paul's speech is not simply a straight defense to charges. The former charges are already dismissed by the judge: "King Agrippa and all who are present with us, you see this man about whom the whole Jewish people petitioned me, both at Jerusalem and here, shouting that he ought not to live any longer. But I found that he had done nothing deserving of death" (25:24–25). The focus of

the trial shifts from specific charges to a judgment on Jewish "controversies" (*zētēmata,* 25:19; 26:3). The focal *point of judgment*[54] is the issue of God's raising the dead:

26:6 I am being *judged* for hope in the promise made by God to our fathers.

26:8 Why is it *judged* incredible by any of you that God raises the dead?

This is similar to the *point of judgment* in other Pauline trials:

23:6 *I am being judged* with respect to the hope and the resurrection of the dead.

24:21 *I am being judged* today with respect to the resurrection.

2. As regards Paul's credentials as a witness, the recounting of Paul's very strict Jewish education in 26:2–3 serves to establish his character as a trustworthy witness. Unlike Peter and John, who were dismissed because of their lack of education (4:13), Paul is acknowledged as learned (26:4–5, 24), and therefore trustworthy. This resembles the function of Paul's earlier testimony before the Jewish assembly (22:3).

3. The recounting of Paul's persecution of the Way (26:9–12) functions as did the comparable report in 22:4–5 to show that Paul is a "reluctant witness"[55] on Jesus' behalf, thus adding to his credibility as a witness.

4. As regards Paul's account of Jesus' appearance (26:13–18), this functions here as it did in 22:6–11 as the basis for Paul's eyewitness experience of the risen Jesus. This experience constitutes him as an official witness, even as one commissioned to testify to this event. Jesus explains: "For I have appeared to you for this purpose, to appoint you to serve and bear testimony to the things in which you have seen me" (26:16).

We are advised, then, to see Acts 26 as a forensic speech, similar to Paul's other forensic speeches.

Although other Pauline forensic speeches contain testimony on Jesus' behalf, Acts 26 has a singular summary of Pauline witnessing to Jesus. Paul argues in typical Lukan fashion that Jesus is the fulfillment of "what Moses and the prophets said would come to pass: that the Christ must suffer, and that, by being the first to rise from the dead, he would proclaim light both to the people and to the Gentiles" (26:22–23). Elsewhere in the speech, Paul testifies that he is commissioned on Jesus' behalf "to open their eyes, that they may turn from darkness to light, and from the power of Satan to God" (26:18). Paul, then, testifies that Jesus is God's foreordained Christ; he is the unique savior of all humankind; in him one gains access to God, with all of one's sins forgiven. All of this rests on the prime testimony that Jesus is raised from the dead (26:23). Acts 26, then, is special in Paul's speeches for the strong testimony it bears on Jesus' behalf.

The judges of this trial are not Jewish judges, and so this trial of Paul is not a trial of Israel. The judges, nevertheless, are also on trial. The *point of judgment* (26:6, 8) is how Festus and Agrippa will judge the resurrection. Paul's testimony on Jesus' behalf is aimed at winning their assent, as Agrippa realized: "In a short time you think to make me a Christian!" (26:28). This is Paul's stated intent: "I would to God not only you but also all who hear me this day might become such as I am" (26:29). The judges, then, are on trial. In one sense they judge justly, for they acquit Paul: "This man has done nothing to deserve death or imprisonment" (26:31). But they obviously did not accept Paul's testimony on Jesus' behalf; and in this they judge unjustly and so come under judgment. The trial of Jesus in Acts 26 has resulted once more in judgment on his judges.

Chapter Four

JESUS' ADDRESS
TO THE WOMEN OF JERUSALEM
(LK 23:27–31)

The interpretation of Lk 23:27–31 has been anything but unanimous. Totally contradictory understandings of it and diverse methodological approaches to its interpretation, moreover, have not yet indicated the way to a surer exegesis. In keeping with the approach of this study, I will first attempt to explain the passage relying on redaction-critical observations. One important clue surely must be the appreciation of the passage in the context of the rejection of Jesus in 23:13–25. And so I suggest that the address to the women of Jerusalem must be evaluated in this context as a judgment pronounced on unbelief. Finally, the Lukan themes and patterns in the passage must be seen in the light of comparable motifs in the rest of Luke-Acts.

I.
Exegetical Problem in Lk 23:27–31

The interpretation of 23:27–31 is controversial. Let us examine some of the major exegetical positions taken in regard to the difficult issues found in the text. First who are these women ("daughters of Jerusalem")? They have been identified as real figures, part of Jesus' general feminine following, actual sympathizers from Jerusalem, curious women,[1] or as women who administered drugged wine to condemned criminals.[2] As symbolic figures, they have been said to represent Jerusalem or Israel.[3] Present trends in interpretation consider them as symbolic figures.

Second, according to the form critical approach to this passage,

Bultmann alluded to Jewish parallels to it and an Aramaic form which lies behind it (biographical apophthegm), and surmised that it "derives from an Aramaic original."[4] More recently it has been argued that only vv. 27–28 and 31 come from Luke's source and that he added vv. 29–30 himself.[5] Thus all or the major part of the passage is said to be part of a pre-Lucan passion narrative.[6]

Third, various Old Testament and Jewish sources have been suggested as the background for individual verses in the passage. Zec 12:10–14 has often been cited as the background/source of v. 29.[7] Although most commentators identify Hos 10:8 as the source of v. 30, a recent German critic argued for Is 54:1, 10 as the relevant parallel for vv. 29b and 30b.[8]

Finally, the total impact of the passage has been difficult to interpret: some say it is a prophetic doom word,[9] a cry for vengeance; others say it is a word of compassion;[10] and still others, a call to repentance.[11]

My hypothesis is that the passage should be form-critically described as Luke's own collection of diverse popular and biblical sayings, the total impact of which is a prediction of the city's doom. It is a formal prophetic oracle of judgment. The important comparative parallels which I will suggest come from the prophetic lawsuit material of the Old Testament. Evidence in support of my suggestion will come mainly from a careful redaction-critical investigation of the passage and from a comparison with similar themes and expressions in Luke-Acts.

Commentators have already suggested parallels in language between Lk 23:27–31 and other passages in Luke's Gospel, but this was done haphazardly and without concern for the form of the material.[12] The observation that Jesus wept over the city when he first entered it (19:41–44) and when he finally left it[13] deserves to be repeated and I will use this observation as my starting point; for it is evidence that Luke, to whom these two passages are unique in the Synoptic tradition, had a creative hand in their composition.

II.
EXEGESIS OF LK 23:27–31

A. The Crowd of "the People" and Women (23:27)

In 23:27 it is stated that Jesus is followed by a crowd containing elements of the people and women: "There followed him a great multitude of the people, and of women." Insufficient attention has been paid to the fact that the text contains two elements here: (1) "a great multitude of 'the people' " and (2) "and of women." Why the double notation? Are these synonymous or is a distinction implied?

In general, Luke refers to the people of Israel as the object of God's saving word in Jesus (1:17, 68, 77; 2:10) and as the object of Jesus' own preaching (9:13; 19:48; 20:1). But with the approach of the passion, the evaluation of "people" changes. On the one hand Luke seems to distinguish the people from their leaders during this Jerusalem narrative, so that "the people" remain favorable to Jesus (19:47–48; 20:1–6, 19, 26, 45; 22:2; 23:5; 24:19–20).[14] Even at the cross, the leaders scoff at Jesus while "the people" merely look on (23:35). Yet as we saw in the last chapter, there is no gainsaying the fact that Luke portrayed this people as rejecting Jesus (23:13).[15] Nevertheless, the guilt of permanently rejecting Jesus and the Christian preachers is not charged as such to "the people," inasmuch as many of this same "people" are ultimately converted in Acts and become the new "people of God."[16]

Yet there is a stream of material which presents Jerusalem and its people in a negative light. In Lk 21:23 "this people" is the object of God's judgment, "for great distress shall be upon the earth and wrath upon *this people*." The cause of this is surely found in Jerusalem's rejection both of God's messengers (13:33–34) and of Jesus' own ministry (19:44). There tends to be, then, a negative portrayal of Jerusalem, yet a more positive view of "the people" in Luke.[17]

In the statement, "a great multitude of the people, and of women," it seems clear that "the people" should not simply be considered synonymous with "the women." As Luke tells the story, a distinction is ultimately made between "the people" and Jerusalem. Many of the "people" will repent and convert (Lk 23:48; Acts 2:41–42; 5:12–14); but Jerusalem is another matter. It is the daughters of Jerusalem—as distinguished from "the people"—who are formally addressed in 23:27–31. They symbolize the element of Israel which continually rejected God's messengers.

It has been suggested that "daughters of Jerusalem" is a symbolic remark,[18] but symbolic of "the people" or Jerusalem? While the phrase "daughters of Jerusalem/Zion" occurs frequently in the Old Testament in prophetic oracles of both joy and woe,[19] in Luke the personified Jerusalem has twice earlier been addressed by Jesus in indictments of the city: "Jerusalem, Jerusalem, killing the prophets . . ." (13:34) and "he saw the city and said, 'Would that even today you knew the things that make for peace' " (19:41). In light of the distinction noted above between "the people" and Jerusalem, "daughters of Jerusalem" should not simply be equated with Israel, but should be seen as identifying that element of Israel which consistently rejected God's messengers, i.e., the prophets, Jesus, and the apostolic preachers.[20]

B. Jesus Turns to the Women (23:28)

In 23:28 Jesus "turns" and addresses the women. This seemingly innocent physical action of Jesus, however, is distinctively Lukan and would seem to belong to a characteristic pattern of describing Jesus. Often Luke notes that "Jesus turned and . . ." in connection with praise or blessing (7:9, 44; 10:22); his "turning" might also be used in combination with a demand (14:25) or a rebuke (9:55). When considered alongside 22:61, one might tend to see a parallel between Jesus' turning to Peter and to the women; in the former case, the turning might be interpreted as a call to repentance,[21] so that, on analogy, the turning to the women should likewise be understood as a call to repentance. In 22:61, however, the effect of Jesus' turning to Peter is to remind him of the prediction of his denial; his sin is dramatically brought home to him. We read further of Peter's tears and repentance, a thing never said of Jerusalem.

Perhaps the best Lukan analogy for Jesus' "turning" in 23:28 might be the description of God's action in Acts 7:42. Because of the people's rejection of God's messenger, Moses (7:35, 39), "God turned and gave them over to the worship of the host of heaven." Paul, after his rejection by the Jewish synagogue in Antioch, "turned" to the Gentiles (Acts 13:46), which turning is a judgment upon the unbelieving crowd. Jesus' turning thus could be understood as belonging to an act of judgment resulting from the Jews' rejection of God's messengers. Jesus' turning in 23:28, then, is not necessarily a call to repentance, but may be an act of judgment.

Could not the command to weep (23:28) be understood as a command to repent? Weeping in Luke is good and productive of salvation (6:21). Those who weep are ultimately consoled (7:13; 8:52) or forgiven (7:38; 22:61 in the light of 22:32 and 24:34). Yet Jesus himself wept over

Jerusalem (19:41) as part of a lamentation for its doom. And it is far from obvious that the women weeping over Jesus are analogous to the weeping prostitute in Simon's house. She actually weeps over Jesus in repentance for her sins; the daughters of Jerusalem are not now weeping over Jesus, nor are they ever told to. They weep for the ruin of their children. Jeremiah's oracle in 9:17–22 to the women of Jerusalem seems to afford a useful example of the kind of weeping enjoined in 23:28.[22] The professional mourners are summoned to lead the mourning in Israel: "Hear, O Women, the word of the Lord, teach your daughters a lament, and each to her neighbor a dirge" (9:20). This is weeping occasioned by God's judgment on sinful Jerusalem (Jer 9:13–16).

C. Days Are Coming (23:29)

The address of Jesus continues with an ominous phrase, "Days are coming . . ." In Luke "the coming days" are carefully distinguished from the day of the Son of Man and from the final day of judgment. In passages unique to Luke, "the coming days" refer specifically to the destruction of Jerusalem. For example, in the lament over Jerusalem in 19:43, "the days shall come upon you" refers to the ruin of the city in 70 A.D., brought upon the city for its rejection of its Savior. And in chapter 21, Luke added significant phrases to Mark's account which are relevant to our point. In 21:6 Luke added to Mark's text the phrase "days will come"; in 21:22 Luke clarified the meaning of the earlier addition: "for these are days of vengeance." The context is clearly the destruction of Jerusalem in 70 A.D., for v. 20 says, "when you see Jerusalem . . ." and v. 24 continues with "Jerusalem will be trodden down." Compared with Mt and Mk, Luke has notably more interest in the judgment of Jerusalem. If, then, we read 23:29 in the light of 21:22, the days which are coming on the women of Jerusalem are days of retribution and wrath.

The weeping of the women in fact is an ironic reversal of many points of Luke's presentation of salvation history. The poor, the hungry, and the weeping are blessed (6:21); even persecuted members of the group are blessed (6:23). Of course "blessing" is something which comes upon believers: upon those who believe the angelic message (1:45), who hear the word of God (11:27), who see what the apostles see (10:23). Alternately, the barren are blessed—with children (1:7, 36). But in 23:29, all of this is reversed. Those who weep are *not* blessed; they are not believers and their weeping is not the result of their faith in Jesus. Those with children will weep because their children are perishing. No salvation here! Rather, 23:29 begins to sound like the cry of lament, "Would that we were never born."

D. Fall on Us, Cover Us (23:30)

The meaning of 23:30 is greatly clarified by comparison with Hos 10:8. In the passage from Hosea, a prophetic judgment is pronounced against the idolatrous northern kingdom. As that destructive judgment unfolds, those caught up in it cry "Cover us . . . fall on us" (10:8), a cry to escape judgment. This text of Hosea is apparently cited in a similar context in Rev 6:16. A "day of wrath" (6:17) is proclaimed from heaven, a day on which the sixth seal will be broken and retribution will be visited upon those who slew the martyrs, whose souls are now under the heavenly altar (6:10–11). When that "day of wrath" comes, those responsible for the slaughter of Christians will cry: "Fall on us and hide us from the face of him who is seated on the throne" (6:16). They are crying to escape the deserved judgment which is coming upon them. As the following synopsis indicates, Lk 23:30 seems to contain an allusion to Hos 10:8.

LK 23:30	HOS 10:8	REV 6:16
Then	and	and
they will begin to say	they will say	they will say
to the mountains	to the mountains	to the mountains
"Fall on us"	"Cover us"	and to the rocks
		"Fall on us"
and to the hills	and to the hills	and cover us
"Cover us."	"Fall on us."	from the face of
		the one who sits
		on the throne and
		from the wrath of
		the lamb . . ."

The context of the saying in Lk 23:30 is the same as it is in Hos and Rev; the guilty cry out as God's judgment comes upon them. They seek to hide from God's wrath at the time of judgment and to escape retribution for their crimes.

E. If They Do This in the Green Wood (23:31)

Based on comparison with similar Jewish materials, 23:31 has conventionally been interpreted as a judgment saying. The exact meaning of the saying in Luke is difficult to state with exactness because the identity of the referents in the sentence is imprecise ("if *they* do these things . . ."). A range of logical possibilities has been offered by commentators. Plummer suggested both the Romans and the Jews as possible choices:

(1) If the *Romans* treat Me, whom they admit to be innocent, in this manner, how will they treat those who are rebellious and guilty?
(2) If the *Jews* deal thus with One who has come to save them, what treatment shall they receive themselves for destroying Him?[23]

And in his recent commentary on Luke, F.W. Danker suggested a third explanation, with God as the subject:

(3) If *God* permits this to happen to one who is innocent, what will be the fact of the guilty?[24]

Precisely because 23:31 is no doubt a popular a fortiori aphorism, it can so easily apply to a variety of situations.[25]

Nevertheless, using Luke's treatment of Jerusalem as our criterion, I think Plummer's second suggestion was correct. The particular sense of the aphorism in 23:31 seems to imply that in the phrase "if they do these things," the identity of the subject ("they") refers to the Jerusalemites; the phrase "do these things" indicates their rejection of Jesus; and "in the green wood" points to their present unbelieving situation.[26] Comparably in the apodosis, "in the dry wood" would then refer to a future situation of the Jerusalemites, viz., their permanent rejection of Jesus and the apostles as seen from the perspective of Acts. "What will happen?" would then refer to the destructive judgment of Jerusalem in 70 A.D. Later passages in Jewish literature, while not exact parallels to Lk 23:31, confirm the use of this language in contexts which treat of death and judgment.[27]

III.
PROPHETIC JUDGMENT ORACLES

The next step in determining the meaning of Lk 23:27–31 is to compare it with other passages in Luke which contain similar themes and perhaps even a common form (13:33–35; 19:41–44; 21:20–24).

The lament over Jerusalem in 13:33–35, of course, comes to Luke from the Q source which he shares with Mt 23:37–39. The setting in Luke, however, seems quite artificial, since Jesus is distant from Jerusalem and its conflicts at this point in the Gospel, while an attempt by Herod to capture Jesus is recorded as the occasion for Jesus' remarks.[28] No, it is not Herod who will kill Jesus, but Jerusalem who characteristically kills God's prophets. Jesus' remarks formally contain an address to the guilty city (13:34a), a statement of its crimes (13:34b, 33) and a sentence-curse for those crimes (13:35).

The sentence-curse in 13:35 ("your house shall be abandoned") is not identical with anything in the Scriptures. The closest parallel is Jer 22:5. Blessings and curses are presented to the people of Jerusalem by the prophet in 22:4–5. They are told that "if you do not heed these words," then judgment will come upon you and the city: "this house shall become a desolation." Confirmation for seeing Lk 13:35 as a general reference to an Old Testament text of judgment comes from Acts, where Ps 68:26LXX is cited in judgment upon Judas' treachery. It, too, alluded to a "desolate house," as the following synopsis shows:

Lk 13:35   "Your house shall be abandoned."

Acts 1:20   "Let his habitation become desolate."

Jer 22:5   "This house shall become a desolation."

Thus judgment on unbelieving Jerusalem and upon the treacherous Judas is expressed by reference to their "desolate houses."

As we shall see in this chapter, Luke tends to allude to Old Testament texts when expressing God's judgment upon sinners, thus making it probable that there is an allusion to Jer 22:5 in Lk 23:31. The Old Testament contains numerous judgments against the "house" of Israel (see Jer 12:7 and 1 Kgs 9:7). There are, moreover, many parallels to Lk 13:35 in Jewish traditions closer in date to the writing of the Gospels. Hillel the Elder, for example, is reported to have issued a blessing/curse in a terse talio formula:

If thou wilt come into my house, I will come into thy house;
if thou wilt not come into my house, I will not come into thy
house.[29]

Furthermore, the "house" spoken of in Luke is not primarily the temple
but Jerusalem and its people.

According to these comparisons, then, the sentence-curse in Lk
13:35 should be understood as a judgment on the city for rejecting God
and his agents.[30] The sentence-curse, moreover, seems to be expressed
in language which, if not a direct citation of Scripture, at least is strongly
allusive of Old Testament prophetic judgments on Jerusalem. Luke himself insists in 21:22 that the future ruin of Jerusalem is predicted and
seemingly described in Scripture. Jerusalem's fate in 70 A.D. will be a
judgment of God; as in 586 B.C., so in 70 A.D.

The second passage for comparison, Lk 19:41–44, is distinctive to
Luke. It, too, is structured in a form identical with the Q passage, 13:33–
35. The guilty city is addressed: "if only you knew . . ." (19:41); its
crimes are cited: "you did not know the time of your visitation . . ."
(19:44b, 42); and a sentence-curse is pronounced: "your enemies will
throw palisades around you . . ." (19:43–44a). The sentence-curse is
more descriptive here than in 13:35; and, like it, 19:44 seems either to
be alluding to prophetic judgment texts or at least to be employing language evocative of them. Luke's statement, "and dash you to pieces, you
and your children," contains language used exclusively in descriptions
of Jerusalem's previous ruin. Although the exact text of Lk 19:44 is not
found in the Old Testament, Hos 10:14 is a suggestive parallel. A prophetic judgment is pronounced against the northern kingdom. The crime
is stated in 10:13, "For you have plowed iniquity, you have reaped in-
justice" (10:13); the sentence-curse follows, "As Shalman destroyed Be-
tharbel, mothers were dashed in pieces with their children, thus it will be
with you, O house of Israel" (10:14). Hosea as well as other Old Testament texts indicates that "to dash to pieces" is a term used exclusively
in descriptions of divine judgment against Samaria or Jerusalem.[31]

The form of 19:41–44, moreover, is not simply an accidental bor-
rowing or imitation of the Q passage found in 13:33–35, for the form
even of that passage is similar to typical Old Testament prophetic judgment oracles. There is a type of disclosure in the prophetic literature

which form critics call the *rib* pattern or prophetic lawsuit.[32] Acting as God's agent, the prophet conducts a trial: he gathers witnesses, summons the defendants, cites their crimes in an indictment, and pronounces a sentence-curse. For forsaking God's covenant, the nation is cursed with ruin. Luke, I maintain, was alert to this form and used it expressly in the composition of 19:41–44, differing from the classic prophetic judgment oracles only in the simpler form he employed (no witnesses are summoned). The sentence-curse in Luke, moreover, differs from that found in the prophetic lawsuits in that it seems to allude to scriptural materials from earlier traditions concerning Jerusalem's ruin, which now function as support for the present verdict on the city as divine judgment. "According to the Scriptures" is not an argument exclusively employed vis-à-vis Jesus' death and resurrection (see Lk 24:26–27, 44–45). As Luke makes abundantly clear in 21:22, it can function apropos of divine judgment on Jerusalem.

A third passage in Luke, while it is not a direct address to Jerusalem, contains the same basic pattern of crime and punishment found in the formal oracles against the city. In the midst of the eschatological discourse in Lk 21, the evangelist inserted special materials in the Markan source for this discourse.[33] According to Luke, in 21:20 it is not the presence of the "desolating sacrilege" (see Mk 13:14) which serves as the temporal clue, but the sight of Jerusalem encircled by siege armies, "When you see Jerusalem surrounded by armies, then you know the time" (21:20a). This, then, signals that "its desolation is at hand" (21:20b), a remark not found in the Markan source. Mark's terse advice to flee the city is greatly expanded in Luke. There are clear warnings actually to vacate the city, "Let those who are inside the city depart" (21:21b) and warnings to forestall flight into it for safety, "Let not those who are out in the country enter into it" (21:21c). And an explanation is added by Luke, "for these are days of vengeance" (21:22). This last remark is best understood by cross-reference to 13:34 and 19:42, as the Roman siege of Jerusalem in the war of 70 A.D. (see Lk 11:47–51; 20:16, 18; and Acts 7:51–53). A further explanatory note is appended to this material; these days of vengeance are happening as it was predicted in Scripture: "These are days of vengeance *to fulfill all that is written*" (21:22). This implies that by being predicted in Scripture, the judgment on those who reject Jesus and God's prophets is a most serious crime indeed. As judgment came upon Jerusalem in 586 B.C., so God's judgment will be repeated. The Scripture is used by Luke as precedent for judgment and as proof that God acts against the house of Israel.

After the condemnation in 21:20–21, a sentence-curse is pronounced, viz., the fall of the city (vv. 23–24a), which contains an interpretative note explaining the significance of the disaster, "wrath upon this people" (v. 23b). The wrath must surely be God's, since the city will fall "in fulfillment of all that is written." This "wrath" is identical with the "vengeance" mentioned in v. 22.

In the more formal prophetic judgment oracles in 13:33–35 and 19:41–44, the doom of the city was sealed with an allusion to Scripture. The present prophecy makes unmistakable reference to this key element (v. 22), and even seems to allude to phrases from prophetic oracles in its own description of the coming ruin. For example, in 21:22a, "days of vengeance" sounds quite similar to Hos 9:7 LXX: "The days of vengeance are come, the days of recompense are come." Hosea spoke this when he announced that God remembers inequity and requites sin (v. 9).[34]

In 21:24, the prediction that "Jerusalem will be trodden down by the Gentiles" resembles the sentence passed on Jerusalem by the prophets of the Old Testament. According to Is 10:6 LXX, Assyria will act as God's agent of wrath when it comes against Jerusalem: "I will send my wrath against a sinful nation . . . to trample the cities." And in Zec 12:3 LXX, the MT was changed so that God's specific judgment against Jerusalem was predicted, and not just God's wrath on his enemies. Jerusalem itself becomes a stone to be trampled on by all its foes: "And it shall come to pass in that day that I will make Jerusalem a trodden stone to all the nations; every one that tramples on it shall utterly mock it."

It can be noted, moreover, that "to trample" in the LXX refers to trampling by enemies (Pss 7:9; 55:1–2; 56:3; Is 16:4; 18:2, 7), but especially to the trampling of Israel's sacred cities by foreign enemies (Is 28:3; 41:25; Ez 26:11); even God tramples them in his wrath (Is 63:3, 6). "To trample" is the distinctive term in later Jewish literature for describing the destroyed condition of Jerusalem during the Maccabean period (see 1 Mac 3:45, 51; Dan 8:13 LXX), and it comes into Christian usage in this same sense in Rev 11:2. Whether Luke had a particular scriptural passage in mind in 21:24 is impossible to determine. But he clearly used a phrase which is especially found in prophetic sentences against Jerusalem and in historical accounts of the city's ruin. Clearly he sees in that expression "the fulfillment of all that is written" (21:22).

Hence the prediction in 21:20–24, while it is not a formal oracle of judgment addressed to Jerusalem, as are 13:34–35 and 19:41–44, nevertheless contains many of the same formal elements found in those prophetic judgments: identification of the city, sentence of destruction, and the use of scriptural tradition as proof of divine condemnation.[35]

When we assess 23:27–31 in this light, the passage is seen to be formally similar to the prophetic judgment oracles found in two other places which treat of Jerusalem's fate. The wicked city is addressed ("Daughters of Jerusalem . . . ." v 28); sentence is pronounced ("days are coming . . ." v 29) and a text of Scripture/tradition is cited which both describes the coming disaster and serves as warrant for the divine nature of the judgment against the city (" 'Fall on us . . . hide us' " v 30). In this light I consider the popular saying in 23:31 to function as the crime which brings on this judgment ("if *they do this* in the green wood"). Thus alongside Lk 13:34–35 and 19:41–44, the address to Jerusalem in 23:27–31 should be understood as another example of the prophetic oracle of judgment against Jerusalem, together with the more descriptive approach to this material in 21:20–24. The full force of the oracle form may be grasped by the following synopsis for the four Lucan examples.

The context of the passage in the flow of the Gospel narrative also contributes to a proper interpretation of it as a judgment oracle. It has been noted that when Jesus first entered Jerusalem (19:41–44) he wept over it; he assessed its crimes and pronounced judgment against it. Balancing that is the present passage in which weeping is again prominent— weeping, however, not for Jesus but for Jerusalem's children. Its crimes are exposed and judgment is pronounced. Lk 19:41–44 and 23:27–31, then, form an *inclusio* around Jesus' activity in Jerusalem, both passages telling the same story of crime and punishment.

The position of 23:27–31 following 23:13–25 is likewise important. As we saw, Israel has made a formal choice in 23:13–25, albeit this choice is a rejection of Jesus and a choosing of his death. In Luke's perspective, this is a formal crime; and judgment upon that crime follows immediately in 23:27–31.

The Prophetic Judgment Oracle in Luke

formal elements	Lk 13:33–35	Lk 19:41–44	Lk 21:20–24	Lk 23:27–31
address	Jerusalem, Jerusalem,	Would that you knew the things that are for your peace	(identification: "when you see Jerusalem")	Daughters of Jerusalem, weep not for me but for yourselves and for your children
crime	killing the prophets, and stoning those sent to her. How often would I have gathered your children . . . and you would not	. . . because you did not know the day of your visitation	Then DAYS OF PUNISHMENT will these be, to fulfill all that is written	For if they do this in the green wood, what will happen in the dry?
sentence	Behold, YOUR HOUSE SHALL BE ABANDONED	for days will come upon you and your enemies will throw up palisades around you and surround you and press you in from all sides. And THEY WILL CAST you and YOUR CHILDREN in you TO THE GROUND. And they will not leave one stone upon another in you.	Alas for those carrying in the womb and to those nursing in those days. For a great necessity will be on the land and wrath to this people. They will fall by the sword and be led away captive among all nations. And JERUSALEM WILL BE TRAMPLED ON BY ALL THE GENTILES	Behold, days are coming, in which they will say: Blessed are the barren, the wombs which never bore, the breasts which never nursed. They will begin to SAY TO THE MOUNTAINS: FALL ON US! AND TO THE HILLS: COVER US!

N.B. Scriptural allusions are identified by the use of upper case letters.

SUMMARY

The foregoing discussion suggests the following conclusions. The address of Jesus is not a call to repentance at all, but another example of Luke's prophetic oracle of judgment against the city for rejecting God's prophets. As a *vaticinium ex eventu*, it interprets the fall of the city in 70 A.D. as an act of divine retribution upon unbelieving Jews. Those Jews who accepted Jesus would have been warned to flee the city in 21:20–24, so that presumably anyone left in the city by the time of its fall may be considered an unbelieving Jew. The Q tradition was certainly suggestive to Luke on this point (see 11:50; 13:34–35). But as a *vaticinium ex eventu* the text functions as a judgment oracle and not as a call to repentance—it is simply too late!

Form critically the passage should be acknowledged as the creation of Luke himself and does not come from the pre-Luke source. While the archetype of this form (13:34–35) is found in the Q source, Luke appreciated it for what it was and consciously employed it again and again: in 19:41–44, when he composed another oracle against Jerusalem, and in 23:27–31, when the rejected Messiah leaves the city for his death.

IV.
JUDGMENT PATTERNS IN LUKE-ACTS

The thematic importance of Lk 23:27–31 gains in clarity when seen in comparison with similar motifs in Luke-Acts. The judgment pronounced in 23:27–31 follows upon the rejection of God's prophet in 23:13–25. These two motifs, rejection of prophets and judgment of their rejectors, are important themes which are extensively found in Luke-Acts.

A. "Division" Among the People

Luke has repeatedly presented in his work a *schism* in the audiences as a result of Christian preaching: i.e., a division of the crowds according to favorable or unfavorable reactions to Jesus.[36] Some of this material comes to Luke from Mark's Gospel: (a) the parable of the sower tells of diverse reactions to the sowing of "the word" (Lk 8:4–8//Mk 4:14–20) and (b) the rich young man rejects Jesus' teaching on possessions, while the apostles respond favorably (Lk 18:18–30)//Mk10:17–31). The Q source presented the parable of diverse reactions to the invitation to the great banquet (Lk 14:15–24//Mt 22:1–10). But the bulk of this material is distinctive to the third evangelist and displays his editorial bent.

The first mention of this *schism* motif is thematically located in the solemn prophetic utterance of Simeon at the very beginning of the Gospel: "This child is set for the fall and rising of many in Israel" (Lk 2:34–35).[37] Simeon's prophecy is fulfilled over and over:

1. Simon the leper treats Jesus with little courtesy, while the sinner woman weeps over his feet (7:49–50).
2. Zacchaeus repents at Jesus' word, while the crowd reacts with hostility to Jesus' eating with a sinner (19:1–10).
3. The crowds acclaim Jesus at his entry into Jerusalem, while the Pharisees seek to silence their acclaim (19:38–40).
4. The two thieves crucified with Jesus react quite differently to him (23:39–43).

The thematic prophecy of Simeon, moreover, is influential even in Acts. Diverse reactions to the apostolic preaching are liberally recorded.[38]

5. Juxtaposed to the Sadducean rejection of the apostolic preaching (Acts 4:1–3) is the note that five thousand persons believed (4:4).
6. Positive reaction to the Christian preaching (5:12–16) is again contrasted with legal proceeding against Peter (5:17–32).
7. Rejection of Stephen (chs. 6–7) and persecution of the Church (8:1–3) are balanced by success in Samaria (8:4–8).
8. Failure in regard to Simon the magician (8:9–24) is juxtaposed to the conversion of the Ethiopian eunuch (8:26–38).
9. Paul's preaching at Antioch in Pisidia leads to diverse reactions: acceptance (13:42–43) and rejection (13:44–47, 50–51).
10. Contrasting results of Christian preaching at Thessalonica are recorded: success (17:2–4) and failure (17:5–9). Similar reactions occur in Beroea (17:12–13) and in Corinth (18:5–11).
11. Sadducees and Pharisees divide over the issue of the resurrection (23:6–9).

Luke, then, repeatedly tells us that "the crowds were divided" (*eschisthē*, Acts 14:4) at the word of the Christian prophets. And he concludes Acts of the Apostles on this note, commenting that at Paul's preaching in Rome, "Some were convinced . . . while others disbelieved" (28:24).

Besides the recording of a *schism* in the crowds at the hearing of the Christian preaching, Luke tells as well of outright rejection of God's prophets. Jesus' inaugural preaching in Nazareth's synagogue results in the tragic rejection of God's new prophet (Lk 4:22–24). This event, because of its strategic importance at the beginning of Jesus' ministry, is prophetic of the way Jesus' and the Church's preaching will fare. Other examples of rejection quickly follow. For example, a healing on the sabbath precipitates a plot to do away with Jesus (6:11). Jesus' followers are themselves consoled for a mission of rejection; "blessed" are they when their audiences "hate you, exclude you, and revile you" (6:22). For thus were the prophets of old treated as well (6:23, 26). Jesus' exorcism produced a request that he leave the territory (8:37). Missionaries who are rejected are given clear instructions on what to do (10:10–12) and woe is proclaimed on cities which reject the testimony of Jesus (10:13–15). Rejection of Christian missionaries is interpreted as rejection of Jesus himself and of the one who sent him (10:16). A story is told about a householder who would not open his door to guests seeking entrance; they refused to come earlier at his invitation and so are declared "unknown" (13:24–30). In fact, those first invited, who refused to come in, will be last (13:28–30). The failure of Jerusalem to know the day of its visitation is lamented by Jesus (19:41–44). Finally the Jewish trials of Jesus record a solemn rejection of him (22:66–71; 23:15–25). The prophecy of Simeon is painfully, but amply fulfilled.

The rejection of the Christian prophets in Acts can be traced through the many notes of Jewish persecution of the Church. Peter *et al.* are arrested and silenced (Acts 4–5); Stephen's testimony leads to his rejection and death (Acts 6–7); the Church is persecuted in Jerusalem and Damascus (Acts 8–9). Paul, the new Christian prophet, is plotted against in Damascus (9:23–25) and in Antioch (13:45, 50). He is stoned in Iconium (14:19), chased from Thessalonica (17:10), hounded in Beroea (17:12–13), and opposed in Corinth (18:6). Finally in Acts 21–26, Paul is arrested and tried; his assassination is repeatedly plotted (Acts 23:12–22; 25:3).

In both the Gospel and Acts, then, Luke tells of the fulfillment of Simeon's prophecy.

B. Judgment on Those Who Reject God's Prophets

What happens to those who reject God's prophets? A negative judgment on God's witnesses brings a condemning judgment on the judges. For rejecting Jesus and the Christian preachers, judgment and condemnation are proclaimed. The bulk of this material comes to Luke from the Q tradition. John the Baptizer describes Jesus as waving a winnowing fork, separating wheat (believers) from chaff (unbelievers) and casting the chaff into a furnace (Lk 3:17//Mt 3:12). Judgment is pronounced against the cities of Jesus' ministry for their unbelief: "Woe to you, Chorazin! Woe to you, Bethsaida!" (Lk 10:13–15//Mt 11:20–24). The cause of judgment, indifference in the face of Jesus' prophetic works (10:13), will weigh heavily "in the judgment." Capernaum, the city which rejected Jesus' miracles, will be condemned (10:15). The queen of the South and the city of Nineveh will "arise at the judgment and condemn" this generation; they accepted the words of Solomon and Jonah, but this generation rejects the words of the one who is "greater than Solomon . . . greater than Jonah" (11:30–32//Mt 12:38–41). The door will be shut against those who did not enter the narrow way at the preaching of Jesus. They will be declared excommunicated from Israel and condemned: "I do not know you" (13:24–30).[39] Those who refused the first invitation to the great feast are condemned for their refusal: "I tell you, none of those who were invited will taste my banquet" (14:24).

Traditions from Mark's Gospel reinforce this theme of judgment in Luke's Gospel. In a classic pronouncement of judgment, Jesus proclaims to unbelievers:

Whoever is ashamed of me and my words
of him will the Son of Man be ashamed
when he comes in his glory and the glory
of his Father and of the holy angels (Lk 9:26//Mk 8:38).

Again in the explanation of the parable of the vineyard, what will the owner of the vineyard do to those who rejected his prophets and his beloved one? "He will come and destroy those tenants" (Lk 20:16//Mk

12:9). In another place, failure to hear the prophetic word is described as a biblical scandal, a stumbling block: "Every one who falls on that stone will be broken to pieces, but when it falls on any one it will crush him" (Lk 20:18).

Besides keeping all this judgment material from earlier sources, Luke added his own contribution to this theme, which indicates how important this motif was for his perspective. To the traditional parable of the talents, Luke added the note that as the nobleman was about to leave to receive a kingdom, "His citizens hated him and sent an embassy after him saying, 'We do not want this man to reign over us' " (Lk 19:12–14). This rejection brings a severe judgment when the royal nobleman returns to settle accounts: "But as for those enemies of mine, who did not want me to reign over them, bring them here and slay them before me" (19:27). To this should be added the first half of this chapter, which studied Luke's judgment oracles against Jerusalem. Materials, then, which came to Luke from Mark and Q lost none of their immediacy, probably due to the Roman-Jewish war of 70 A.D. To these Luke added his own materials on the judgment which comes upon rejection and unbelief. It should be noted, moreover, that the judgment which Luke records comes precisely as condemnation for rejecting God's prophets, Jesus and the Christian preachers.

The theme of judgment upon unbelievers is also found in Acts. Luke comes at the topic of judgment in a different way in three speeches in Acts.

1. In Acts 3, Luke continues to develop the theme of prophecy-fulfillment when he sees the fulfillment of Dt 18:15–16 in Jesus, the prophet like Moses. Yet the speech contains a dire threat of judgment as well, for Luke continues the prophecy from Deuteronomy which warns: "And it shall be that every soul that does not listen to that prophet *shall be destroyed from the people*" (Acts 3:23/Dt 18:19). At this point, Luke has intensified the LXX word for judgment, changing *ekdikēso* to *exolethreuthēsetai*. The point is that Luke records the judgment of Scripture against those who reject God's prophets, a move comparable to the use of Scripture in the prophetic woe oracles against Jerusalem.

2. Stephen's speech records another judgment on those who refused to obey the prophet Moses. After noting that "Our fathers refused to

obey him (Moses), but thrust him aside" (7:37), Stephen tells how God brought judgment upon the unbelievers: "But God turned and gave them over to the host of heaven" (7:42).[40] Then Stephen cites Am 5:25–27 as the scriptural warrant for God's judgment, describing how God has always dealt with this rebellious nation: "I will remove you beyond Babylon" (7:42).

3. In still a third place, Luke records in the apostolic preaching a warning judgment against those who reject God's prophets. After testifying to Jesus, Paul told the synagogue at Antioch: "Beware lest there come upon you what is said in the prophets, 'Behold, you scoffers, and wonder and perish; for I do a deed in your days, a deed you will never believe, if one declares it to you' " (13:40–41). The warning is realized when the crowds reject Paul's preaching in 13:44–45, 50. In three speeches, then, Luke records the threat of judgment against those who reject God's prophets. The judgments, moreover, are formally presented through a citation of Scripture, which serves to prove that divine judgment shown against Israel and Jerusalem in biblical history will continue in the present time. Prophecies await fulfillment. The Scriptures, then, serve as the warrant for Lukan theodicy.

C. Jesus as Judge

In still another vein Luke expresses the theme of judgment in Acts. Peter tells Cornelius of Jesus' role as judge: "God commanded us to preach that he (Jesus) is the one ordained by God to be judge of the living and the dead" (Acts 10:42). And Paul proclaims to the Athenians, "God has fixed a day on which he will judge the world in righteousness by a man whom he has appointed" (17:31). During his trials, Paul twice alludes to judgment: he tells Felix that he and his Jewish accusers agree about a resurrection into judgment (24:15), a point which he reiterates to Felix in later conversations: "He argued about justice, self-control, and future judgment" (24:25). In proclaiming Jesus as Judge, Luke is apparently reflecting a traditional confessional formula about him (see 1 Pet 4:5, 2 Tim 4:1).[41] But the designation of Jesus as Judge is a very important theme in Luke-Acts as well.

Jesus is the Judge who separates the wheat from the chaff (Lk 3:17). He pronounces judgments of woe against unbelieving cities (10:13–15).

He shuts the door on those who refuse his invitation (13:25). He executes judgment against those who would not have him reign over them (19:27). In each case, Jesus' judgment comes upon those who reject him as God's prophet and refuse to believe in him. In Luke-Acts, then, Luke presents Jesus as the judge of God's covenant people. Seen against this background, the woe oracles against Jerusalem are still more examples of Luke's consistent presentation of Jesus as Judge. The address to the women of Jerusalem (23:27–31), then, fully reflects Luke's typical presentation of Jesus as one who pronounces judgment on those who reject God's prophets.

CONCLUSION

This investigation indicates that Luke presents Jesus as a Judge in his passion narrative. It is not just that Jesus utters prophetic woe oracles, for judgment is a key element in Luke's Christology. First, as the rejected Son of Man, Jesus becomes the Judged Judge. Second, it belongs to God's Lord and Christ to exercise judgment over God's covenant people. And since from his birth Jesus is the heir of David's throne (Lk 1:32–33), it belongs to this ruler of God's covenant to exercise judgment.

It may be disturbing for some to find Luke presenting such a view of Jesus in the passion narrative. We have tended to see Jesus as the victim in these circumstances, as one who is the recipient of judgment and hatred. Jesus's suffering, moreover, is popularly understood as ''on our behalf'' and ''in our stead.'' We have never thought of Jesus acting aggressively against sinners in this context, although we know that this is part of the evangelist's portrait of him in his ministry. Judgment goes against the popular grain. But in fairness to Luke's redaction of Jesus' passion narrative, we must look to the text for our clues. First, Jesus' judgment in 23:27–31 completes the narrative begun in 23:13–25. Israel once more rejected, denied, and sought to destroy God's prophets; such a crime brings judgment. Second, Jesus' judgment is not all negative, for he will pronounce a saving judgment on the repentant criminal in Lk 23:43.

There is a sense in which Jesus' judgment here seems premature or incomplete. Only in Acts do we learn of Israel's repeated and conclusive rejection of Jesus and his witnesses. One needs Acts to make Lk 23:27–

Chapter Five

THE CRUCIFIXION SCENE:
THE SAVED SAVIOR

No reader of the Synoptic accounts of Jesus' death can fail to note the distinctiveness of Luke's version. This chapter aims at recovering Luke's redaction[1] of this episode in Jesus' passion by a careful identification of the omissions, additions and changes made to the Markan account and by identifying distinctive Lukan themes and patterns. An attempt will then be made to assess the drift of Luke's redaction: What distinctive description of Jesus is Luke communicating and what soteriology[2] is expressed by this presentation? The approach to Luke's text in this chapter is basically descriptive. The next chapter will more systematically investigate what model of soteriology Luke is employing in his presentation of Jesus' death. But for the present, let us investigate Lk 23:32–49 to recover Luke's particular redaction of the crucifixion scene.

I.
LUKAN REDACTION

Although Luke had the Markan version of Jesus' crucifixion, he omitted a number of items from Mark in his own presentation of Jesus' death. For example, the Hebrew word for "the place of the skull," Golgotha, is left out of Lk 23:33 (cf. Mk 15:22); nor is drugged wine offered to Jesus (cf. Mk 15:23); nor is there an initial time reference (cf. Mk 15:25). In the taunting of Jesus which follows his crucifixion, the crowds in Lk 23:35 do not "wag their heads" and blaspheme him (cf. Mk15:29a); nor do they chide him about destroying the temple (cf. Mk 15:29b; 14:58); nor do the crowds repeatedly demand that Jesus "come down from the cross'' (cf. Mk 15:30, 32b). In the narration of Jesus' death, Ps 22 is absent in Lk 23:46, as well as the reference to Elijah and the expectation of that prophet's rescue of Jesus (cf. Mk 15:34–36). Finally, the temple veil is not rent "from top to bottom" in 23:45 (cf. Mk 15:38b).

Significant among Luke's additions is the note about "the people"[3] looking at Jesus' crucifixion (23:35). These folk are probably to be linked with Luke's addition of bystanders who "saw what had taken place" and returned home, beating their breasts (23:48). An important addition, then, has been made in shifting the crowd's reaction from rejection of Jesus to repentance, which reaction balances the intensely negative reaction of the rulers and soldiers in 23:35–37. Although Mark merely noted that "those crucified with him reviled him" (15:32), Luke added a full account of this dialogue with Jesus in 23:39–43. Luke expanded the Markan note about "darkness over the whole land" (15:33) with the explanation of a solar eclipse, "the sun's light failed" (23:45).[4]

Luke changed many elements in Mark's account. Those crucified with Jesus are generic "criminals" (23:33), not "thieves" (Mk 15:27). In place of Mark's remark that only "high priests" mocked Jesus (15:31), Luke notes in more inclusive terms that it was "the rulers of the people" who reviled him (23:35b), probably intending this as another formal example of Israel's rejection of God's Christ, comparable to the formal rejection in 23:13, 18–25. The substance of the rulers' taunting in Luke's version focuses more explicitly on Jesus' relationship to God, probably an emphasis on Jesus' holiness and sinlessness which has been a Lukan theme throughout the passion narrative. Instead of mocking Jesus as "Christ, King of Israel," the Lukan rulers taunt him as "the Christ of God, his chosen one."

MK 15:31–32	LK 23:35
He saved others; himself he cannot save.	He saved others; let him save himself
Let *the Christ, the King of Israel* come down now from the cross.	if he is *the Christ of God, his chosen one*.

Luke's designation of Jesus as "Christ of God, his chosen one" (*ho eklektos*) seems to be echoing God's proclamation of Jesus at the transfiguration where he was acclaimed "my Son, my chosen" (*ho eklelegmenos*, 9:35). The one whom God chooses is rejected by Israel's rulers (Acts 3:14; 4:11); and so in their verdict on Jesus, the rulers "are found opposing God" (Acts 5:39). But even as Jesus is rejected by humanity, Luke ironically insists on God's closeness to Jesus.

Although Mk 15:29–32 noted that two Jewish groups mocked Jesus (passersby and chief priests), Luke presents a more inclusive picture of Jewish rulers and Gentile soldiers mocking Jesus in 23:35–37. This is probably to be linked with remarks in Acts where the "Gentiles rage" against God's Christ (Acts 4:25–27). In Acts 4, Luke interprets Ps 2 as referring to the time when Herod and Pilate "with the Gentiles and the people of Israel" gathered together against God's holy servant. Both in form and in content, the soldiers' mocking remarks in Lk 23:37 basically duplicate[5] the mockery of the Jewish rulers in 23:35, indicating how the two groups joined together against God's servant.

LK 23:35	LK 23:37
(Jewish rulers)	(Gentile soldiers)
He saved others; let him *save himself if* he is the *Christ of God*, his chosen one.	*Save yourself if* you are the *King of Israel*.

The most notable substitution by Luke is the prayer of the dying Jesus. Instead of Mark's remarks that Jesus cried out according to Ps 22, Luke reports in 23:46 that Jesus prayed from Ps 31, a point to which we will return shortly. And in place of the centurion's acclamation that Jesus was "Son of God" (Mk 15:39), Luke has him proclaim Jesus as innocent and saintly (23:47).

Luke's redaction is not just an occasional substitution or addition, but a structural reworking of the scene. As we noted above, the mocking of the two groups in 23:35–57 is more tightly drawn in Luke: (a) it is clearly inclusive, for Jewish leaders and Gentile soldiers join together in taunting Jesus, and (b) they both mock his identity and mission in their ironic remarks about him saving himself because he is God's holy and chosen one. But Luke, who does things in twos, balanced this mockery with the addition of the conversation between Jesus and the two criminals in 23:39–43. The first criminal repeats the basic mockery found in 23:35–37:

LK 23:35, 37	LK 23:39
He saved others let him *save himself* if he is *the Christ of God,* his chosen one.	*Save yourself* and us; are you not *the Christ?*

But this mockery is juxtaposed with the other criminal's confession of Jesus' innocence: "This man has done nothing wrong" (23:41). Balancing the criminal's mockery of Jesus' inability to save himself is the petition from the repentant criminal for "remembrance in your kingdom" (23:43). Luke, then, has restructured the Markan text to present two contrasting scenes of rejection and acceptance.[6]

The repentant criminal's reaction to Jesus, moreover, is joined in Luke by other positive reactions: (a) a centurion's declaration of Jesus' innocence (23:47), (b) the crowd's beating of its breast (23:48), (c) the burial of Jesus by the "good and righteous Joseph . . . who was looking for the kingdom of God" (23:50–53). The contrast is intentional and dramatic: for some, Jesus is a sinner and a fraud; he cannot be God's Christ. But for others he is innocent and saintly, even God's Christ. Some mock his powerlessness, while others beg his favor. While some soldiers revile Jesus (23:36–38), another soldier acclaims him as a saint (23:47). Structurally, then, there are three mockeries of Jesus (23: 35, 37, 39) which are juxtaposed to favorable reactions to Jesus (23:40–43, 47, 48, 50–53). As we noted earlier, Luke frequently presents in a narrative a "division" in reactions to Jesus. He is, after all, "set for the rise and fall of many" (2:34).

From this structural reworking of Mark's account, Luke has highlighted a "salvation" theme.[7] "Salvation" is the ironical subject of the triple mockery: "He *saved* others, let him *save* himself" (23:35) . . . "*save* yourself" (23:37) . . . "*save* yourself and us" (23:39). This mockery of Jesus as Savior is in stark contrast with the heavenly proclamation of Jesus as "the Savior, Christ the Lord" at his birth (2:11). The mocking remarks at the crucifixion are ironic for, while the mockers deny that he is Savior, God affirms that he is. And "salvation" becomes the substance of Jesus' proclamation to the repentant criminal (23:43) and the hope of the repentant crowd in 23:48. As well as Jesus' salvation of others is focused upon, his own salvation by God is highlighted by Luke in 23:46. "Salvation," then, is a key Lukan theme in his redaction of the crucifixion scene. Jesus becomes the Saved Savior.

Jesus' relationship to God is still another important redactional theme here. Jesus' evident faith in God and his prayer from the Psalms in 23:46 certainly stresses his holiness. Ironic as it may seem to some, Jesus' relation to God as "the Christ of God, his chosen one" (23:35) is just that, as we saw by comparing 23:35 with God's own pronouncement at the transfiguration (9:35). Jesus' innocence and the piety with which he dies are grounds for his acclamation as a saint (23:47). He certainly was not a sinner or God's enemy. His true identity as God's chosen one, his sinlessness, and his saintliness are affirmed again and again.

The drift of Luke's redaction, then, points to contrasting judgments about Jesus, judgments which mean salvation or rejection for God's people. There is, moreover, intense concern with "salvation" as well as with Jesus' faith and holiness.

II.
Jesus' Death and Lukan Eschatology

It is simply inaccurate to assert that there is no soteriology in Luke's passion narrative. Building on the redactional clues noted above, I propose to discuss four points which surfaced as part of Luke's redaction of the crucifixion scene and which have a direct bearing on the Lukan soteriology expressed in that scene:

1. "he saved others"
2. the Christ cannot save himself
3. faith saves
4. Jesus' faith in God

The focus of this contribution to Lukan soteriology is twofold. In an apologetic vein, it is important to call attention to the saving language which is so abundant in the crucifixion scene and to the salvation theme which is a major Lukan element of the death of Jesus. More positively, insufficient attention has been given to the Lukan theme that faith saves, even the faith of Jesus.

A. "He Saved Others" (Lk 23:39–43)

Despite the fact that Lk 23:32–49 depicts Jesus as a passive victim being put to death, there is in this scene a surprising amount of language which speaks of saving activity—Jesus' own salvation and his salvation of others. We noted earlier that Luke's redaction of the crucifixion retained Mark's comments about salvation (23:35) and that he expanded those remarks especially in the dialogue of the two criminals (23:39–43). In part the remarks about salvation are ironic; enemies taunt Jesus for saving others but not being able to save himself; and a genuine criminal rails at Jesus to "save yourself and us." The remarks are ironic because according to Luke *it is true* that Jesus saved others and would save even a criminal, if he would but repent. Yet the greatest irony lies in the fact that Jesus' death, a moment of weakness, is par excellence the saving moment, an experience of power. God will indeed save him. Irony, then, should not distract us from the truth contained in the taunts. And in part the remarks about salvation are unmistakably clear. Jesus judges the repentant criminal, declaring his sins forgiven and promising him life (23:43). He saves others. Let us look more closely at the major redactional change in the dialogue between the criminals and Jesus. It is here that Luke seems to have presented his strongest case for the saving significance of the death of Jesus.

Lk 23:39–43 contains a considerable number of characteristically Lukan themes and phrases, all of which have a bearing on the theme "he saves others." First, as regards the structure of Luke's addition to the Markan text, the dialogue of the two criminals exemplifies the Lukan tendency to do things in pairs. The two sets of mockers in 23:35 and 37 are balanced by two criminals in 23:39–43. Second, the criminals represent contrasting attitudes to Jesus. They differ in the tone of their remarks to Jesus and in the content of their requests of him. One continues the mockery of Jesus, taunting him to "save yourself and us." Inasmuch as his words are identical with those of Jesus' enemies in 23:35, he is presented as one who rejects Jesus as God's Christ. The second criminal speaks of Jesus' innocence and joins himself to Jesus in his request to be remembered. In contrast to the first criminal, he may be said to accept Jesus. And so we have another example of a "division" in the Lukan narrative.

A third theme comes to mind in 23:40, when the rejecting criminal is described as one "who does not fear God." In the Old Testament when someone is described as "not fearing God," that person is said to indulge in evil deeds, not expecting God's just judgment (Ps 36:1; Gen 20:11;

Eccl 8:13; Rom 3:18; Lk 18:2,4). Yet judgment comes upon such a person. The unwise, who spurned the voice of Lady Wisdom and "hated knowledge and did not choose the fear of the Lord," received a severe judgment (Prv 1:29). The wicked before whose eyes there is no fear of God (Ps 36:1) and who act wickedly (vv. 2–4) will come to a sure judgment (v. 12). The criminal who mocks Jesus, then, is truly one who did not fear God, who acted wickedly, and so comes to judgment. His wickedness is compounded by not recognizing God's salvation which came to him in Jesus, God's Christ (see 19:44). In contrast, the other criminal is experiencing a conversion which will lead to salvation and life. He joins the ranks of those who "fear God." And, Luke insists: "the mercy of the Lord is upon those who fear him" (1:50). The two criminals are finally contrasted in terms of their eschatological fates; one experiences the just judgment of God and the other finds salvation in God's Christ.

Fourth, the second criminal is probably to be associated with other sinful figures in Luke's Gospel who turn to Jesus and find forgiveness and salvation. The sinful woman who came to Jesus in 7:37–50 has her sins forgiven, as does Zacchaeus (19:9–10). The repentant criminal, moreover, petitions Jesus for a blessing. In Luke we find numerous people petitioning Jesus for healings and favors. Simon's family besought healing for Simon's sick mother-in-law (4:38–39); a leper begged a cure (5:12–13); a centurion petitioned for his slave (7:3–4, 8–9). Jairus begged for his daughter (8:41–50), the father for his epileptic son (9:38), and the blind beggar in Jericho for himself (18:37–42). Exceeding what he found in his sources, Luke in many of these episodes has stressed the petitionary aspect of these encounters: instead of merely speaking to Jesus about the feverish mother-in-law, they explicitly *petition* Jesus for her (*erotēsan peri autēs*, 4:38); the leper formally *petitioned* Jesus (*edeēthe*, 5:12); the father of the epileptic boy *requested* a cure (*deomai*, 9:38) for his son. Luke intends these redactional changes to give truth to Jesus' words on petitionary prayer in 11:9–10. In ch. 11 Luke collected and edited many statements of Jesus on prayer. First, Jesus teaches the Our Father (11:1–4); then, a parable on prayer is given (11:5–8). Luke appends several traditional logia to the parable (11:9–17), including a remark on petitionary prayer: "Ask, and it will be given to you; seek, and you will find; knock, and it will be opened to you" (11:9). And so, the criminal's petition to be remembered should be seen in light of the Lukan pattern of people who petition Jesus for healing help. To be sure, this prayer will be answered.

Fifth, the criminal's petitioning takes on a fresh look when he is compared with other figures in Luke who look for salvation and deliverance. Simeon "looked for the consolation of Israel" (2:25); likewise Anna spoke to all "who looked for the redemption of Israel" (2:38). Joseph of Arimathea is described by the Lukan redactional touch as one "who was looking for the kingdom of God" (23:51). There is, then, a body of holy and righteous figures in Luke who look for God's salvation. The criminal is in the process of conversion and turning to God's anointed one for salvation, and so he deserves to be put alongside Simeon, Anna, and Joseph. Those who "seek" for salvation "find it" (11:9).

Sixth, the thematic difference between the two criminals is found in their contrasting reactions to Jesus. Instead of mocking Jesus, the second criminal makes an extraordinary statement about Jesus' innocence. This is clearly not an empirical statement based on private, inside information, nor one which is psychologically motivated by the narrative. It is an abrupt, bold, and clear statement suggesting that the criminal is not scandalized by Jesus' cross; Jesus' crucifixion does not preclude his being God's Christ. Rather it is tantamount in Luke to a confession of faith in Jesus as God's Christ and Chosen One. The statement seems to dissociate him from those who reject God's prophets and seek their ruin; it dissociates him from those who think Jesus to be sinful (11:15). Alternately it links him with figures who confess Jesus as holy (4:34; Acts 3:14; 4:27), as God's anointed one (9:20; 19:38; Acts 10:38), and as righteous (23:47; Acts 3:14). Attestation of Jesus' innocence means confession of him as God's holy messenger of salvation. This forms the narrative basis in Luke's account for the subsequent request for remembrance in Jesus' kingdom.

Seventh, we should attempt to read the request for remembrance in Jesus' kingdom from Luke's perspective rather than from the restricted historical perspective of what an actual criminal could have meant by this language prior to Jesus' resurrection. Luke's viewpoint, at least, is accessible and it offers a rich source of insight into the meaning of the scene. It is well known that Jesus is acclaimed King in his crucifixion (23:2, 3, 37, 38). Like the remarks about "the Christ" who "saved others," the proclamation of Jesus as King is highly ironic. Jesus indeed is God's anointed one, a point mockingly conceded by those who reject him, but conceded nonetheless. Although Jesus was designated as God's anointed one at his baptism (4:18; Acts 10:38), the death and resurrection of Jesus are perceived as the moments in which God established him as King and Lord (Acts 2:36; 13:33). Vindicated by God and enthroned at God's right hand, Jesus assumes kingly reign not at his parousia[8] but ironically on the cross and in his resurrection. From Luke's perspective, the remarks of the repentant criminal constitute faith in Jesus as ruler of God's covenant people. He is acclaiming faith in Jesus according to the formula which Peter preached on Pentecost (Acts 2:36) and which Paul preached in the synagogue of Antioch (Acts 13:22–23, 32–34). The criminal, then, takes his place with those in Acts who confess faith in Jesus and so are saved.

Eighth, if we may say that Luke presents the repentant criminal as a converted sinner and even as a believer, then it follows that we look carefully at his faith. Luke frequently tells us: "Your faith has saved you." Besides the two instances where Luke retains Mark's report that "your faith has saved you" (8:48; 18:42), Luke has added this concluding judgment to numerous other stories of healing and forgiveness. The public woman in 7:50 is forgiven, not just because she loved much (7:47) but because of her faith (v. 50); Jairus is told, "Only believe and she will be saved" (8:50); the healed leper hears Jesus' words, "Your faith has saved you" (17:19). Likewise in Acts, a cripple in Lystra is healed as Paul sees that "he has the faith to be saved" (14:9), and the jailer at Philippi is told: "Believe and you will be saved" (16:31). This Lukan perspective is verified also in the case of the repentant criminal; for, in response to his faith, Jesus promises that he will be with him in paradise (23:43).

Ninth, the climax of this scene is Jesus' remark: "Today you will be with me in paradise" (23:43). According to Luke's overall perspective, Jesus' remark proclaims two things: (a) the man's sins are forgiven, for sinners are excluded from paradise, and (b) the man is promised eschatological life: he will surely die on the cross, and paradise is not a place of death. Much scholarly discussion has been given to the meaning of "today" in Jesus' remark, especially whether this refers to the final judgment[9] after a long stay in some intermediate state.[10] It is important to ask what Luke means by these words, rather than to speculate on what the historical Jesus could have meant by them. The Lukan understanding of them is accessible to us and we do well to concentrate on that.

Luke's Gospel contains numerous examples of the proclamation of immediate salvation: the angels announce to the shepherd, "Today is born to you a Savior" (2:11); to the repentant Zacchaeus Jesus proclaims, "Today salvation has come to this house" (19:9). "Today" saving prophecies are fulfilled (4:21), "today" sins are forgiven (5:26), and "today" demons are cast out (13:32). Luke's Gospel, then, insists that salvation is not simply a radically future experience but a thing of the present.[11] So when Jesus proclaims to the repentant criminal, "Paradise . . . today," we should take that pronouncement of salvation in terms of Luke's consistent sense of immediacy.

The preceding examples all have to do with living people who experience God's immediate salvation in their lives. In Luke's perspective, the dead are also said to know immediate rewards and punishments. In the parable in 16:22–23, Lazarus is immediately taken at his death to Abraham's bosom, while the rich man is immediately tormented in Hades. It will not do to maintain that Luke describes the "intermediate state" here, for immediate rewards and punishments which are permanent are announced. In another place Judas is said to have "gone to his place," a phrase echoing the fate of Balaam in Num 24:25; the midrash on this text says that Balaam went to hell. Judas, then, immediately experienced his eschatological fate. In regard to another text, Jacques Dupont maintains that Lk 12:16–20 reflects the Lukan perspective of an individual, immediate judgment.[12] The statement to the sinner there is the mirror copy of what Jesus says to the repentant criminal:

| 12:20 | Fool, this night | your soul | is required of you. |
| 23:43 | Today | you | will be with me in Paradise. |

A fourth example is the martyr Stephen, who sees the enthroned Son of Man and asks Jesus to "receive his spirit" (Acts 7:59), just as Jesus prayed to God to accept his spirit (Lk 23:46). As Jesus' prayer was answered in his resurrection, so it is implied that Stephen's prayer will be immediately answered.[13]

The Lukan perspective that some are given eschatological life at Jesus' death is reinforced by comparison with the Matthean account of

Jesus' death. For in Mt 27:51–53 the evangelist speaks of an immediate giving of life in connection with Jesus' death. Among the marvelous signs recorded in connection with Jesus' death, Matthew tells of one great sign. (a) "The earth was shaken" (27:51b); earthquakes are traditional biblical descriptions of eschatological events[14] and visitations of God. (b) "The rocks were split" (v. 51c), which is likewise seen as an act of God (see 1 Kgs 19:11; Ps 114:7; Is 48:21), and even as an eschatological event according to Na 1:5–6. (c) "The tombs were opened and many of the bodies of the saints were raised" (v. 52). These "saints" are Old Testament figures and they experience a resurrection in that "their bodies were raised." But this immediate experience of eschatological life is surely not the parousia nor the final resurrection and judgment.

This report in Mt 27:51–53 is judged by D. Senior to be a symbolic, not a journalistic report. It speaks of a new beginning—the advent of the eschaton. It is especially a manifestation of power at Jesus' death and as such it indicates a distinctive soteriological aspect of that death.[15] For our purposes it is important to note that it speaks of an immediate grant of life as a consequence of Jesus' death.

Mt 27:51–52 and Lk 23:43 are surely not reporting different versions of the same event. In Matthew, saints are raised from the dead at an earthquake; in Luke, a criminal is promised paradise with Jesus. Yet they both speak of a gift of new, eschatological life, which is immediate, which is connected with Jesus' own death and resurrection, and which symbolically tells of the soteriological effects of Jesus' death. Indeed, Jesus saves others. To judge from Mt 27:51–52, it is not strange to find a gift of immediate eschatological life given as a result of Jesus' death.

One final redactional point deserves attention. In 23:43 Jesus' remark is neither a prediction nor a promise. His remark is best understood according to Luke as a judicial pronouncement. As we noted in the last chapter, Jesus is proclaimed in Acts as "judge of the living and the dead," a function which Jesus exercised throughout his ministry (see Lk 5:20; 7:48; 19:9).

Judgment, of course, belongs to God's Christ and to the King of Israel. And he exercises it accordingly. The designation of Jesus as Christ and King of Israel is not limited to some abstract identity of Jesus but functionally describes his proper activity vis-à-vis God's covenant people.[16] Jesus, proclaimed as Christ by God's heavenly messenger (1:32–33), is acclaimed as such as he dies (22:67; 23:2–3, 35, 37). Ironically he is such, and as such he exercises judgment when he pronounces both woes (23:27–31) and saving blessing (23:43).

In summary, then, 23:39–43 is characteristic of Luke in its language and themes. And the substance of this redactional addition to the crucifixion scene by Luke is a thoroughgoing statement of soteriology. The second criminal embodies all the basic patterns in Luke associated with salvation from Jesus:

(a) he accepts Jesus as God's Christ;
(b) he is not scandalized by the cross;
(c) he petitions for a blessing and his prayer is answered;
(d) he looks for salvation and finds it.

According to Luke, he has faith in Jesus and this faith is salvific. Jesus' own remark in 23:43 is itself a saving judgment on that sinner. It is eminently true, therefore, to say of the crucified Jesus that "he saves others."

B. The Christ Cannot Save Himself

The Lukan crucifixion narrative calls attention to the dying Jesus as "the Christ," especially in connection with salvation language. Although the Markan text mentioned this but once (15:31–32), Luke has amplified it:

23:35 He *saved* others, let him *save* himself
if he is the *Christ of God,* his Chosen One.
23:37 If you are the *King* of the Jews
save yourself.
23:39 Are you not the *Christ?*
Save yourself and us.

Luke is focusing here on the polemic[17] against the Christian claims for Jesus, a polemic which was pervasive and deeply troubling (see Gal 3:13; 1 Cor 1:24). Is Jesus God's anointed one? Is he holy, consecrated, near to God? Is he God's appointed prophet? Is he the chosen and commissioned agent of God? Surely a holy and divinely appointed leader could exercise power from God, either by miracle or by prayer, and so escape from the hands of his enemies (see Dan 3; 6; Esther). Inasmuch as some assumed that "the Christ would remain forever" (Jn 12:32–34), Jesus' death would argue that he cannot be God's chosen and holy one.

Unlike the Markan text, Luke has ironically turned polemic into apology. In his perspective the argument works just the opposite way: the proof that Jesus is God's Christ lies precisely in his rejection and death. First, Mark speaks about the necessity of the death of the Son of Man (Mk 8:31), a point repeated in Lk 9:22, 17:25 and 24:7. Luke's focus, however, is primarily on the identification of Jesus as "the Christ" (1:31–33, 35) and so he speaks as well about what "the Christ must suffer." Again and again Luke argues that "the Christ must suffer" (24:46; Acts 3:18; 4:25–28; 26:23). And this suffering is not proof that Jesus is a sinner, abandoned and punished by God; on the contrary he suffers according to God's providence, that is, "according to the Scriptures" (Lk 24:26–27, 45–47; Acts 18:28). Jesus, then, is portrayed as obedient to God's plan and as faithful to God's directives in his death. So, Jesus *cannot* escape death since he is holy and appointed. If he is truly God's Christ, he cannot save himself.

The Christ does not save himself, but it is unthinkable that the Christ is not saved. Whence comes his salvation? God saves Jesus by raising him from the dead. But the text of Luke is quite nuanced in insisting that God raised "the Christ." For example the messianic Pss 16 and 110 in Peter's Pentecostal speech are cited apropos of "the resurrection of the Christ" (Acts 2:31). The person whom God vindicated was God's designated "Leader and Savior" (Act 5:31). Jesus' heralded role as "Savior of Israel" (Lk 2:11) is vindicated by God's saving him. God is saving the Savior of Israel.

Luke makes still a third point: the Saved Christ becomes the Savior. It is as the enthroned "Lord and Christ" that Jesus pours out God's Holy Spirit (Acts 2:33–36). The rejected and vindicated "Author of Life" is the power operative in the healing of the crippled man (Acts 3:15). In the name of the risen Jesus signs and wonders are done for Israel (Acts 4:30). The Christ whom God raised from the dead brings forgiveness of sins and salvation from everything from which the law of Moses could not save (Acts 13:38–39). The raised Jesus, the first to rise from the dead, proclaims light to the people (26:23).[18] But as Luke tells the story, Jesus could never be Savior to others were he not saved by God. His holiness and obedience, which constitute him as God's Christ, will ultimately be salvific for himself in his resurrection and will constitute him as Savior of others.

The crucifixion scene in Luke is necessarily terse. But it is full of clues and hints of Luke's broader theological attitudes. If one but finishes the story and follows out Luke's clues in Acts, then one sees that for Luke Jesus' death as Christ is theologically motivated: (1) it is as the holy and righteous one that Jesus dies; (2) Jesus *cannot* save himself, for, according to Luke, this would mean opposing God's plan and will; (3) Jesus is saved nevertheless in a salvation which confirms him as God's holy and appointed one; (4) as Saved One he becomes Savior to others. The statements in Lk 23:35, 37, 39 are intensely ironic, for Jesus is proved to be the Christ only if he does *not save* himself and yet by *not saving* himself he will in fact save others.

C. Faith That Saves

One of the most striking redactional changes in Luke's crucifixion scene is his replacement of Jesus' dying words. According to Mk 15:34, Jesus cried out "My God, my God, why have you forsaken me?"—a cry based on Ps 22. Luke replaced that cry with a prayer to God, "Father, into your hands I commit my spirit" (23:46), a prayer based on Ps 31:5. Whatever one may say of Ps 22 in the Markan account,[19] Ps 31:5 in Luke is more evidently a prayer, and more clearly expresses Jesus' faith in God. To appreciate the full weight of Luke's redactional change, we propose to investigate Jesus' dying words in Lk 23:46 as a supreme act of faith in God and to see this prayer in the light of the Lukan theme of "faith that saves."

There is a general theological axiom operative in Luke-Acts that "faith saves," which is an appropriate place to begin this discussion. We noted above in connection with the petition of the repentant criminal in 23:42 that Luke often speaks of a "faith that saves" (7:50; 8:48, 50; 17:19; 18:42). Thus in Luke's Gospel, the "faith that saves" is seen as acceptance of Jesus as the source of life and blessings, even acceptance of him as God's Christ (9:20; 23:42).

This pattern is continued in Acts with even greater clarity. (1) In Acts 2:21 Peter cited Jl 2:32 to the effect that those "who call upon the name of the Lord are saved."[20] Later in Acts we learn that Christians are those "who call upon his (Jesus') name" (9:14, 21). Paul was baptized and "called upon his name" (22:16). Those who acclaim Jesus and pray in his name are saved; faith saves. (2) Faith in the name of Jesus is the power whereby the crippled man is made to walk (Acts 3:6, 16; 4:10). (3) The Scriptures in fact teach: "Everyone who believes in him receives forgiveness of sins through his name" (10:43).

In Paul's homily in the synagogue of Antioch of Pisidia, this theme takes a new turn. A "word of salvation" is preached (Acts 13:26), a word about the risen Jesus as the fulfillment of God's great promises. Those who believe in this Jesus receive forgiveness of sins (13:38) and deliverance from all from which the law of Moses could not free them (13:39). But this homily indicates that faith explicitly includes belief in God's promises as fulfilled in Jesus (Acts 13:22–23, 32–35). Thus in Acts, the "faith that saves" is both faith in Jesus as God's Christ and faith in God who fulfills his promises of salvation in Jesus. This faith is saving in that it leads to healing, forgiveness of sins, radical deliverance from uncleanness, and the fullness of God's promised eschatological blessings in Jesus. Luke and Acts thoroughly agree on this point, that "faith saves."

In Luke-Acts, however, faith is a much broader religious phenomenon and it includes as well belief in the Scriptures, the prophecies and promises of God, and the words of God's angelic messengers. For example, Mary is blessed because she believed "that there would be a fulfillment of what was spoken to her from the Lord" (1:45). What she believed was the angelic message about the birth of Jesus and also that God's promises concerning the Son of David were being fulfilled in Jesus (see 1:32–33). Her own response was to magnify God for remembering his mercy and fulfilling the promises "as he spoke to our father, to Abraham and his posterity" (1:54–55). Although Zechariah is censured for *not* believing the angelic message about his son John (1:14–17, 22), he is eventually restored as a believer who blesses God for raising up a horn of salvation, "as he spoke by the mouth of his holy prophets of old" (1:70). For God has "performed the mercy promised to our fathers" (1:72); he has kept "the oath which he swore to our father Abraham" (1:73). Simeon, a devout man looking for the fulfillment of God's promise (see "consolation," 2:25), was promised that he would not die "before he saw the Lord's Christ" (2:26). And he prayed to God in gratitude, for he saw the "salvation" which God prepared (2:30–32).[21] The holiness of these towering saints of Luke's infancy narrative rests primarily on their faith, viz., their belief in God's immediate fulfillment of his promises to Abraham and David.

On Easter, the main function of the angelic messenger and of Jesus himself was to awaken faith in the disciples in God's promises in the Scriptures concerning Jesus. Although there is surely an apologetic strain to these texts, what separates believers from unbelievers is the belief that Jesus fulfills the Scriptures, not just the suffering aspects, but the promises of salvation as well. The women at the tomb are charged with "remembering how he told you. . . that the Son of Man must be delivered . . . crucified and on the third day rise" (24:6). Jesus himself instructs the Emmaus disciples to see that "the Christ must suffer and enter into his glory" (24:25–26). Finally the risen Lord reminds the disciples: "These are my words which I spoke to you while I was still with you, that everything written about me in the law of Moses and the prophets and the psalms must be fulfilled" (24:44–46). Belief in these prophecies and promises of God leads to full discipleship, and hence to salvation.

In Acts, belief in the fulfillment of God's promises in Jesus is a central theme. As Nils Dahl has shown so clearly in regard to Stephen's speech,[22] the central issue which unifies the speech in Acts 7 is the "promise of God to Abraham" that Israel would "come out and worship me in this place" (7:7). Although "the time of the promise drew near, which God had granted to Abraham," (7:17), Moses and his deliverance of Israel did not fulfill it. Nor was it fulfilled in Solomon's temple (7:47–50). The promise was fully and exclusively fulfilled in Jesus, the prophesied Righteous One whom the Jews murdered. True belief in God's promises to Abraham and how these are fulfilled in Jesus, then, constitutes the saving faith which characterizes God's people and separates them from the stiff-necked and uncircumcised of heart and ears (7:51).

Likewise in the preaching to the Antioch synagogue, Paul proclaims that God has indeed fulfilled the promises to Abraham and David in Jesus, Israel's Savior (13:23). The essence of his proclamation rests in the proclamation: "We bring you the good news that what God promised to the fathers, this he has fulfilled for us their children by raising Jesus" (13:32–33). Belief that the risen Jesus is the fulfillment of the promises to Abraham and David is the critical issue, acceptance of which brings forgiveness of sins and freedom (13:38–39), but rejection of which leads to ruin (13:40–41). This "faith" clearly saves.

Finally, in Paul's trials, Luke repeatedly insists that Paul is "on trial for hope in the promise made by God to our fathers" (26:6). Although we have seen that the "promise to Abraham" was understood as the raising up of a son in whom God's blessings would come upon the people (see Acts 13:32–33), the faith of Abraham also included deep faith in God's promise to raise the dead. For example, in Rom 4 Abraham is promised a son (4:17), but the obstacle to the fulfillment of this promise was the "dead" bodies of Abraham and Sarah ("he considered his own body as good as dead," 4:19). His faith extended, then, to God's promise to give life to the dead. And if one may include the sacrifice of Isaac, especially if the midrash on the Binding of Isaac existed in Christian times and influenced texts such as Rom 8:21,[23] them Abraham's faith included belief in God who raises the dead, i.e., the sacrificed Isaac. And so, Paul could maintain that the essential confession of faith was to say "God raised Jesus from the dead" (Rom 10:9).

Apart from his trials, Paul is also presented in Acts as a figure who believed in the revelations and prophecies which God sent to him. For example, when in prison in Corinth, the Lord appeared and gave Paul an encouraging message to support his faith and his ministry: "Do not be afraid, but speak and do not be silent; for I am with you . . ." (18:9). Paul knows of predictions of his imprisonment and afflictions (20:23); as the prophet Agabus bound Paul symbolically with a cord, he prophesied: "So shall the Jews at Jerusalem bind this man" (21:11). Paul's response here is highly significant. A prophecy may evoke belief and even obedience; in Paul's case, he demonstrated his faith with the phrase "The will of the Lord be done" (21:14). Faith, then, may be expressed as obedience. Other revelations point to Paul's salvation from the death plots of the Jews so that he might "bear witness at Rome" (23:11). He is symbolically promised deliverance from death for himself and the whole crew with the revelation, "Do not be afraid, for you must stand before Caesar, and God has granted you all those who sail with you" (27:23). Again his response is noteworthy: "I have faith in God that it will be exactly as I have been told" (27:25). Paul, then, believes the promises of God that he would be saved from death and protected. His response is faith and obedience.

It cannot be doubted, then, that belief in the fulfillment of God's promises to Abraham and David and belief in the promises of God to raise the dead constitute the paramount religious acts of the holy figures in

Luke-Acts. Faith, moreover, is belief in the God who fulfills these promises, and such faith is salvific.

III.
JESUS' FAITH

What has this to do with Jesus? Does Luke present Jesus as having faith, a saving faith? One of the most striking redactional changes in Luke's account of Jesus' death is the Lukan version of Jesus' dying words. Mark recorded that as Jesus died, he said, "My God, my God, why have you forsaken me?" (Mk 15:35); but Luke records Jesus saying "Father, into your hands I commit my spirit" (Lk 23:46). Luke's redactional change is all the more striking when one notes that in John's Gospel, Jesus utters a different dying word. The following synopsis brings out these differences;

Jesus' Dying Words in the Four Gospels
A. Mk 15:35   "My God, my God, why have you forsaken me?"
B. Mt 27:46   "My God, my God, why have you forsaken me?"
C. Jn 19:28   To fulfill the Scripture perfectly, he said: "I thirst."
D. Lk 23:46   "Father, into your hands I commit my spirit."

The evangelists have put different sets of words on the lips of the dying Jesus. This might be explained in various ways. One might argue that in fact Jesus said all of these words, in a sequence which we cannot recover. One might argue that there is an authentic and inauthentic version of Jesus' dying words. These and similar arguments are based on a bias that the Gospels are in some sense history and that historical explanations of Jesus' life and death can solve the differences in the various Gospels. But this approach is quite narrow in scope and can lead to frequent dead ends.

An important factor in evaluating the issue of Jesus' dying words is to start with the formal observation that in each case Jesus cites a phrase from the Scriptures, and, in particular, the Psalms.

A. Mk 15:35   Ps 22:1
B. Mt 27:46   Ps 22:1

C. Jn 19:28   Ps 22:15
D. Lk 23:46   Ps 31:5

This immediately suggests that we bracket consideration of Jesus' emotions or his psychology in the face of death. All the Gospels portray him citing the Psalms. Yet form implies function. Why do the evangelists put Psalms on Jesus' lips as he dies? What function is implied?

John 19:28 formally indicates that Jesus is "fulfilling Scripture" when he says "I thirst": "After this Jesus, knowing that all was now finished, said (to fulfill the Scripture), 'I thirst.' " This belongs with other formal statements in John that Jesus fulfilled the Scriptures when he died (see 19:24/Ps 22:18; 19:36/Ex 12:46; 19:37/Zec 12:10). John's choice of Jesus' dying words is governed by his concern to show that Jesus replaces Jewish cultic feasts and sacrifices[24] and that his death is Jesus' own "laying down of his life" (see Jn 10:17–18).

Turning to Luke, we continue our formal analysis by noting that Jesus' dying words from the Psalm are a prayer, not unlike the other prayers of Jesus in Luke-Acts.[25] The function of Luke's redaction is both pastoral and theological. By dying with a prayer to God on his lips, Jesus shows the new covenant community the proper way to die, viz., with faith in God to save him from death.[26] This is confirmed in Acts in the depiction of Stephen imitating Jesus' death. As Jesus died praying "Father, into your hands I commit my spirit," so Stephen died with a like prayer on his lips: "Lord Jesus, receive my spirit" (Acts 7:59). Inasmuch as Stephen is the first Christian martyr to die, his death is of great interest. It is pastorally significant that his death be modeled on Jesus' death. Like Jesus, he shows faith, saving faith.

Luke was also making an important theological statement when he recorded that Jesus prayed a psalm at his death, a prayer of faith in God. As I hope to show, Jesus' dying words are an expression of faith which is explicitly faith in *God-who-raises-the-dead*. First, Lk 23:46 should be seen alongside Jesus' other remark from the cross, the proclamation to the repentant criminal that he would be with Jesus in paradise (23:43). That proclamation implicitly contains a belief that the imminent deaths of Jesus and the criminal are not final and that there is a future victory over death. Jesus' dying prayer in 23:46, likewise, contains explicit faith in God that Jesus' imminent death is not final, and that God will sustain him through it. Formally, then, Lk 23:43 and 46 are fundamental statements of Jesus' faith in God to rescue him from death. Because they are constrained by the shape of the narrative, these statements of Jesus' faith are highly compacted. They are unfolded and confirmed in Acts, where considerable attention is devoted to faith in God-who-raises-the-dead.

It is in Luke's treatment of Ps 16 in Acts 2 and 13 that we find a fuller exposition of the faith contained in Lk 23:46/Ps 31:5. The first mention of Ps 16 occurs in Peter's Pentecostal speech in Acts 2.[27] This speech is highly rhetorical in that it makes serious attempts to persuade. The speech contains many arguments, such as the preliminary argument that the apostles' strange behavior is *not* due to drunkenness but to the outpouring of the Spirit (Acts 2:14–21). That settled, Peter begins his persuasive exposition of the fact and significance of Jesus' resurrection. First, he proclaims Jesus' ministry (2:22) and death (2:23), facts well known and requiring no proof. Then Peter proclaims Jesus' resurrection (2:24), a fact that needs considerable proof and extensive arguing. Precisely at this point Peter states his main point: "But God raised him from the dead," and he proceeds to marshal his best arguments in support of his assertion. God raised Jesus "because it was not possible for him to be held by it" (i.e., death, 2:24b). But why was it "not possible"? The proof lies in God's scriptural promise in Ps 16 to raise the dead, even the Christ. So Luke begins a formal argument which scholars call the "proof from prophecy."[28] The pivot of the argument rests in showing that the speaker of the Psalm (David) died and that his tomb (full of bones and dust) is with us today (2:29). The Psalm, then, cannot reflect David's faith or fate. The true speaker of the Psalm must be someone else, namely, God's Christ. Peter argues that David was but a prophet who "foresaw and spoke of the resurrection of the Christ" (2:31), who is the true speaker of the Psalm. Ps 16, then, functions as a formal argument for the resurrection, a proof from prophecy. As we shall see, Ps 16 makes several statements of great importance to Luke: (a) a statement about God, who raises the dead (2:27–28) and (b) a statement about the faith of the Christ in God-who-raises-the-dead (2:25–26).

As regards God, the Psalm contains a clear assertion that *God raises the dead*. In Acts 2:27–28, the psalmist proclaims: "Thou wilt not abandon my soul to Hades nor let thy Holy One see corruption." Luke interprets these words as referring to God's resurrection of the Christ from the dead, as he explains later in the speech: "He [David] foresaw and spoke of *the resurrection of the Christ,* that he was not abandoned to Hades nor did his flesh see corruption'' (2:31).

PS 16 AS CITED (ACTS 2:27–28)	PS 16 AS INTERPRETED (ACTS 2:31)
	He spoke of the resurrection of the Christ,
For thou wilt not abandon my soul to Hades,	that he was not abandoned to Hades
nor let thy Holy One see corruption (Acts 2:27).	nor did his flesh see corruption (Acts 2:31).

Luke uses Ps 16 a second time in Paul's speech in Acts 13. Ps 16:10 is again cited and an interpretative remark similar to Acts 2:31 is made that David, who spoke the Psalm, ''fell asleep . . . and saw corruption'' (Acts 13:36). But ''he whom God raised up'' saw no corruption (13:37), proving that God both promised and fulfilled his promise to raise the dead. As the following synopsis shows, Ps 16 is clearly interpreted by Luke as proclaiming and proving that God raises the dead:

PSALM 16 IN ACTS 2	PS 16 IN ACTS 13
1. *Identification of Scripture*	1. *Identification of Scripture*
''For David says concerning him . . .'' (2:25)	''He [David] says in another psalm . . .'' (13:35a)
2. *Text of Psalm as Prophecy*	2. *Text of Psalm as Prophecy*
''Thou wilt not abandon my soul to Hades,	''Thou wilt not
nor let thy Holy One see corruption'' (2:27).	let thy Holy One see corruption'' (13:35b).
3. *David as Prophet*	3. *David as Prophet*
''Being therefore a prophet . . . he foresaw and spoke of the Christ'' (2:30–31).	''For David, after he served the counsel of God in his own generation . . .'' (13:36a).

4. *David's Death*
"I say to you confidently of the patriarch David that he died and was buried and his tomb is with us to this day" (2:29).

4. *David's Death*
". . . fell asleep, and was laid with his father, and *saw corruption*" (13:36b).

5. *Fulfillment: God Raised Jesus*
"David foresaw and spoke of the resurrection of the Christ, that he *was not abandoned to Hades* nor did his flesh *see corruption*. This Jesus God raised up (2:31b).

5. *Fulfillment: God Raised Jesus*
"But he whom God raised up *saw no corruption*" (13:37).

Ps 16, then, is one of the premier Lukan scriptural proofs that God has promised to raise the dead. Luke argues through Psalm 16 that God has promised that his Holy One "will not see corruption," and God has fulfilled that promise: "God raised up Jesus." The Psalm, then, confirms one point: God raises the dead.

According to Acts 2, Psalm 16 makes another thematic statement, this time a statement about the faith of the Christ. In contrast to Acts 13, Acts 2 cites Psalm 16 in rather great detail.

PSALM 16 IN ACTS 2
I saw the Lord always before me,
for he is at my right hand that
I may not be shaken;
therefore my heart was glad,
and my tongue rejoiced;
moreover my flesh will dwell in hope.
For thou wilt not abandon my soul to Hades,
nor let thy Holy One see corruption.
Thou hast made known to me the ways of life;
thou wilt make me full of gladness with thy presence (Acts 2:25–28).

PSALM 16 IN ACTS 13

Thou wilt not let thy Holy One see corruption (Acts 13:35).

In combination with remarks about what God will do (i.e., raise the dead), additional verses of the Psalm are cited which describe what the speaker does: "Seeing God always . . . not being shaken . . . heart being glad and tongue rejoicing . . . dwelling in hope." These are all expressions of faith in God, even faith in God's promise to raise the dead. For God will raise the dead not simply in virtue of his promise but also because of the faith which the speaker of the Psalm expresses. Since the speaker of the Psalm is the Christ, Luke intends us to hear Jesus speaking these words of faith to God: "Thou wilt not abandon my soul to Hades nor let thy Holy One see corruption." Psalm 16, then, expresses two points: (a) the faith of God's Christ, who is Jesus, and (b) faith in God-who-raises-the-dead.

Formally, then, the content of the Psalm which Jesus prays when he dies (Ps 31:5) is the same as the content of the Psalm attributed to Jesus in the formal arguments of Acts (Ps 16). Both express a belief of the Christ which is a belief in God's power and promise to raise the dead:

Lk 23:46   Father,   into your hands I commit my spirit
Acts 2:27   Thou   wilt not abandon my soul to Hades, nor let thy Holy One see corruption.

In Luke and Acts, then, the evangelist is clearly intent on presenting Jesus as a believer in God, especially under the rubric of God's promise to raise the dead. This is what faith means in Luke-Acts.

There is a third factor of faith in Luke-Acts which we should attend to. The believer trusts in God as the one who raises the dead. This, however, is a response to a previous promise on God's part that God indeed intends to raise the dead. We turn our attention now to the data in Luke-Acts where we find Luke speaking of God's formal promise to raise the dead.

One of the fundamental elements of Luke's portrayal of Jesus is his knowledge of God's promises of salvation, especially those relating to his career. This is most evident in Luke's articulation of this theme at the climactic moments of Jesus' career. First, Jesus' inaugural public appearance in Nazareth's synagogue portrays him as knowing the prophetic oracles of salvation and believing in their fulfillment "today" (Lk 4:18–21). This episode is programmatic for Luke's narrative not only in terms of Jesus' healings but also in terms of the pattern of prophecy-fulfillment.

It presents Jesus as the prime figure who knows of God's promises of salvation and believes in their immediate fulfillment.

At the conclusion of Jesus' career, Luke characteristically presents the risen Jesus proclaiming: "These are the words which I spoke to you while I was still with you, that everything written about me in the law of Moses and the prophets and the psalms must be fulfilled" (Lk 24:44). Luke insists here that Jesus was continually aware of the Scriptures which he would fulfill and continually referred to these in his teaching. And the center of this teaching was that "the Christ should suffer and *on the third day rise from the dead*" (24:46). By this Luke signals that Jesus spoke often of God's promise of his resurrection as this is understood in the Scriptures. This is no isolated instance of this theme, for it is also the substance of Jesus' instruction to the Emmaus disciples. Jesus interpreted to them in all the Scriptures how "the Christ should suffer and *enter into his glory*" (Lk 24:26). The fact that it is Jesus who recalls the Scriptures and explains their predictions about himself should not be lost. Luke insists that Jesus is the one who knows and believes God's promises.

In addition to Jesus' own discourses on Easter about God's promises, the angels at the tomb remind the women of Jesus' frequent comments on God's promises concerning himself: "Remember how he told you, while he was still in Galilee, that the Son of Man must be delivered . . . *and rise*" (Lk 24:7). Jesus, then, is the premier figure who knows God's promises about the Christ, not only the predictions of his death, but also the promises of his resurrection.

In connection with this, it should be pointed out how frequently Luke notes that Jesus knows of God's promise that the rejected Christ would be raised from the dead. The so-called "passion" predictions of Mark's Gospel are repeated in Luke (see 9:22, 44; 18:32); but it should be noted that these prophecies also contain a prediction that the rejected one would "rise on the third day":

Lk 9:22 The Son of Man must suffer many things . . . and *on the third day be raised*.

18:31–33 Everything written of the Son of Man by the prophets will be accomplished . . . and *on the third day he will rise*.

In addition to these prophecies, Jesus predicts to the Sanhedrin: "From now on the Son of Man will be seated at the right hand of the power of

God'' (Lk 22:69), a statement which refers to Jesus' resurrection (see Acts 2:36). The teachings of the risen Jesus on Easter all contain references to prophecies of his resurrection, how the Christ will ''enter his glory'' (24:26) and how ''on the third day he will rise from the dead'' (24:46). Jesus' proclamation to the repentant criminal about paradise (Lk 23:43) and his dying prayer to God (Lk 23:46) also express Jesus' faith in God's promise of life after death. There are, then, eight instances in the Gospel where Luke proclaims that Jesus predicted his resurrection: 9:22; 18:33; 22:69; 23:43, 46; 24:7, 26 and 44–46. Jesus' predictions, moreover, are grounded on his knowledge of God's promises in the Scriptures that ''his Holy One would not see corruption'' (Ps 16).

This description of faith in Luke-Acts can be confirmed by a brief study of Paul's defense speeches in Acts 23, 24, and 26. Luke again emphasizes that belief in God's promises to raise the dead is the chief characteristic of Christian faith. According to correct forensic procedure, Paul ignores the charges against him and demands that his judges judge another issue, the resurrection.[29] Before the Jewish Sanhedrin, Paul insists that the ''issue to be judged'' is the resurrection; ''With respect to the hope and the resurrection of the dead I am on trial'' (Acts 23:6). Before Felix, Paul insists that ''I . . . have a hope in God which these themselves accept, that there will be a resurrection of the just and the unjust'' (Acts 24:15). Finally, before Festus and Agrippa, Paul insists that his trial is about one issue only: ''I am being judged for hope in the promise made by God to our fathers'' (Acts 26:6). That ''promise'' is the resurrection: ''Why is it judged incredible by any of you that God raises the dead?'' (Acts 26:8). Luke had already portrayed Paul arguing from Ps 16 in defense of Jesus' resurrection in his speech to the synagogue in Antioch of Pisidia in Acts 13. In summary, then, Luke presents a consistent description of faith in his work: (a) true Jews are recognized by their belief or hope *in God,* (b) who *raises the dead,* (c) even as God *has promised in the Scriptures.*

We should situate Jesus' dying prayer (Lk 23:46) in this context as a statement of faith in God who raises the dead. It is not accidental, then, that Luke portrays Jesus praying from the Psalms, for God's promises of the resurrection are formally contained there (see Lk 18:31–33; 24:7, 44–46; Acts 2:25–31 and 13:35–37). Jesus, then, has faith.

Jesus' faith in the promises of God, even promises of salvation, is not mere academic knowledge, as the chief priests displayed when they advised Herod in Mt 2:3–6. They knew the Scriptures, but this knowledge did not make them believers. Jesus, however, is presented as a believer. His acceptance of God's promises took the form in Luke's narrative of faithfulness and obedience in the face of knowledge of his rejection and death (recall Lk 22:42). The same is true of Paul in Acts. His reaction to Agabus' predictions of his sufferings (Acts 22:11) was faithful obedience: "The will of the Lord be done" (21:14). Analogous to Jesus' faith in God's promises of resurrection is the faithful reaction of Paul to heavenly dreams and revelations about his rescue from prison and danger (see Acts 18:9–10; 22:17–21; 27:23–26). The faith of those who believe God's promises of salvation is indicated in Luke-Acts. And such faith saves.

In this vein, Luke includes Jesus among the righteous figures in Luke-Acts who believe in God's fulfillment of his promises of salvation. Simeon, a righteous and devout prophet who "looked for the consolation of Israel" (2:25), believed God's promise: "It had been revealed to him that he should not see death before he had seen the Lord's Christ" (2:26). His faith was vindicated as he took Jesus into his arms and praised God for fulfilling his promise: "Mine eyes have seen thy salvation" (2:30). Anna, a prophetess, spoke of Jesus to all "who were looking for the redemption of Israel" (2:38). We noted earlier how Mary and Zechariah believed angelic messengers and accepted a present fulfillment of God's promises of salvation to Abraham and his posterity. And so in Luke there are many holy and devout people who believed in God's fulfillment of his promise. Righteousness, then, might be said to consist in belief in God's promise of salvation. As such, Jesus would be portrayed as a singularly righteous figure, one full of faith.

CONCLUSION

1. Luke's major redactional changes in Jesus' crucifixion scene are easy enough to identify. The two which most interested us were the addition of the dialogue between Jesus and the two criminals (23:39-43) and the change of Jesus' dying words (23:46).

2. The drift of the redactional changes points in two complementary directions: (a) salvation language and (b) faith in God.

3. In assessing the thrust of Luke's redactional changes vis-à-vis his larger canvas, we saw that they should be seen apropos of several major themes which pervade Luke-Acts: (a) he saved others, (b) the

Christ cannot save himself, (c) faith saves, and (d) Jesus exhibits faith in God.

4. In this context Luke portrays Jesus in his crucifixion and death as the Saved Savior. The one who had faith in God-who-raises-the-dead was ultimately saved because of his faith and obedience. And in being saved and exalted, the Saved One became the Savior of others, just as the Lukan Gospel has always proclaimed.

It remains now to assess what model of soteriology is operative in Luke's accounts, but that is the purpose of the next chapter.

Chapter Six

JESUS' FAITH:
OUR SALVATION

In the last chapter we saw that the Lukan redaction of the crucifixion scene is by no means devoid of salvation language. There is much talk, albeit ironic, of Jesus saving others and being saved himself: Jesus promises paradise to the criminal (Lk 23:43) and believes in his own salvation by God (Lk 23:46). In particular Luke notes that it is Jesus' faith and obedience which saves him (Lk 22:42; 23:46). Since the questions there were those of Luke's redaction, the critical method was appropriately literary and descriptive.

In the present chapter the critical question is no longer: What redactional changes did Luke make? Rather, we now ask: What model of soteriology is operative in Luke's passion narrative? and How is Jesus' faith and obedience salvific of others? I assume that Luke employs some model of soteriology to explain the significance of Jesus' death for God's people.[1] This is a valid assumption, for Luke calls Jesus the *unique* Savior of the world (Acts 4:12) and the *universal* Savior of all (Acts 13:38–39). Our present task is to investigate what model of soteriology undergirds these assertions. As the questions change, so does the critical method. We will now pursue a more systematic investigation of Luke's thematic understanding of Jesus as Savior.

I.
MODELS FOR INTERPRETING JESUS' DEATH

Although New Testament scholars may prefer one or another model of soteriology, they all readily admit that the New Testament contains many models and metaphors for explaining the saving significance of

Jesus' death.[2] Jesus' death may be seen both in terms of his relationship to God and in terms of the effects of his death on us.[3] As regards the former, Jesus is the rejected stone which God raised up (Lk 20:17; Acts 4:11–12); he is the Son of Man rejected by his enemies on earth but vindicated by God in heaven (Lk 22:69). His death may be described in line with the death of God's prophets who were always rejected by Israel (Lk 4:24; 11:47–51; Acts 7:52). His death may be seen as fulfillment of the prophecies in God's Scriptures: "Was it not necessary that the Christ suffer and so enter into his glory, and beginning with Moses and all the prophets, he interpreted to them in all the Scriptures the things concerning himself" (Lk 24:26–27).[4] These interpretations of Jesus' death are basically apologetic explanations supportive of Jesus' identity as God's Holy One; they do not directly explain the significance of his death for us.

Jesus' death, however, is seen as having effects and consequences on the lives of Christians. Even here there is considerable variety in the modeling of the effectiveness of his death. (1) Sacrificial terminology[5] may be employed: Jesus' death may be a *covenant* sacrifice which effects our union with God as his new, holy people (Lk 22:20; 1 Cor 11:25); it may be a *passover* sacrifice which effects our liberation from sin and slavery (1 Cor 5:7); it may be an *atonement* sacrifice which purifies us from our sins and consecrates us as God's holy people (Heb 9; Rom 3:25).[6] (2) The Good Shepherd lays down his life for his sheep, protecting them from the attacks of the wolf (Jn 10:11–16). (3) The Suffering Servant of Isaiah is a substitutionary Lamb who was "wounded for our transgressions and bruised for our offenses" (Isa 53:5; 1 Pet 2:24). (4) The Grain of Wheat dies, but brings forth a great harvest (Jn 12:23–25), a pattern which if followed leads Jesus' disciples to life (see Mk 8:35–36). (5) The rejected stone may become the head of a new temple (Mk 12:10–11; 14:58) or the stone which joins two contrasting walls into one (Eph 2:14, 20).[7] (6) Jesus' death may be understood as a liberating redemption (1 Cor 6:14; 7:23), a reconciliation (2 Cor 5:18–20), a peace which ends hostility (Rom 5:1), or as justification (Rom 4:25). (7) Jesus' death may effect the end of the era of sin and slavery and the beginning of an era of the fulfillment of God's promises of redemption (Gal 3:13–14).[8] (8) Finally, the death of the obedient second Adam may undo the disobedience of the first Adam, thus effecting life and justification for all who have faith (Rom 5:12–21).[9] Unlike the explanations of Jesus' rela-

3. Salvation, which was prophesied but absent, is available "today" in Jesus: Lk 4:21; 19:9; 23:43. Jesus' "today" marks a different and definitive period of salvation history.
4. Paradise, long since closed, is open according to Jesus' judgment (Lk 23:43).
5. The reign of Satan, which began in Adam and lasted up to the present time, is ended in Jesus: "I saw Satan fall like lightning from heaven" (Lk 10:18). Jesus, furthermore, proves by his exorcisms that he and his followers do not live in the kingdom of Satan but rather "the kingdom of God has come upon you" (Lk 11:20).
6. Most basically, eras and periods of history are structured by Luke in terms of "prophecy and fulfillment." The former age is only an age of prophecy, of waiting, of need; the present age represents God's definitive fulfillment of the ancient prophecies and the arrival of the blessings and benefits heralded in those prophecies.
7. In Acts 2:16–21, Peter explains that the outpouring of God's spirit indicates that these are "the last days." Former days are contrasted with the eschatological "last days" of biblical prophecy.

Second, Luke's periodization of history yields a *sense of two contrasting ages*.[12] In the course of Luke-Acts, Luke carefully suggests how discontinuous Jesus' period of history is with the former age and how superior it is, as the following chart shows:

Contrasting Ages in Luke-Acts

THE PRE-JESUS AGE	THE AGE OF JESUS
1. a time of sin and disobedience (Lk 13:33; Acts 7:52)	1. a time of faithfulness and obedience (Lk 4:1–13; 22:42; 23:46)
2. the kingdom of Satan (Lk 10:17–20; 13:16; Acts 10:38; and 26:18)	2. end of Satan's kingdom; beginning of God's kingdom (Lk 11:20; 17:21; Acts 1:3)
3. death	3. resurrection and eternal life
4. need for and expectation of salvation (Lk 2:25 & 28)	4. "today" salvation is present (Lk 2:11; 4:21; 19:9; 23:43)
5. paradise closed	5. paradise opened (Lk 23:43)

6. age of prophecy	6. age of fulfillment (Lk 4:16–21; 24:25–26)
7. age of Adam	7. the "last days" (Acts 2:16–21)

B. Jesus as a Foundational Figure

In relation to the period of history that Jesus begins, Luke describes him as a *foundational figure,* who is not the first in time, but the cause and source of the new age. Twice in Acts, Luke speaks of the distinctiveness of Jesus as the unique Savior of the world. Before the Sanhedrin, Peter summarizes the basic proclamation about Jesus: he is the one whom the Jews crucified, but whom God raised from the dead (4:10). Jesus is, moreover, the *cause* of something new and special, the healing of the paralytic: "By the name of Jesus . . . by him this man is standing before you well" (4:10b). This same Jesus, the stone rejected by the builders, has become "the *head* of the corner" (4:11). Of course this is an allusion to Ps 118:22, and can be traced to the use of Ps 118 in Mk 12:10 and Lk 20:17. In citing this Psalm, Mark primarily stresses Jesus' rejection and vindication, for his citation concludes with not just Ps 118:22 ("the stone rejected by the builders") but v. 23 as well ("This is the Lord's doing"). "The Lord's doing" (i.e. Jesus' resurrection) will be stressed in Mk 12:18–27 and 35–40. Lk 20:17 cites only Ps 118:22 ("the stone rejected by the builders"); and in the subsequent verse he explains his use of this citation: "Every one who falls on that stone will be broken to pieces; but when it falls on any one it will crush him" (Lk 20:18). At this point Luke stresses human judgment about Jesus and the radical consequences of that judgment: Jesus is the stone of scandal—as one judges Jesus so one is judged in turn. If Jesus is rejected, his rejector will be crushed in judgment.

In Acts 4:10–12, Luke again cites the Psalm, this time identifying the unbelievers in the Sanhedrin as "you builders" who reject God's stone. Yet Luke is more intent here on drawing out the implications of the second part of Ps 118:22, viz., ". . . has become the head of the corner." Neither Mk 12:10–11 nor Lk 20:17–18 did anything with this phrase, but Acts 4:12 interprets it in a significant way: "There is salvation in no one else, for there is no other name under heaven given among us by which we must be saved" (4:12). Jesus is the unique source of salvation. Luke, then, uses Ps 118:22 in two radically different ways: (a) to point out Jewish rejection of Jesus and its recompense (Lk 20:17–18) and (b) to point to Jesus as the head or unique Savior of the world (Acts 4:12).

The uniqueness of Jesus is stressed again in Paul's speech to the synagogue at Antioch in Pisidia. The speech begins by recounting an important slice of Israel's history which climaxes in a composite citation of two prophecies: "I have found David" (Ps 89:20) and ". . . a man according to my own heart" (1 Sam 13:14). These two texts of Scripture are cited together in Acts 13:22 as prophecies of God's great promise to David (2 Sam 7), concerning an ancestor to sit on David's throne (see Lk 1:32–33, 69–70). According to Acts 13:33, Jesus is the unique fulfillment of that promise: "Of this man's posterity God has brought to Israel a Savior, Jesus, as he promised." Luke spells out what he means by Jesus as "Savior" at the end of his speech, in 13:38–39. Jesus is Savior from our sins which could not otherwise be forgiven: "By him everyone who believes is freed from everything from which you could not be freed by the law of Moses" (13:39). Jesus is Savior, then, not in the sense of a Davidic warrior-king who could defeat Israel's enemies and liberate the land; he is the unique source of holiness for God's people. Acts 13:38–39 states that (a) the law of Moses could never free sinners—a radically hopeless situation, but (b) Jesus is the unique Savior from just those sins and hopelessness.

There is a third passage in Acts which has a bearing on Jesus as the unique Savior according to Luke. A healing is narrated in 3:1–10, an event which leads to an explanatory sermon. Peter proclaims that the paralytic was healed by faith in Jesus' name (3:16; see 4:10). In the course of his exhortation, Peter explains how it is that Jesus' name has saving power. Jesus is the Holy and Righteous One whom the Jews denied (3:14); he is the Author of Life whom they killed (3:15). The term "Author" (*archēgos*) has been translated both as "leader" and as "source." Although it is important to note that Jesus is also presented in Luke-Acts as leader of "the Way," and as model to be followed,[13] there is no hint of this in the argument in Acts 3. Peter does not ask the paralytic to believe, to repent, or to follow any pattern. On the contrary, the healing is a naked act of power. It functions as a rhetorical proof[14] that Jesus is God's established "Lord and Christ" (Acts 2:36): God raised him from powerlessness (death) and made him the source of saving power for others. In the context of this argument, *archēgos* is best translated as *source* of healing and salvation.[15]

Help in interpreting this term comes from two quarters. First, in Acts 5:31, Jesus is proclaimed as *archēgos kai sōtera* (''leader/source and savior''). He is so constituted by God to ''give repentance to Israel and forgiveness of sins.'' Since Jesus is the Holy and Righteous One, he does not need forgiveness of sins for himself; he is not establishing a pattern or serving as a model here. Again, the issue in Peter's speech is not the imitation of Jesus who is *archēgos* and Savior, but acceptance of him as God's Christ that is the source of repentance and forgiveness. Space does not allow us to explore the soteriological model encoded in ''Savior.'' F. Danker's recent works do this admirably.[16] He argued that a leader was a savior or ''benefactor,'' not because of the pattern he established for moral living, but because of his gifts of peace and prosperity to his subjects. And so a ''benefactor'' is a source of salvation. Luke claims that Jesus' benefaction is ''to give repentance and forgiveness of sins,'' that is, eschatological blessings. *Source,* then, captures the sense of Jesus as Savior and Benefactor. As Holy and Righteous One and Author of Life, Jesus is the source of these for others. He is the source of holiness in that he gives the Holy Spirit (Acts 2:33) and forgiveness of sins (Acts 13:38–39); he is the Source of Life in that sick and dying people are saved through his name. *Archēgos,* then, may be translated in the Lukan narrative as *source.* Admittedly the full explanation of how this occurs is unexpressed and only implied in Acts 3–4, the full explanation of which is the task of this chapter. But the claim in Acts 5:30–31 that Jesus is divinely constituted as source of repentance and forgiveness of sins implies that the old ways of attaining these through temple sacrifice, etc., are inadequate, and so are replaced by Jesus (see Acts 13:38–39). Jesus, then, is constituted as the unique source of holiness, life, and forgiveness of sins.[17] This reading of Acts 5:31 colors our reading of *archēgos* in Acts 3:15, and suggests that *source* is the correct interpretation there as well.

In a second place, the Letter to the Hebrews, Jesus is twice called *archēgos:*

2:10 ''It is fitting that he . . . should make the *archēgos* of their salvation perfect through suffering.''

12:2 ''Let us look to Jesus, the *archēgos* and perfecter of our faith.''

In 2:10, Jesus might be said to be *leader* (or ''pioneer'') of our salvation by his faithfulness in suffering; he would then be a model or pattern of the way to salvation (see 2:18; 4:15; 5:7–8). And imitation of Jesus constitutes an important element in the exhortation of Hebrews. But *source* is an equally valid interpretation of *archēgos* because of what is subsequently said in two places. Jesus is *source* of salvation because "He destroyed him who has the power of death, that is, the devil, and delivered all who through fear of death were subject to lifelong bondage" (2:14–15). He is *source* of salvation, that is "Author of Life," because he destroys death and death's lord, Satan. And through his sufferings, this same Jesus "became the cause/source (*aitios*) of eternal salvation" (5:9). It is not enough to say that *archēgos* means *leader* or "pioneer" in the sense that Jesus established a saving pattern to be followed. In Heb 2–5, Jesus is proclaimed as the very *source* of salvation: he conquered death and the devil, and he is the very cause (*aitios*) of eternal salvation.[18]

C. Jesus' Radical Holiness

Besides Luke's sense of time, clues to the model of soteriology can be found in the way Luke insists on *the radical holiness of Jesus*: his sinlessness, his innocence, and his closeness to God. Jesus' radical holiness is never in doubt in Luke-Acts, a holiness which is expressed in a variety of ways:

1. God's holy angels herald his coming (Lk 1:32–35; 2:10–11).
2. His birth is attributed to the power of God's Holy Spirit; and so, "the child to be born will be called holy, the Son of God" (Lk 1:35).
3. As Jesus fulfills the commands of God's law concerning his circumcision (Lk 2:21) and his dedication (2:22–24), he achieves the purpose of the law, his consecration to God: "Every male that opens the womb shall be called holy to the Lord" (Lk 2:23/Ex 13:2, 12).
4. Unclean spirits know that he is *not* one of them, but of God's realm: "I know who you are, the Holy One of God" (Lk 4:34).
5. In the preaching of Acts, Jesus is again and again called "Holy." He is "the Holy One" whom God will not let see corruption (Acts 2:27; 13:35/Ps 16:10). Jesus is "the Holy and Righteous One" whom the Jews denied, but whom God raised up (Acts 3:14). He is "the Holy Servant" against whom Herod and Pilate plotted (Acts 4:27, 30).

Luke portrays Jesus as one who is innocent of all crime and evil-doing, the Righteous One:

1. Jesus is acquitted of all charges by Pilate (23:4, 14–15, 22); a criminal crucified with Jesus proclaims him innocent (23:41), as does his executioner (23:47).[19]
2. Jesus' innocence is acclaimed by Peter and Stephen as an essential part of their preaching. Jesus is "the Righteous One" whom the Jews denied (Acts 3:14), and whom they betrayed and murdered, as they did all God's prophets (Acts 7:52).
3. Ananias, himself a righteous man, announced to Paul that God had favored him "to know God's will, to see 'the Righteous One' and to hear a voice from his mouth" (Acts 22:14).
4. And if one is known by the company one keeps, there were always righteous people associated with Jesus: (a) Zechariah and Elizabeth (Lk 1:6), (b) Mary (1:28, 30), (c) Simeon the prophet (2:25), and (d) Joseph of Arimathea (23:50).
5. Jesus is always presented as Satan's most dogged opponent and his conquerer (Lk 4:1–13; 10:16–20; Acts 10:38).

In still other ways, Luke indicates Jesus' radical holiness by his closeness to God:

1. Jesus is always linked with God's Holy Spirit: he is born through the Spirit's power (Lk 1:35); he receives a great infusion of God's Spirit at the beginning of his ministry (3:22), which is the power behind his preaching and miracles (4:18). Finally, Jesus himself pours out God's Holy Spirit on his followers (Acts 2:33). By this God declares him his holy associate.
2. Jesus is God's "Chosen One" (23:35), the one of whom God himself says: "Thou are my beloved Son; with thee I am well pleased" (3:22; 9:35).
3. Peter proclaims of Jesus that "God was with him" (Acts 10:38), which is a topic statement for the whole of Jesus' career:
   (a) God was with him through his spirit (Lk 1:35),
   (b) in special theophanies (3:21–22; 9:34–35), and
   (c) in his death and resurrection. God did "not abandon" his Holy One to see corruption (Acts 2:27; 13:35). And Stephen sees this same Jesus "standing at the right hand of God" (Acts 7:55). From birth to death and beyond death, God was ever with Jesus.

4. Jesus, moreover, is the one whom God vindicates, raises to life, and enthrones at his right hand: (a) the stone rejected by men is raised up by God (Acts 3:15; 4:10–12; 5:30–31); (b) the Author of Life, whom they killed, God raised from the dead (Acts 3:15); (c) God's Chosen One is "exalted at God's right hand" (Acts 2:33) and made Lord and Christ by God (Acts 2:36). Especially in Jesus' death is God "with him."

From the beginning of his career to the last stages of his ministry, Jesus is ever close to God. In life and especially in death, he is favored by God.

In summary, these four clues suggest that Luke sees Jesus as inaugurating a new period of salvation history which stands in sharp contrast to the previous one. Jesus, moreover, is a radically holy figure. He is also a foundational figure, a unique cause and source of blessing to his descendants and followers. These surface clues invite a further investigation of one of the models of soteriology which underlies this view of history and Jesus. My hypothesis is that Luke proclaims Jesus as the New Adam.

III.
LUKE'S MODEL OF SOTERIOLOGY:
JESUS AS THE NEW ADAM

The only explicit mention of Adam in Luke-Acts occurs in the genealogy where Jesus is ultimately linked with "son of Adam, son of God" (Lk 3:38). It has been very popular in biblical commentaries to remark that Luke here intended a Jesus-Adam comparison. But this connection is never made explicit by its proponents or sufficiently argued. For example, Jeremias argued the connection on very shaky grounds: Mk 1:13 speaks of Jesus being honored by beasts and angels, motifs which, according to Jeremias, echo elements of Adam's story.[20] But without so much as another word, he extended the Adam-Jesus likeness based on Mark's version of the temptations to Luke's comment in the genealogy that Jesus is linked with Adam. No wonder M.D. Johnson was quick to criticize this,[21] for the reference to beasts and angels, so important in Mark's account of the temptations, is not found in the Lukan temptation story. Hence, it is asked, what have Adamic allusions in Mark's temptation to do with Luke's genealogy? Jeremias' argument was clearly defective. The case has yet to be seriously argued for an Adam-Jesus relationship in Luke.[22] But I would like to attempt that argument now.

The basic data for an Adam-Jesus comparison in Luke-Acts comes in rhetorically significant places in the narrative. I propose to investigate how Jesus is linked with Adam both at the beginning of Jesus' career (genealogy and temptation) and the end of his life (garden and cross). As we shall see, it is Luke himself who indicates that we link these two moments.

A. *The Genealogy*

A number of points must be taken into account in interpreting Luke's genealogy: (a) the context and position of the genealogy vis-à-vis Luke's narrative, (b) the unusual mention of figures from Abraham to Adam, (c) the substance of the connection between the first and last figures, and (d) the function of the genealogy in Luke's overall perspective.

First, it is generally conceded that the position of the genealogy in Luke's narrative is critical for its proper understanding.[23] Unlike Matthew's list of ancestors, which is placed at the beginning of the Gospel, Luke's genealogy occurs between the baptism and the temptations of Jesus. These three passages are stitched together by the repeated reference to "son of God":

Baptism: " Thou art my beloved Son" (3:22)
Genealogy: ". . . being the son (as it was supposed) of Joseph" (3:23)
           ". . . the son of Adam, the son of God" (3:38)
Temptations: "If you are the Son of God . . ." (4:3)
           "If you are the Son of God . . ." (4:9)

What God readily asserted in 3:22 ("Thou art . . .") Satan calls into question in 4:3, 9 ("If you are . . ."). The genealogy provides the link between assertion and question; it provides the context in which to assess the meaning of "son of God." While Jesus is not the first to be so named, Luke suggests that he is the one most fittingly called "son of God."

Second, as regards the substance of the connection between Jesus and specific figures in the genealogy, in Matthew's list Jesus was said to be related especially to two figures who are named with Jesus in the rhetorically significant places in the list, at the very beginning and end of the list, Abraham and David:

Mt 1:1   The book of the genealogy of Jesus Christ, the son of David, the son of Abraham.

1:17   So all the generations from Abraham to David were fourteen generations, and from David to the deportation to Babylon fourteen generations, and from the deportation to Babylon to the Christ fourteen generations.

It is relatively unimportant that Jesus is descended from Aminadab (v. 4) or Ahaz (v. 9) or Achim (v. 14); the focus is on Jesus as "son of David, son of Abraham." The relationship might be pointing to Jesus as the fulfillment of the "covenants of promise" made to Abraham and David,[24] a covenant celebrated in Eph 2:21, Gal 4:24, Rom 1:3 and Acts 13:22–23. The full explanation for Matthew's linking of Jesus with specific figures need not detain us here.

In Luke's genealogy, Jesus is likewise linked with two specific figures, David (3:31–32) and Abraham (3:34). The Lukan narrative is intent on showing that Jesus is the fulfillment of God's great promises to David and Abraham:

David: Lk 1:32–33, 68–71; 2:11; 18:38–39
          Acts 13:22–23, 34–37; 15:16–18
Abraham: Lk 1:55, 73; Acts 7:3, 7

Luke's genealogy, however, does not terminate with David or Abraham, but goes back to Adam (see 1 Chr 1:1). What purpose is served by this extension? William Kurz[25] suggests two reasons for Luke's inclusion of figures from Abraham to Adam. (1) Luke is intent on showing that the event of Jesus and his apostles did not happen "in a corner" (Acts 26:26), but belongs to the context of world history as Luke repeatedly indicates (Lk 1:5; 2:1–2; 3:2–2). (2) Luke's understanding of the time line of history is as broad as it can be: from creation (see Adam, Lk 3:38; Acts 17:24) to judgment (Acts 10:42; 17:31). We may add to Kurz's arguments a third point. Jesus is not just another event on the time line for Luke, but is the pivot of salvation history. With Jesus' coming, one age ends and another begins. The age which ends includes Jesus' contemporaries all the way back to the first human, Adam—truly an inclusive age (see Rom 3 for other examples of inclusiveness). Jesus does not fulfill any promise

made to Adam, as was the case with David and Abraham. Rather, he is
the pivotal figure who marks the turn of the two ages. His association
with Adam serves to indicate the complete extent of the age which has
just ended.

The principle of specifically linking first and last figures in the genealogy is important for Luke. What have Jesus and Adam in common?
The end of the age beginning with Adam does not exhaust the Lukan
purpose for mentioning Adam in the genealogy, for both the first and the
last figures in the genealogy share a common title, "son of God." But
how does the designation "son of God" apply to them? The Scriptures
speak of Adam in two ways: (a) as made in God's image and likeness and
given dominion over the earth (Gen 1:26), and (b) as a sinner who was
subsequently excluded from God's paradise (Gen 3). Adam, then, is
either saint or sinner.

The designation of Adam as "son of God" is extremely rare. When
Philo speaks of God as Adam's father, he does so in the tractate *De Vir-
tutibus,* in the context of a discussion of nobility. While not all nobility
is related to birth and pedigree, Adam's was: for he was "judged worthy
to receive his soul not from any other thing created but through the breath
of God" (*Virt.* 203). The fatherhood of God, moreover, is perceived of
in moral terms: "His Father was no mortal but the eternal God, whose
image was in virtue of the ruling mind within the soul" (*Virt.* 204). Although nobility came to Adam by birth, he was "son of God" because
of his moral uprightness and because of the rule of reason.

The designation "son of God," moreover, seems to imply a distinctive moral relationship to God. In the Hebrew Bible, the title refers
to (a) heavenly or angelic beings, (b) Israelites, and (c) the kings of Israel.[26] But in post-biblical Judaism, the designation "son of God" is
more frequently given to the righteous and the obedient. Philo, for example, in discoursing on the text "Ye are the sons of the Lord your God"
(Dt 14:1), explains the title on the basis of obedience to God: "This promise of mine is confirmed by the law, where it says that they who do 'what
is pleasing' to nature and what is 'good' are sons of God" (*Spec. Leg*
i.318). Philo is faithful to the context of Dt 14:1 in interpreting the phrase
"son of God" in relation to obedience (see 13:18). Not all who are Israelites by birth are sons of God. In Dt 32:7–9, Philo sees a distinction
between those who are merely "sons of Adam" and those who are truly
"the lot . . . portion of the Lord." The distinction has a moral basis: "lot

. . . portion'' are the names given to ''the character who has eyes to see Him and accords Him genuine devotion,'' whereas ''sons of Adam'' refers to those ''incapable of following the guidance of right reason'' (*Plant.* 59–60). Finally in *Q. Gen.* I. 92, Philo remarked that only ''good and excellent men'' are called ''sons of God.'' Philo, therefore, links the title ''son of God'' with morally upright, obedient, and righteous Israelites.

The same linkage between moral uprightness and the title ''son of God'' is found in other post-biblical literature.

1. In Sir 4:1–10, the author lists the good deeds proper to the wise and righteous Israelite, deeds which stress concern for the needy, beggars, orphans, and the poor. Whoever is wise in this way (see Dt 15:7–11) is properly called a ''son of God'' (4:10).

2. In the Wisdom of Solomon, a plot is hatched by the wicked against ''the righteous man'' (2:12, 17), who ''professes knowledge of God'' (2:13). This righteous man opposes the actions of the wicked and reproaches them for their sin (2:12); his manner of life is totally different from that of the wicked (2:15), for he avoids the way of the wicked as ''unclean'' (2:16). The plot against him is a challenge to his moral uprightness: ''For if the righteous man is God's son, he will deliver him'' (2:18). Later in 5:1–8, the fate of the righteous man is commented on. The wicked despised him and thought to defeat him; so in amazement they ask, ''Why has he been numbered among the sons of God?'' (5:5).

3. In the prologue to the book of Jubilees, Moses first recounts the sins of Israel. Then God speaks about the salvation which he will effect on Israel when he circumcises their hearts, creates a holy spirit within them, and ''cleanses them so that they shall not turn away from me from that day until eternity'' (1:23). God continues: ''Their souls shall cleave to me and to all my commandments and they shall fulfill my commandments and I will be their Father and they shall be my children'' (1:24–25).

4. According to Ps. Sol. 17:28–30, the expected son of David shall gather a holy people unto God who shall become his sons in virtue of their righteousness:

> And he shall gather together a holy people,
> whom he shall lead in righteousness;

and he shall judge the tribes of the people
that has been sanctified by the Lord his God;
and he will not suffer unrighteousness
to lodge any more in their midst;
nor shall there dwell with them
any man that knoweth wickedness.
For he shall know them,
that they are all *sons of their God*.

And so, we see that "son of God" is a designation taken basically from Dt 14:1 and applied in a moral sense to the righteous, obedient, and holy ones of Israel.[27]

When Luke links Jesus, "son of God," with Adam, "son of God," the thrust of this surely does not link Jesus with Adam as sinner, but rather with Adam as one created in righteousness and head of God's creation. While Adam is the first to be called the "son of God," he is not ultimately known as God's son because of his sin and disobedience. The appropriateness of Jesus' designation as "son of God" remains to be tested in his temptations and even afterward. But if this parallel material is of any help, it suggests that according to Luke, the content of "son of God" in Lk 3–4 is linked with Jesus' holiness and obedience. First and last figures, then, are joined in comparison and contrast as heads of their respective ages.

Third, concerning the total number of generations listed, although scholars count the number of generations in Luke's genealogy differently, seventy or seventy-two seem to be the total number.[28] This is often seen in the light of the Jewish understanding of the seventy nations of the world, based on Gen 10. The seventy generations suggest both the fullness of human time as well as some form of periodization of history. Something is happening in Jesus which sets him apart from the Adam-through-Joseph period of history and which juxtaposes him to it. Ultimately Luke will explain Jesus as Savior of the whole world (see Acts 4:12) indicating that he has a position vis-à-vis the whole world comparable to that of Adam, but salvific rather than sinful.

Fourth, as regards the function of genealogies, Raymond Brown[29] listed five possible functions of genealogies:

1. they are passports for membership in the tribe and its privileges;
2. they undergird status;

3. they structure history into epochs;
4. they authenticate office holders;
5. they imply collective personality whereby something of the ancestor appears in the descendant.

The five functions do not all apply equally to the Lukan genealogy, at least not the first. There is never any question of Jesus' Jewishness or of his belonging to God's covenant people (see Lk 2:21, 22–27). The genealogy only serves in part to undergird Jesus' status as "son of David." Jesus' link with David comes through Joseph, who was "of the house of David" (1:27; see 2:4); but Joseph is not the true parent of Jesus (3:23), and so the link with the house of David is tenuous. The angelic oracle to Jesus' mother states that God will give Jesus "the throne of his father David" (1:32), which is a much firmer link between the two. This would account, however, for only half of the genealogy, inasmuch as David's name is mentioned in the midpoint of the list.

In Luke, the fourth function is meaningless, for the heavenly messenger does a far better job than the genealogy of authenticating Jesus' special role as covenant leader (1:32–33, 35; 2:11). And the *bat kol* at Jesus's baptism (3:22) is certainly superior to the genealogy as a pronouncement of Jesus' status.

But the third and fifth functions are highly suggestive. Luke does in fact structure history into periods. In the case of Luke's narrative, there is a definite break between the period of Israel and the period of Jesus. Jesus is not just one more name in a long list of figures, but stands in discontinuity with the period listed in the genealogy. As we saw earlier, in the course of Luke-Acts, Luke indicates that the pre-Jesus age and the age of Jesus are sharply contrasted as periods of sin/grace, prophecy/fulfillment, and the kingdom of Satan/the kingdom of God. And so, according to Luke's periodization of history, Jesus stands in discontinuity with the earlier period of his ancestors.

As regards the fifth function, the genealogy should imply a sense of collective personality[30] whereby some important characteristic or trait of the ancestor is found in the latest descendant. Here again, we noted that both Adam and Jesus are called "son of God." Both begin their lives as "son of God," especially beloved of God. But in the case of Adam, this trait was quickly lost and not handed on to his descendants. Adam handed on instead disobedience and death. As Luke shows, Jesus neither inherits

Adam's disobedience nor does he die for the same reason that Adam dies. The only thing which Jesus inherits from his ancestor is the title "son of God," which he restores to the clan and tribe. And with the title comes the blessing of that relationship with God, victory over death.

The genealogy, therefore, specifically links Jesus with Adam in terms of comparison and contrast. The first and the last figures in the genealogy are specifically linked; both are "sons of God," but only Jesus is properly so called. Both are heads of periods of history: Adam, head of Israel's history of sin, and Jesus, head of a period of salvation. What makes Jesus different from Adam is his fundamental and lasting obedience to God. It is, then, suggested by the genealogy that Jesus is an Adam-like figure whose obedience will have saving significance for his tribe or nation.

B. The Temptations of the New Adam

In the baptism a claim is made on Jesus' behalf that he is "son of God." As we saw, in the context of Lk 3–4 that designation is not messianic, but points to a singular righteousness and obedience which is unlike that of another "son of God," Adam, who failed to live up to that relationship to God as "son." In the account of the temptations which follow upon the baptism, the claim which is made on Jesus' behalf is tested and proved true. He is God's son in virtue of his singular obedience, a holiness which is both imputed to him (1:35; 3:22) and now verified.

The materials in the temptation narrative come to Luke from the Q source, yet Luke redacted this traditional material in ways which serve his Christological purposes. Luke's first and most evident redactional change is the juxtaposition of the genealogy (3:23–38) with the temptations (4:1–13). "Son of God" is the title given to Jesus when God's spirit rests on him (3:21–22), which title is contrasted with the use of that name for Adam, "son of God" (3:38), and which is proved true in Jesus' case with his fidelity to God in his temptations as "son of God" (4:3, 9). The context of the temptations, then, suggests a conscious attempt to confirm the special meaning of "son of God" when applied to Jesus.

The background of the narrative is likewise changed by the new context given it by Luke. It is often claimed that in Matthew's version of the temptations, Jesus is presented as the new Moses and so the background of the temptations is explained by allusion to the Exodus period and by explicit citations from Moses' own book, Deuteronomy. This is not evidently the case with Luke. Except for a parallel between Jesus and Moses as rejected prophets (Acts 7:20–40, 52), Luke is not interested in presenting Jesus as the giver of a new Torah. Moses is not even mentioned in the genealogy. Even the allusion to Dt 18:15 in Acts 3:22 implies that Jesus is like Moses in terms of his rejection by the people (see Acts 3:23).

It is a fact that in Lk 4:1–13 Jesus repeatedly quotes from Deuteronomy. This does not necessarily imply a Moses-Jesus comparison, for the citation of Deuteronomy could just as readily underscore the presentation of Jesus as a thoroughly obedient and faithful person, a holy son of the covenant. The Exodus story, moreover, does not mention that Israel or Moses was ever tempted by a Satan figure, although one midrash notes that Moses was confronted by the Angel of Death and bested him by repeatedly citing Scripture (*Deut. R* XI.5). The substance of the temptations, moreover, does not reflect an Exodus theme, except perhaps in the case of bread, if the murmuring for food in Ex 16 is relevant. But in Lk 4:1–4, Jesus is not murmuring against God for bread; on the contrary, he refuses bread when proffered. Moses and Exodus are not the correct background for understanding Jesus' temptations.

In the light of the Adam reference in 3:38, I suggest that Luke gives us a clue to the proper background to his interpretation of Jesus' temptations. By the mention of Adam he suggests a Genesis background to them, contrasting Jesus' reaction to Satan's temptations with that of Adam's. This suggestion has been made before[31] and deserves a fresh and fuller consideration. The argument goes as follows:

First Temptation:

Adam was tempted by Satan to eat the proscribed fruit; his eating was disobedient; he sinned, became Satan's subject, and lost his status as "son of God" (Gen 3:1–7).

Jesus was tempted by Satan to turn a stone into bread for eating purposes ("for he was hungry," 4:2). This bread would not be lifegiving according to Jesus' understanding: "Not by bread alone will man live" (4:4). Rejecting what was evidently "good for food and a delight to the eye" (Gen 3:6), Jesus remained totally free of any influence of Satan. Unlike Adam, he does *not* eat. And so, he remains truly "son of God."

Second Temptation:

Adam was given dominion over all things by God (Gen 1:26–30); yet Satan offered him a way to greater power. By eating of the fruit, "you will be like God, knowing good and evil" (Gen 3:5). In following Satan's suggestion, Adam lost even the power he already had, as he became subject to sin and finally death (Gen 2:17, 3:19).

Jesus is offered all power over the whole world by Satan (4:5–6). In rejecting this, Jesus refuses Satan's demand to "worship me" (4:7), and so become subject to Satan. On the contrary, Jesus openly proclaims his radical fidelity to God: "You shall love the Lord your God and him only shall you serve" (4:8). Jesus remained unconditionally God's "son," subject only to God's will.

Third Temptation:

Adam was created immortal and deathless.[32] Since death came as a result of sin, as long as Adam was sinless, he would never die: "On the day you eat it you shall die" (Gen 2:17; 3:3, 19). In tempting Adam to sin, Satan lied when he promised Adam that eating would not bring death: "You shall *not* die" (Gen 3:4). Adam ate, sinned, and died: "You are dust and to dust you shall return" (Gen 3:19).

Jesus is tempted to defy death when Satan suggests that he leap from the temple. Implied in this temptation is a lie similar to that told to Adam: a son of God should be deathless, in Jesus' case because God has commanded the angels to guard him. Jesus rejects this lie, and allows God to remain the Lord of life (and death) for him. His statement of obedience to God means that he will not put himself in any way at variance with God's will (Lk 4:12).

A Genesis background, then, is quite plausible for the Lukan temptation scene, especially in light of the Adam-Jesus contrast in the genealogy (3:38). We remember in this context Luke's structuring of history into periods. Jesus is evidently contrasted with Adam's and Israel's period of history. Biblical history records that Israel was repeatedly unsuccessful in resisting temptation, certainly not during its desert exodus (Ex 16–17;

Ps 95:8–11; 1 Cor 10:6–11; Jude 5). Adam is known primarily as one who succumbed to temptation. Jesus, as the one who resists temptation and remains obedient, belongs to a different period of history than Adam or Israel. Indeed he inaugurates it. He is a head or foundation figure. The parallels between the Genesis narrative and the Lukan temptation scene suggest this sense of history more clearly.

Lukan redactional touches can be discerned especially in the third temptation. Whereas in Mt 4:5 Jesus is brought to the "holy city," in Lk 4:9 it is more clearly stated that he was taken to Jerusalem. In Mt 4:6, Ps 91:11 is cited as proof that Jesus would not be harmed; in Lk 4:10–11 the same Psalm is cited but with the addition of the comment, "He commanded his angels *to guard you*," an intensification of the divine command that Jesus not be harmed. The temptation has less to say about a wonder-working epiphany of Jesus and more about the promise that Jesus will be guarded by God's angels so that *he not die in Jerusalem*. It is judged by commentators, moreover, that Luke changed the original order of the temptations in Q and put this third temptation in the climactic, final position.[33]

The thrust of these slight redactional changes, seemingly insignificant in 4:1–13, is clarified by noting the symbolic importance of "Jerusalem" in Luke's narrative, as well as Luke's insistence that Jesus' death is God's will and plan. First, Jerusalem is the aim of Jesus' great journey: "He set his face to go to Jerusalem" (9:51) and "He went on his way . . . journeying toward Jerusalem" (13:22). His conversation with Moses and Elijah centered around "the *exodus* which he was to accomplish at Jerusalem" (9:31). Jerusalem, then, is the climactic place of Jesus' career, just as it is foreshadowed in the temptations.

Second, Jerusalem is the place of Jesus' death: "Behold we are going up to Jerusalem and everything written of the Son of Man will be accomplished" (18:31–33). No prophet, moreover, ever perished outside Jerusalem (13:33–34). Jerusalem, then, is the place where Jesus will most certainly die, not escape death.[34]

Third, Satan says that it is God's will that Jesus not die in Jerusalem, for God has commanded the angels "to guard him" from harm. This perspective clashes with the Lukan presentation of Jesus' death as God's will and according to God's plan. In a variety of ways, Luke insists that Jesus dies according to the divine will:

1. "The Son of Man *must* (*dei*)³⁵ suffer many things" (9:22); this phrase is a circumlocution for God's will (see 17:25; 24:7, 26; Acts 14:22; 17:3).
2. Luke openly says that Jesus suffered and died "according to the definite plan and foreknowledge of God" (Acts 2:23; 4:27–28).
3. God's will, moreover, is expressed in the Scriptures; Jesus dies "according to the Scriptures," fulfilling all God's plans in his regard: "Beginning with Moses and all the prophets, he interpreted to them in all the Scriptures the things concerning himself" (24:27).
4. Finally, in Gethsemane, Jesus' death in obedience to God's will and plan is clearly acknowledged and accepted: "Father, if you are willing, remove this cup from me; nevertheless not my will, but thine, be done" (22:42).

It is *not* God's will, then, that Jesus escape death at Jerusalem. Satan is telling a lie.

The Lukan story, then, points to Jerusalem as the place of Jesus' death, a death which is explicitly described as God's will and plan. The climactic temptation proposes that since Jesus is the "son of God" (i.e., sinless), *he will not die*. The Lukan story on the contrary maintains that because he is truly "son of God" and completely sinless, *he will die* in obedience to God's will.

There is one final redactional touch to Luke's version of the temptations, viz., 4:13. Luke omits the reference found in Mark to "ministering angels" who attended Jesus after the temptations (see Mk 1:13). And instead of the simple notation that "the devil left him" (Mt 4:11), Luke remarked: "The devil left him *until an opportune time*." Scholars generally see some connection between 4:13 and the passion narrative when Satan is described as active again.³⁶

In summary, Luke's presentation of Jesus' temptations yields five points:

1. The genealogy and temptations are joined through a common, yet important title, "son of God."
2. The temptations validate the title, proving that Jesus is completely obedient to God. In this he is unlike the common ancestor of all, Adam.

3. The proper background for the temptations is Genesis 1–3, not Israel's desert experience.
4. The climactic temptation is Satan's lie that God will protect Jesus from death in Jerusalem.
5. In 4:13, Luke indicates that Jesus' temptations will be resumed at a future time, which I suggest must be the time of Jesus' passion and death.

C. The Garden and Jesus' Obedience

From Luke's redactional comment in 4:13 that Satan left Jesus "until an opportune time," Luke insists that Jesus' temptations would continue. In various places in this book I have suggested that Satan returned to his task in the Lukan passion narrative ("Satan" is mentioned explicitly in 22:3, 31, 53). More specifically, I suggest that the episode of Jesus in Gethsemane (22:39–46) fulfills that prophecy. This assertion is based on three related arguments.

First, the substance of the Gethsemane episode is almost identical with the contents of Jesus' third temptation (4:9–12). Satan enticed Jesus to risk death by jumping off the temple. He lied that God would guard Jesus from death. Had Jesus jumped, the readers of Luke would realize that Jesus was in some way under Satan's power; and if Satan were successful in his lie, Jesus would in fact die in the fall. His death, then, would be both punishment for sin and proof that he was under Satan's power. The point of 4:1–13 was to prove that Satan failed completely and that Jesus remained ever faithful and obedient to God. But the issue of his death remains.

In 22:39–46, we find this discussion of Jesus' death and of his relationship to God continued, as the following synopsis shows:

4:1–13
1. Jesus is "son of God," proved obedient (4:3, 9)
2. Jesus was promised by Satan that he would not die; such is God's will (4:9–11)

22:40–46
1. God is "Father" (22:42) and Jesus is the obedient son
2. Jesus is commanded to die; this is God's will (22:42)

3. Jesus shows complete obedience: "You shall worship the
Lord your God, and him only
shall you serve" (4:8)
4. Temptation (*peirasmos*, 4:2,
13) from Satan
5. Jesus' victory: Satan has no
power over him

3. Jesus shows total obedience:
"Not my will but thine be
done" (22:42b)
4. Contest (*agonia*, 22:44) from
unnamed assailant
5. Jesus' victory: although he will
die, Satan has no power over
him

Jesus will indeed die. But according to Luke, that death in no way indicates that Satan has any power whatsoever over Jesus. Jesus' faithfulness to God's will is both stated (22:42) and tested (22:43–44). There is no sin in Jesus, as was noted earlier in this chapter.

Second, in the desert as well as Gethsemane, Luke highlights Jesus' absolute faithfulness to God. As we saw earlier in Chapter Two, Jesus is quick to search out God's will and firm in pledging himself to it: "Not my will, but thine, be done" (22:42). This obedience of Jesus is the dramatic climax of Jesus' lifelong faithfulness to God; it is the moment in Luke-Acts when all the prophecies of Jesus' death are accepted by him; it is the time which indicates the profundity of Jesus' loyalty to God, for it is "obedience unto death" (Phil 2:8). Inasmuch as Luke emphasizes Jesus' radical holiness, innocence, and closeness to God, Jesus' obedience in 22:42 is a highly significant act,[37] one that contrasts him with all other people. If, as we have suggested, Luke portrays Jesus as the obedient new Adam in 4:1–12, then this parallel dramatization of Jesus' obedience to God is likewise the faithfulness of the new Adam.

Third, the Gethsemane episode is the time when Satan returns to resume his temptations of Jesus. We noted earlier that Satan's temptations have a double edge in the passion narrative. Luke is explicit that Satan is the force behind the plot to kill Jesus. As the catalyst of the death plot against Jesus, Luke notes that Satan entered Judas and so set the plot in motion (22:3). The arresting party is linked with this demonic power, as Jesus noted: "This is your hour and the power of darkness" (22:53). Satan, then, is active in the passion narrative as the dark power which is working Jesus' death. Luke implies by this the common assumption that sinners die and are subject to death: death means being in Satan's power. Luke, of course, counters this in Acts where Ps 16 is cited as proof that even in his death, Jesus was *not* in Satan's power, for "God did not abandon my soul to Hades, nor let his Holy One see corruption" (Acts 2:27, 31). This is the final word in the drama, but in 22:42 we are investigating only the first word, how Satan seeks Jesus' death to have power over him.

Satan's activity in the passion has a second aspect. When it is remarked that Satan desired to sift Peter and the others (22:31), Satan is not attempting to use Peter as an agent of Jesus' death as was the case with Judas. This remark speaks of a temptation to faithlessness. Satan works not only death in the passion narrative, but sin as well. I argued earlier in regard to the episode in the orchard that Jesus both protests obedience to God as his faithful son and is tested in this. He sought God's will (22:42) but was also found in an *agonia* which tested his obedience. And so, Satan resumes his activity, tempting to unfaithfulness and working death.

As was predicted in 4:13, Satan returns in the passion narrative. He continues to tempt to unfaithfulness and to work death. And so he attempts to work Jesus' death through Judas and Jesus' enemies; and he attempts to work sin through his assault on Jesus' faithfulness in the orchard. The full significance of Jesus' obedience in 22:42 lies in its character as the confirmation of his earlier faithfulness to God. At the beginning of his career and at the end, Jesus was always obedient to God; he was always the sinless "son of God." If the temptations and Jesus' obedience were presented as proof that Jesus is the new Adam, then the resumption of Jesus' temptations and his renewed obedience in 22:39–46 should also be seen as Luke's confirmation of Jesus as the new Adam.

D. The Cross and Jesus' Faithfulness

Turning once more to Jesus' crucifixion scene, we note three aspects of this narrative which indicate its place in Luke's Adam-Jesus comparison.

1. There are formal similarities between 23:32–49 and 4:1–13, indicating that Satan's suspended temptations are also resumed in the crucifixion scene.
2. Jesus indicates that access to "paradise," denied since Adam, is now open to God's creatures (23:43).

3. Jesus' faithfulness to God, so pivotal in his earlier temptations, is dramatically confirmed, especially his acceptance of death as God's will (23:46).

First, one might see a resumption of the temptations in the crucifixion scene itself. Three different groups come up to Jesus in succession and say to him:

A. "Let him save himself
   if he is the Christ of God, his Chosen One" (23:35).
B. "Save yourself
   if you are the King of the Jews" (23:37).
C. "Save yourself and us!
   Are you not the Christ?" (23:39).

These three suggestions to Jesus are not identical with the temptations in 4:1–13 in that Satan is not speaking to Jesus on the cross nor are the suggestions made formally structured according to Gen 1–3, as was the case in 4:1–13. But there are remarkable formal similarities between 4:1–13 and 23:35–39.

1. In each case, *three suggestions* are made to Jesus by his enemies.
2. Both the temptations in 4:1–13 and the suggestions in 23:35–39 make their point on the basis of *Jesus' relationship to God*:
   4:3, 9 "If you are the son of God . . ."
   23:35 "If you are the Christ of God,[38] his Chosen One . . ."
3. As the climactic temptation in 4:9–12 suggested that *Jesus should not die,* so all three suggestions on the cross propose that Jesus save himself from death. The mockers at the cross are telling Jesus substantially the same thing as Satan did. Jesus' escape from death because he is God's Chosen One is the issue in 23:35–39 as well as 4:1–12.
4. Although Satan is not himself speaking to Jesus on the cross, Luke has already linked Jesus' antagonists with Satan (22:53); and Satan is active in Judas to work Jesus' arrest and death. *Satan is not absent or inactive* in Jesus' passion narrative.

These formal similarities strongly invite the reader to see the crucifixion scene as related to the temptations. Satan's return "at an opportune time" would include Jesus' crucifixion as well.

Second, in the previous chapter we indicated that Jesus' remark to the repentant criminal (23:43) contained an important statement about Lukan soteriology. When Jesus says, "Today you will be with me in paradise," two things are implied: (a) forgiveness of sins and (b) conquering of death. If the criminal is to be "with me," he cannot still be a sinner; his sins must be somehow forgiven if he is to be with the holy Jesus in God's holy place. And if he is to be with Jesus "in paradise," he will not be dead, but in some way conquer death, for the dead are unclean and cannot come into God's holy presence. In this chapter we are continuing to explore the possible Adam allusions contained in Luke's version of Jesus' death, and so we re-examine 23:43 precisely in terms of the phrase "with me in paradise" to see what is denoted by it.

The question is simple: What is meant by "paradise" in 23:43? We are all well aware of the bewildering diversity of viewpoints concerning afterlife in post-biblical Judaism. As George Nickelsburg[39] reminds us, "There is no single Jewish orthodoxy on the time, mode and place of resurrection, immortality, and eternal life . . . a unitary view is pure fiction." But to what type of tradition or stream of speculation would "paradise" belong? Even if it were true to say that "paradise" denotes no more than an "intermediate state," the full import of even being in that "intermediate state" needs clarification. For example, martyrs are said to experience immediate vindication and to enter the heavenly realm; the suffering martyrs of the Maccabean period, the Son of Man, approach God's very throne (Dan 7) and the Christian martyrs are said to be already under the altar of God in the center of heaven (Rev 6:9). But "paradise" is not the term used to designate the place to which suffering martyrs go. And the criminal in Lk 23:43 is hardly a martyr; he suffers justly for his crimes (23:41). "Paradise," then, does not belong to traditions about martyrs or the suffering righteous.

"Paradise" seems to belong in more speculative traditions about afterlife. It commonly designates the future abode of the righteous.[40] And it belongs to a long-standing biblical expectation that "the last time is like the first."[41] The "paradise" of the last age corresponds to or is identical with that of the first age. The opinions about a future paradise are indeed quite varied, but in some way they all harken back to Gen 1–3 and attempt to deal with the issues raised there concerning sin and death.

The future paradise functions in some way as the antidote to the experience of sin and death here on earth. On the one hand, it was recognized that sinners cannot enter paradise: "And that paradise whose fruit endures incorruptible . . . shall be manifest, but we cannot enter it because we have passed our lives in unseemly manners" (4 Ezr 7:123). But it is also expected that the closed gates of Paradise will be reopened. Speaking of a figure who would completely undo the curse of Adam, T. Levi explicitly speaks of a reopening of the closed gates of paradise:

> And he shall open the gates of Paradise
> and shall remove the threatening sword against Adam
> and shall give to the saints to eat from the tree of life
> and the spirit of holiness shall be on them
> and Beliar shall be bound by him
> and he shall give power to his children to tread on
> evil spirits (18:10–12, see T. Dan 5:9–12).

"Paradise," then, is a condensed symbol of the Genesis myth for dealing with sin and death. But as Hanhart remarked, when understanding paradise as the place of future life, one deals with a myth of *Paradise Lost*. "The question is . . . when will the gates of Paradise be open and who has the key?"[42]

When Jesus says to the criminal, "Today you will be with me in paradise," Luke seems to be concerned with both questions. Paradise is lost; but Jesus has the key and the gates will be opened "today." That paradise is closed according to Luke may be inferred from a Lukan remark that Jesus fills a very great need: he frees us from everything from which we could not be freed by the law of Moses (Acts 13:39). That paradise is subsequently opened rests on the place Jesus has in Luke's plan of salvation history. He does not belong to the period of Israel; he inaugurates "the last days" when he pours out God's spirit as Joel prophesied (Acts 2:16–21). Jesus' presence indicates that God's predicted kingdom is already in our midst (Lk 11:20; 19:21). The remark to the criminal indicates that paradise is now regained through Jesus. That Jesus has the key to the gates may be inferred from the Lukan presentation of Jesus as the unique and necessary Savior of the world (Acts 4:12; 13:38–39). Jesus' remark to the criminal in 23:43 is no mere prophecy of future events, but a juridical pronouncement by Jesus the Judge of the living and the dead (Acts 10:42; 17:31).

The full import of Luke's understanding of "paradise" in 23:43 comes when we contrast his description of new life and forgiveness of sins (paradise) with other remarks about the eschatological future in Luke-Acts. Luke uses the generic description of "heaven" for future life when he remarked that the apostles' names are "written in heaven" (Lk 10:20), assuring them of a reward in the future life. Lazarus goes to "Abraham's bosom" after death, a place contrasted with Hades and its torments (Lk 16:22–23). Those who invite the poor, the maimed, and the lame to their banquets will be rewarded at "the resurrection of the just" (14:14). Given these general terms used for afterlife and rewards and retribution after death, the use of "paradise" in 23:43 is all the more striking. It is evocative of Genesis imagery and allusive of an Adam-Jesus comparison.

Luke's use of "paradise" helps us to refine his sense of the periods of history. The "period of Israel" begins with Adam and Adam's sin; it is a period of temptation and disobedience; it is the reign of Satan; and during it, the gates of Paradise were closed. Jesus inaugurates a new period of salvation history, which is a period of obedience to God and in which forgiveness of sins is available only through Jesus; it marks the end of Satan's reign (Lk 10:18) and the despoiling of Satan's kingdom (11:15–22). With Jesus' obedience and faithfulness, paradise is once more opened to God's people. "Paradise," or rather "Paradise Regained," is a condensed and appropriate symbol for certain aspects of the period of history which Jesus inaugurates. It speaks of the lasting consequences of Jesus' career, just as sin and death describe the consequences of Adam's actions.

Third, if "paradise" is a condensed symbol, is there evidence in Luke-Acts that other aspects of the symbol are present? Is "paradise" the only allusion? The earlier citation of T. Levi is important to our argument because it offers a summary of all the saving actions of the predicted hero, giving them all an Adamic reference. Without doing violence to Luke-Acts, these predicted actions of the new Adam are verified in Luke's account of Jesus:

1. "He shall open the gates of paradise"—
   Jesus proclaims to the crucified criminal that paradise is reopened (Lk 23:43).

2. "The spirit of holiness shall be on them"—
   As we have seen, Jesus has God's spirit (Lk 1:35; 3:22; 4:18) as well as gives it (Acts 2:33).
3. "Beliar shall be bound"—
   According to Luke, Jesus defeats Satan (Lk 11:17–19); he looses those whom Satan has bound (Lk 13:16); and he ends Satan's kingdom (Lk 10:18; Acts 26:18).
4. "He shall give power to his children to tread on evil spirits"—
   This is almost identical with Jesus' bequest to his disciples: "'Behold I have given you authority to tread on serpents and scorpions, and over all the power of the enemy; and nothing shall hurt you" (Lk 10:19). Jesus' disciples, moreover, are formally given power over evil spirits (Lk 9:1; see Acts 16:16–18).[43]

Since T. Levi 18:10–12 is a condensed symbol of the myth of the new Adam, this should color the way that the comparable Lukan statements are read about Jesus' saving actions.

We noted earlier that Luke edited Jesus' death scene to emphasize that his dying words be understood as a profound statement of faith and faithfulness. This faith of Jesus consisted of a belief in God's promise that, although the Christ must suffer and die, God would raise him from the dead. This faith, then, was perceived as radical obedience to God, even unto death (see Phil 2:8). Yet Jesus' death ironically is not due to sin as in the case of all other people. We noted earlier how Pilate, the criminal, and his executioner all witnessed to Jesus' innocence, as did God himself. His death in no way indicates that Satan reigned over him as a sinner. Rather, his dying in faith dramatically portrays Jesus' radical obedience to God's will. And so, his death means that God reigns over him, not Satan. Tempted even on the cross, Jesus remained God's Christ and Chosen One. Jesus' faith in God, moreover, definitively constitutes him as God's Son.

IV.
THE SAVING SIGNIFICANCE OF JESUS' FAITH

The obedience (22:42) and faith (23:46) of Jesus are pivotal events in the Lukan perspective of Jesus' death. If, as we have argued, Luke's model of soteriology lies in an Adam-Jesus comparison, then great weight rests on appreciating 22:42 and 23:46 as having saving significance for others as well as for Jesus. It will be helpful in assessing their functional importance in Luke-Acts if we can compare these phenomena with other materials which explicitly use an Adam-Jesus comparison. And so we turn now to a background study, comparing Luke's understanding and use of Jesus' faith and obedience with Paul's discussion of the same in his letters.

From the sheer bulk of references, there is no doubt that Paul's preferred model for interpreting the saving significance of Jesus' death is that of the new Adam:[44]

Adam and Creation References in Paul

1. Rom 5:12–21
2. 1 Cor 15:20–22, 42–49
3. 2 Cor 5:17
4. Gal 3:28
5. Phil 2:6–11

In many places Paul speaks of a "new creation" in Jesus (2 Cor 5:17); he speaks of the abrogation of the divisive effects of sin in the creation of a new Adam (Gal 3:28).[45] Although only snatches of the Adam-Jesus comparison are operative in these two places, they serve as a condensed code for the whole model. It is presumed in these two places, moreover, that there is a general popular appreciation of an Adam-Jesus comparison, a tradition which Paul did not himself originate but could allude to with brief, condensed remarks.[46]

Fuller and more explicit elaborations of the Adam-Jesus comparison are found in later letters of Paul. The risen Jesus is compared to Adam ("as in Adam all die, so in Christ shall all be made alive," 1 Cor 15:22). Finally, in Rom 5 Paul carefully compares Jesus and Adam. The comparison there contains three basic points: (a) there is a head figure who did a most significant and influential action, (b) which action led to important consequences for all of God's people, and (c) which consequences are a matter of life and death for them. Both Adam and Jesus are heads of their respective clans and peoples; they are both founding figures, inaugural persons. As Adam was disobedient, Jesus was faithful (5:19). The consequences of Adam's disobedience was death and judgment for all (5:16); but the result of Jesus' obedience is life and justification. Adam's sin opened the way to death (5:12, 15); "death reigned through that one man" (5:17). But "through the one man Jesus Christ," we reign in life (5:17b), even in eternal life (5:21). The formal contrast of Adam and Jesus clearly shows that with Jesus' obedience the old reign of sin and Satan has ended (16:20). Salvation, forgiveness of sins, and eternal life come to us through the obedience of Jesus, the new Adam. Although in Rom 5:12–21 Paul makes no formal link between Jesus' obedience and the cross, that is surely what is presupposed (see Phil 2:8). Rom 5:12–21, moreover, is but building on the remarks about Jesus' death in 5:6–10.

As Nils Dahl has shown,[47] the material in Rom 5 summarizes the argument which preceded in Rom 1–4. Rom 5:12–21, then, may be considered the clearest, sharpest summary of Paul's understanding of the saving significance of Jesus' death in Romans. It focuses on his obedience, an obedience unto death. But Paul's remarks on the significance of Jesus' death are not confined to Rom 5. Earlier in 3:21–26 he spoke of that death, a passage to which we now turn.

When we turn back to 3:21–26 from 5:12–21, we are quite sensitized by Paul's emphasis on the obedience of Jesus which is salvific. And so our attention is attracted in 3:21–26 to three passages which seem to speak of this same saving disposition of Jesus. The phrase under consideration is *pistis Christou* ("the faith of Christ"):

3:22 *dia pisteōs Iēsou Christou*
(through the faith of Jesus Christ)
3:25 *hilastērion dia pisteōs*
(an expiation through faith)
3:26 (*theon*) *dikaiounta ton ek pisteōs Iēsou*
(God justifying them by the faith of Jesus)

There has been a healthy debate recently over whether *pistis Christou* is an objective genitive ("faith in Christ") or a subjective genitive ("faith of Christ").[48] Until recently it was presumed that the objective genitive was correct, and so Paul was said to maintain that we are saved by "faith in Jesus." This presumption has come increasingly under fire by scholars who suggest that the subjective genitive is both grammatically and theologically correct. Hence, it is argued that we are saved by "the faith of Christ."

The basic grammatical argument in favor of the subjective genitive has been urged by George Howard and the theological argument by Luke Johnson. Howard[49] observed in regard to the proper grammatical reading of the genitive in *pistis Christou:* (1) In Hellenistic Jewish literature, faith/

pistis is rarely, if ever, followed by the non-subjective, personal genitive; when faith *in* someone is expressed, a preposition is employed (e.g., *ten pros ton theon pistin,* Philo, *Mut.* 201). (2) The Latin Vulgate, the Syriac Peshitta, and the Sahidic Coptic translations of Paul's letters all favor the subjective genitive. Johnson[50] recently entered the debate and persuasively showed from a literary analysis of Rom 3:21–26 that the subjective genitive is the only interpretation coherent with the theological argument in Rom 3–5. I am presuming the solid work of these two careful scholars.

If the subjective genitive is correct, what is the theological significance of this observation? We are required to look more closely at Rom 3:21–26. This passage functions in the letter's argument as the antithesis of 1:18–3:20; in that former section of the letter, Paul showed that "God's wrath is revealed" (1:18) upon all sinners; all people, moreover, were proved to be sinners and so under God's just judgment, for "all people, both Jew and Greek, are under the power of sin, as it is written, 'None is righteous, no, not one . . .'" (3:9–10). 3:21–26 begins with an adversative conjunction "But . . ." indicating that it stands in contrast to what preceded. For, in 3:21ff Paul then shows how "God's righteousness is revealed" upon all; all indeed sinned and fell short of God's glory (3:22), but all can be saved. The righteousness of God, moreover, is revealed in Christ's death (3:24–25). Commentators[51] point out that 3:24–25 come from a pre-Pauline tradition, containing ways of interpreting Jesus' death which were unusual in Paul's own letters and which were not picked up elsewhere in his writings. The non-Pauline phrase is the description of Jesus' death as an expiation; the more typical Pauline redactional phrases here are the insertions of *pistis Christou* into the argument. It is not the mere shedding of Jesus' blood nor the mere fact of his death that constitutes it as salvation and righteousness for us. The value of the physical death is contained in Paul's understanding of *who it is* who shed that blood and *what* that figure was doing vis-à-vis God's plan. The one who died was the new Adam and what made his death different from any other death was his singular obedience (5:19). 3:21–26 contain a terse and incomplete statement of the mechanics of our salvation. But when it is seen alongside the fuller, more explicit statement in 5:12–21, then the meaning and importance of the remarks can be more fully grasped. And so, in 3:21–26, Jesus' faith as he died is the locus of God's righteousness, and this faith is salvific of others.

But what is this "faith of Jesus" which is salvific? Paul speaks in Rom 4 about the structure of faith.[52] First, it is stated that faith saves: "Abraham believed God and it was credited to him as righteousness" (4:3/Gen 15:6). Saving faith is directed toward God, under the rubric of believing God's promise of blessings. Second, in Rom 4:17 Paul states that God made a second promise to Abraham about an heir and son (Gen 17:10). Of Abraham's faith Paul says: ". . . in the presence of the God in whom he believed, who gives life to the dead and calls into existence the things that do not exist." Faith is again directed to God, under the rubric of the *one-who-raises-the-dead*. Third, in 4:20–21 we are told that Abraham's faith did not waiver when he considered his and Sarah's withered, old bodies, "as good as dead." Rather, "he grew strong in faith . . . fully convinced that God was able to do what he had promised." Finally, in 4:23–24, Paul notes that the biblical remarks about Abraham's faith were not written for his sake alone but for ours also: "It will be reckoned to us who believe in him who raised Jesus from the dead." Like Abraham, we are called to have faith in God who raises the dead. Faith, then, is:

(a) faith *in God*

(b) who *raises the dead*

(c) as he *promised.*

This is confirmed in Rom 10:9 where Paul specifies the act of Christian faith which saves. If you confess with your lips that Jesus is Lord, and "believe in your heart that God raised him from the dead," you will be saved.

Now it is clear that Abraham's faith in God is but a type. Inasmuch as "*All* fall short of the glory of God" (3:22) and "*All* are under the power of sin" (3:9), Abraham is not excepted. He, too, is ultimately in need of Christ's saving death. Yet Abraham's "faith" is celebrated; it is credited to him as righteousness. His faith, moreover, is to be imitated (4:23–24); they are true descendants of Abraham only if "they share the faith of Abraham" (4:16). And Abraham is to be the father of a nation, the head of a new people of God. But for all that, he is a sinner and needs Jesus' saving death. His "faith," then, should be seen as a type, a prophecy of the faith of the one sinless man, Jesus. The structure of Jesus' saving faith in 3:21–26 is explained through the biblical example of Abraham in Rom 4. And that saving faith is (a) faith in God, (b) who raises the dead, (c) even as he promised. Just as Abraham's faith is prophetic of Jesus', so remarks about Abraham's being the new head of God's people and father of a nation (Rom 4:16–17) are also prophetic of the new Adam. Abraham, after all, was but a sinner. A person who is not a sinner was to come on the scene, a person whose faith is fully canonized by God in the Scriptures. And that faithful person truly became the head of a new people because of his sinlessness, because he is a new Adam.

Rom 3:21–26, then, tells us that Jesus' faith in God was salvific. 4:3–24 describes the structure of that faith and indicates how it constitutes Jesus as the head of a new people. Finally, 5:12–21 draws out quite clearly how this faithful obedience is unique in all the world, what cosmic effect it has on all peoples, and how it truly inaugurates a new period of salvation history. 3:21–26, 4:3–24, and 5:12–21 all stress in varying degrees the same argument:

(a) Jesus' faith and obedience,
(b) the radical, salvific effects of his faith,
(c) the constitution of Jesus as Head[53] of God's people and the beginning of a new period of salvation history.

It should be noted that in Romans, Paul repeatedly links the two phenomena, "faith" and "obedience."[54] At the very beginning of Romans, Paul states that his apostolate is to bring about "the obedience of faith" (1:5); and at the close of the letter, he repeats that God's plan in the Scriptures and Paul's gospel is to "bring about the obedience of faith" (16:26). The inherent connection of "obedience" and "faith" is certainly agreed upon in the critical literature on Paul's understanding of faith. The reader of Romans is thus urged to see how 3:21–26, 4:3–24, and 5:12–21 are all dealing with the same issue: (a) how Christians are saved by Christ's faith (ch. 3) or by his obedience (ch. 5), and (b) how Christ's faith constitutes him father of a nation (ch. 4) or his obedience designates him as the new Adam, head of a new people of God (ch. 5).

A second presentation of Jesus' faith and obedience is found in Hebrews. The author there speaks of Jesus as a "faithful" (*pistos*) high priest (2:17; 3:2, 6), who learned obedience by what he suffered (5:8). This faithful and obedient high priest was indeed tempted in every way as we are (4:15), yet he was ever sinless (4:15). Being made perfect in suffering, he "became the source of eternal salvation to all who obey him" (5:9). The figure of Jesus in Hebrews is called a high priest, not Adam; but in all of the important aspects, the profiles of Jesus in Romans and Hebrews and Luke-Acts are remarkably similar:

ROMANS	HEBREWS	LUKE
1. Jesus has faith (3:22, 25, 26)	1. Jesus is faithful (2:17; 3:2, 6)	1. Jesus has faith (22:42; 23:46)
2. Jesus is obedient (5:12–21)	2. Jesus is obedient (10:5–10)	2. Jesus is obedient (22:42)
3. Jesus is sinless (implicit in 5:12–21 as antithesis of Adam)	3. Jesus is sinless (4:15)	3. Jesus is innocent (23:4, 14–15, 22, 41, 47; Acts 2:27; 13:35)
4. _____	4. Jesus is tempted (4:15)	4. Jesus is tempted (4:1–13; 22:39–46; 23:35–39)
5. Jesus is the head and father of a new people of God (5:18–19)	5. Jesus is the source of eternal salvation (2:10–15; 5:9; 12:2)	5. Jesus is the source of salvation (23:43; Acts 4:10–12; 13:38–39)
6. Jesus' death is the key saving moment (3:24–25)	6. Jesus' death is the focal saving moment (5:9; 9:11–28)	6. Jesus' death is the pivotal moment (23:43, 46)

From this excursus into Romans and Hebrews, we realize that discussions of Jesus' faith and obedience are not incidental to theological explanations of the saving significance of his death.

CONCLUSIONS

1. Chapters 5 and 6 are one more step in correcting the dying consensus that there is no soteriology in Luke-Acts. No, it is wrong to say that Luke has no soteriology at all, no *theologia crucis*.

2. We have concentrated on only one model of soteriology in Luke-Acts, the Adam-Jesus comparison. But it is important to remember that many models of soteriology are operative in Luke-Acts as well as in early Church preaching. It would be a mistake to expect only one model, and a sacrificial or atonement model at that.

3. The Adam-Jesus model may seem rather implicit in Luke; the skeletal substructure of the model may not be as obvious or explicit as

one might want. But a glance at the Pauline use of this same model offers a sage bit of correction. The Adam-Jesus comparison may be present only in a key code phrase which evokes the whole myth. The mere mention of "new creation" (2 Cor 5:17) or of the healing of divisions in the new Adam (Gal 3:28) suggests a fuller symbolic story, which is found explicitly in Rom 5:12–21. A minimum of clues may be effective, as the image of a log cabin at a Republican convention evokes the myth of Abe Lincoln or the playing of "Happy Days Are Here Again" at a Democratic convention summons up the myth of FDR. A lot rides on a little.

4. By the time of the writing of Luke-Acts, the Adam-Jesus model was a commonplace in New Testament writings. It is already an established part of early Church preaching by Paul's time. It is not our intention to make Luke into a disciple of Paul, but the Pauline use of the Adam-Jesus comparison offers a genuine, testable norm against which to measure Luke's data.

5. The essential pieces of the Adam-Jesus comparison in Luke are:

(a) the Adam reference in 3:38 and the subsequent temptation of the new Adam in 4:1–12.

(b) 4:13 is a key Lukan redactional verse which functions as a prophecy linking the earlier material on the new Adam (Son of God, innocence, temptation, and obedience) with the resumption of the attacks on this same figure in his passion and death. Baptism-genealogy-temptation are linked with passion-death by the evangelist.

(c) In his passion, Jesus demonstrates singular obedience and faithfulness to God, even to death on a cross. This is no mere Church paraenesis, but belongs to the core of Luke's Christology. Lk 22:42 and 23:46 are great moments in salvation history.

(d) Jesus effects the reopening of paradise (23:43), completing the end of the reign of Satan and inaugurating the coming of God's kingdom.

The model which holds these pieces together and interprets their full significance is the Adam-Jesus comparison.

6. The Adam-Jesus model is the shaping force which focuses and interprets two streams of Lukan redactional material. (a) Luke the historian sketches a clear picture of salvation history divided into periods: pre-Jesus and post-Jesus. The periods, although linked through prophecy and fulfillment, are still in stark contrast. (b) The Christology of Acts

proclaims Jesus as both the holy, righteous one and as the unique, necessary source of salvation. Both of these clues mesh with and reinforce the Adam-Jesus comparison at every point.

7. We are reminded of one of the central perspectives of this book, the place of Acts in the interpretation of Luke. Small redactional changes in the Lukan Gospel are often made with a view to their impact on and explanation in Acts. Acts is no mere echo of the Gospel, not simply its "confirmation," but its goal and realization. This is never clearer than in Luke's soteriology, where the major Christological statements in Acts 4:10–12, 13:38–39, and 26:23 explain Jesus' role as the unique and necessary Savior, and where the Acts 2:27, 3:15, 5:30, 7:52, and 13:35 stress his innocence, holiness, and righteousness as God's Christ. The small redactional changes in the passion narrative cast long shadows in Acts.

8. According to this presentation, Luke's soteriology is not all concentrated in the passion narrative. Jesus' death serves as the climactic moment when the pattern of obedience and faith reaches its completion and the true character of Jesus as the new Adam is definitively achieved. From his temptations (4:1–12) to his death, the whole career of Jesus expresses the "today" of salvation available in Jesus. But the climax of that salvation and its confirmation are sealed in the final act of obedience of the new Adam.

NOTES

INTRODUCTION

1. *The Theology of St. Luke* (New York: Harper and Brothers, 1960).
2. For example, Helmut Flender, *St. Luke: Theologian of Redemptive History* (Philadelphia: Fortress, 1967); Jerome Kodell, "The Theology of Luke in Recent Study," *BTB* 1 (1971) 115–144; and Joseph A. Fitzmyer, *The Gospel According to Luke I–IX* (Garden City: Doubleday, 1981) 143–270.
3. For example, C.K. Barrett, *Luke the Historian in Recent Study* (London: Epworth, 1961); J. Drury, *Tradition and Design in Luke's Gospel* (London: Darton, Longman and Todd, 1976); David L. Barr and Judith L. Wentling, "The Conventions of Classical Biography and the Genre of Luke-Acts: A Preliminary Study," *Luke-Acts* (ed. C.H. Talbert; New York: Crossroad, 1984) 63–88.
4. The older works of Henry J. Cadbury are still very pertinent: *The Making of Luke-Acts* (London: SPCK, 1927) and *The Style and Literary Method of Luke* (Cambridge: Harvard U. Press, 1920); see C.H. Talbert, *Literary Patterns, Theological Themes, and the Genre of Luke-Acts* (SBLMS 20; Missoula: Scholars Press, 1974); W.C. van Unnik, "Elements artistiques dans l'évangile de Luc," *L'Évangile de Luc* (BETL 32; ed. F. Neirynck; Gembloux: J. Duculot, 1973) 129–140.
5. See E. Pluemacher, *Lukas als hellenistischer Schriftsteller: Studien zur Apostelgeschichte* (Goettingen: Vandenhoeck und Ruprecht, 1972); W.C. van Unnik, "Luke's Second Book and the Rules of Hellenistic Historiography," *Actes des Apôtres: traditions, rédaction, théologie* (ed. J. Kremer; Gembloux: Duculot, 1973) 37–60; and J. Dupont, "La question du plan des Actes des Apôtres a la lumière d'un texte de Lucien de Samosate," *NT* 21 (1979) 220–231.
6. For example, the titles of recent works on Luke reflect this: *Studies in Luke-Acts* (ed. J.L. Martyn and L.E. Keck; Nashville: Abingdon, 1966); *Perspective on Luke-Acts* (ed. C.H. Talbert; Danville: Association of Baptist Professors of Religion, 1978); and *Luke-Acts* (ed. C.H. Talbert, 1984).
7. See *Literary Patterns, Theological Themes, and the Genre of Luke-Acts,* 15–65.
8. "The Paul-Jesus Parallels and the Purpose of Luke-Acts: H.H. Evans Reconsidered," *NT* 17 (1975) 15–45; see Walter Radl, *Paulus und Jesus im lu-*

kanischen Doppelwerk: Untersuchungen zu Parallelmotiven im Lukasevangelium und in der Apostelgeschichte (Frankfurt: Peter Lang, 1975).

9. "'The Book of Acts,' the Confirmation of the Gospel," *NT* 4 (1960) 26–59.

I. JESUS' FAREWELL SPEECH (LK 22:14–38)

1. For a recent survey of the discussion of the sources of Luke's passion narrative, see G. Schneider, "Das Problem einer vorlukanischen Passionserzaehlung," *BZ* 16 (1972) 222–244. See also P. Winter, "The Treatment of His Sources by the Third Evangelist in Luke xxi–xxiv," *SJTh* 8 (1955) 138–172; Vincent Taylor, *The Passion Narrative of St. Luke* (Cambridge: University Press, 1971), and Joseph A. Fitzmyer, *The Gospel According to Luke I–IX* (Garden City: Doubleday, 1981) 63–106.

2. It has been fashionable for some time to identify Lk 22:14–38 as a farewell speech, but very little work has been done in spelling out what formal elements are present in Luke's version; for example, see J. Dupont, "Le logion de douze thrônes (Mt 19,28; Lc 22,28–30)," *Bib* 45 (1964) 355–392 or even H. Schuermann, *Jesu Abschiedsrede Lk 22,21–38* (Muenster: Aschendorf, 1957). Fridolin Keck (*Die Oeffentliche Abschiedsrede Jesu in Lk 20,45–21,36* [Stuttgart: Katholisches Bibelwerk, 1976]) neither discussed what a farewell speech is or how Lk 20–21 is Jesus' farewell, when Luke also records a final speech in 22:14–38. On typical farewell speeches, see Johannes Munck, "Discors d'adieu dans le Nouveau Testament et dans la littérateur biblique," *Aux Sources de la Tradition Chrétienne: Mélanges offert à M. Maurice Goguel* (ed. J.J. von Allmen; Paris: Delachaux et Niestle, 1950) 155–170; and Ethelbert Stauffer, "Abschiedsreden," *RAC* I. 29–35.

3. P. Corssen, "Die Abschiedsreden Jesu in vierten Evangelium," *ZNW* 8 (1907) 125–142; G.-M. Behler, *The Last Discourse of Jesus* (Baltimore: Helicon, 1965); Aelred Lacomara, "Deuteronomy and the Farewell Discourse (Jn 13:31–16:33)," *CBQ* 36 (1974) 65–84; and John Painter, "The Farewell Discourses and the History of Johannine Christianity," *NTS* 27 (1981) 525–543.

4. J.H. Neyrey, *The Form and Background of the Polemic in 2 Peter* (Ph.D. dissertation, unpublished; Yale: 1977), 99–105.

5. *The Covenant Formulary in Old Testament, Jewish and Early Christian Writings* (Philadelphia: Fortress, 1971) 144–161.

6. "The Genre Testament and Forecasts of the Future in the Hellenistic Jewish Milieu," *JSJ* 6 (1975) 57–71.

7. W.S. Kurz, "Luke 22:14–38 and Graeco-Roman and Biblical Farewell Addresses," forthcoming from JBL.

8. *The Lord's Supper* (Philadelphia: U. Pennsylvania Press, 1981) 72.

9. *Ibid.* 79.

10. *Ibid.* 82.

11. *Ibid.* 85.

12. R.E. Brown, *The Gospel According to John* (Garden City: Doubleday, 1966) I. 272–274; A. Feuillet, *Johannine Studies* (Staten Island: Alba House, 1965) 76–101; and Peter Borgen, *Bread from Heaven* (Leiden: Brill, 1965) 147–182.

13. R.E. Brown, *The Gospel According to John,* 517–518.

14. For other Lukan examples of this intensified type of expression, see Acts 5:28; 16:28; 23:10; 28:10.

15. For recent discussions of Lukan eschatology, see E.E. Ellis, "Present and Future Eschatology in Luke," *NTS* 12 (1965–66) 27–41; S.G. Wilson, "Lukan Eschatology," *NTS* 16 (1969–70) 330–347; and A.J. Mattill, "Naherwartung, Fernerwartung and the Purpose of Luke-Acts: Weymouth Reconsidered," *CBQ* 34 (1972) 276–293 and *Luke and the Last Things* (Dillsboro: Western North Carolina Press, 1979).

16. See Luke T. Johnson, "The Lukan Kingship Parable (Lk 19:11–27)," *NT* 24 (1982) 153–159.

17. See Joachim Jeremias, *The Eucharistic Words of Jesus* (London: SCM, 1966) 210–211.

18. In John's Gospel we find a formal "replacement" theme developed, showing how Christian feasts and rites replace Jewish ones; see A. Guilding, *The Fourth Gospel and Jewish Worship* (Oxford: Clarendon, 1960); and J.H. Neyrey, "Jacob Traditions and the Interpretation of John 4:10–26," *CBQ* 41 (1979) 419–437.

19. Johannes Behm, "deipnon," *TDNT* II. 34.

20. J.H. Neyrey, "The Apologetic Use of the Transfiguration in 2 Peter 1:16–21," *CBQ* 42 (1980) 504–519.

21. I am not considering the interpretative word over the cup ("blood of the new testament," 22:20) as testamentary legacy; the whole gift of the Eucharist is intended; see J. Behm, "deipnon," 34–35.

22. J. Wanke, *Beobactungen zum Eucharistieverstaendnis des Lukas, auf Grund der lukanischen Mahlbericht* (Leipzig: St. Benno, 1973) 31–34 and " '. . . wie sei ihn beim Brotbrechen erkanneten.' Zur Auslegung der Emmauserzaehlung Lk 24, 13–35," *BZ* 18 (1974) 180–192; Raymond Orlett, "An Influence of the Early Liturgy Upon the Emmaus Account," *CBQ* 21 (1959) 217; Richard J. Dillon, *From Eye-Witnesses to Ministers of the Word* (AB 82; Rome: Biblical Institute Press, 1978) 149–155.

23. J. Wanke, *Beobachtungen zum Eucharistieverstaendnis des Lukas,* 66–70.

24. For Lukan dependance on Mk 14:18–21 at this point, see H. Schuer-

mann, *Jesu Abschiedsrede,* 3–21 and Jack Finegan, *Die Ueberlieferung den Leidens-und Auferstehungsgeschichte Jesu* (BZNW 15; Geissen: A. Toepelmann, 1934) 8, 13.

25. On Luke's use of *dei* for God's determined will, see E. Fascher, "Theologische Beobachtungen zu *dei,*" *Neutestamentliche Studien fuer Rudolf Bultmann* (BZNW 21; Berlin: Toepelmann, 1954) 245–247.

26. See 2 Pet 3:3; 1 Tim 4:1; 2 Tim 3:1; Mk 13:5–6, 21–23.

27. D.L. Tiede, "No Prophet Is Acceptable in His Own Country," *Prophecy and History in Luke-Acts* (Philadelphia: Fortress, 1980) 19–61.

28. S. Brown, *Apostasy and Perseverance in the Theology of Luke* (AB 36; Rome: Biblical Institute Press, 1969), 82–97.

29. M.-J. LaGrange, *Évangile selon saint Luc* (Paris: Gabalda, 1948) 550.

30. *Str. B.* II. 257–258.

31. Klaus Baltzer, The Covenant Formulary, 148–152.

32. See R. Bultmann, *History of the Synoptic Tradition* (New York: Harper and Row, 1963) 158–159.

33. See Jacob Jervell, "The Twelve On Israel's Thrones," *Luke and the People of God* (Minneapolis: Augsburg Publishing House, 1972) 75–112.

34. See 1 Tim 3:1–13; 4:11–16; Tit 1:5–9.

35. See Karl Georg Kuhn, "Jesus in Gethsemane," *ET* 12 (1952–53) 282–284; this will be dealt with at greater length in the last part of this book.

36. Jacques Dupont, "Le logion des douze thrônes," 355–365.

37. See E. Osty, "Les points de contact entre le récit de la passion dans Saint Luc and dans Saint Jean," *RSR* 39 (1951) 146–154; P. Borgen, "John and the Synoptics in the Passion Narrative," *NTS* 5 (1958–59) 246–259; I. Buse, "St. John and the Passion Narrative of St. Matthew and St. Luke," *NTS* 7 (1960–61) 65–76; A. Kolenkow, "Healing Controversy as a Tie Between Miracle and Passion Material for a Proto-Gospel," *JBL* 95 (1976) 623–638; F. Lamar Cribbs, "A Study of the Contacts That Exist between St. Luke and St. John," *SBL Seminar Papers 1973* II. 1–93.

38. The agency of Satan against Ananias and Sapphira (Acts 5:3, 9) should also be noted here.

39. See G. Staehlins, "exaiteo," *TDNT* I. 194; see Josephus, *Ant.* V. 152.

40. See A.N. Argyle, "The Influence of the Testaments of the Twelve Patriarchs upon the New Testament," *ExpT* 63 (1951–52) 256.

41. I.H. Marshall, *The Gospel of Luke* (Grand Rapids: Eerdmans, 1978) 820–821.

42. S. Brown, *Apostasy and Perseverance,* 68.

43. Pace Staehlins, "exaiteo," 194.

44. See I.H. Marshall, *The Gospel of Luke,* 821–822.

45. Compare with other Lukan passages concerned with the fidelity of leaders: Lk 12:42; 16:10–12; 19:17.

46. Yet see E.F. Suttcliffe, "'Et Tu Aliquando Conversus,' St. Luke 22,32," *CBQ* 15 (1953) 305–310.

47. See Acts 1:15; 2:29; 6:3; 9:17; 10:23, etc.

48. This rapidly became part of the New Testament tradition; see 1 Cor 15:9 and 1 Tim 1:12–18.

49. R.E. Brown, *Peter in the New Testament* (New York: Paulist, 1973) 121.

50. See *Peter in the New Testament,* 40–56; also W. Dietrich, *Der Petrusbild der lukanischen Schriften* (Stuttgart; Kohlhammer, 1972).

51. See also T. Joseph 7:4; T. Dan 1:7; 6:1–3.

52. *The Final Passion Prediction: A Study of Luke 22:33–38* (Ph.D. dissertation, unpublished; Fordham, 1974).

53. *Ibid.* 43–44.

54. *Ibid.* 46.

55. *Ibid.* 55.

56. *Ibid.* 55–61.

57. *Ibid.* 78.

58. *Ibid.* 77.

59. *Ibid.* 75–77; 139–140.

60. *Ibid.* 79–81.

61. *Ibid.* 102–103.

62. *Ibid.* 115–127.

63. *Ibid.* 142–156.

64. *Ibid.* 84–89.

65. *Ibid.* 89–95.

66. *Ibid.* 95–100.

67. *Ibid.* 68.

68. "A Note on Luke xxii 36," *NT* 7 (1964–65) 132–134.

69. Simeon's "Nunc Dimittis" (Lk 2:29–32) is surely his farewell, but it is not a farewell speech.

70. See Walter Radl, *Paulus und Jesus im lukanischen Doppelwerk* (Frankfurt: Peter Lang, 1975); but he claims that there are not extended parallels between Lk 22–23 and Acts 20 (p. 131).

71. Recent commentators on Acts 20 have alluded to parallels between Lk 22:14–38 and Acts 20 on the basis of one item: the blood of Jesus in Lk 22:19 and Acts 20:28. These comparisons have focused on only one item, how the words in Acts 20 may be clarified by cross-reference to Lk 22, and not on common literary form or thematic correspondences; see J. Dupont, *Le Discours de Milet*

(Paris: Cerf, 1962); H. Schuermann, "Das Testament des Paulus fuer die kirche," *Unio Christianorum* (Paderborn: Bonifacius Verlag, 1962) 108–146; and most recently Hans-Joachim Michel, *Die Abschiedsrede des Paulus an die Kirche Apg 20:17–38* (Munich: Koesel, 1973). I am not aware of any study attempting to show formal parallelism between the two Lukan farewell speeches.

72. H.-J. Michel (*Die Abschiedsrede des Paulus an die Kirche Apg 20,17–38* [Munich: Koesel, 1973] 68–71) lists different formal elements, but without suggesting whether they are typical of farewell speeches.

73. See. H. Schuermann, "Das Testament des Paulus fuer die Kirche," 111–121; H.-J., Michel, *Die Abschiedsrede des Paulus an die Kirche,* 97; and O. Knoch, *Die Testamente des Petrus und Paulus* (SBS 62; Stuttgart: KBW Verlag, 1973) 32–39.

74. See G. Klein, *Die zwoelf Apostel* (FRLANT 77; Goettingen: Vandenhoeck und Ruprecht, 1961) 178–184.

2. JESUS IN THE GARDEN
(LK 22:39–46)

1. The issue of authenticity will be taken up in this chapter. Recent commentators tend increasingly to accept them as original for a variety of reasons other than manuscript evidence; see A. Harnack, "Probleme in Text der Leidensgeschichte Jesu," *SAB* (1901) 251–255; Lyder Brun, "Engel und Blutschweiss, Lc 22:43–44," *ZNW* 32 (1933) 265–276; T. Lescow, "Jesus in Gethsemane bei Lukas und in Hebraeerbrief," *ZNW* 58 (1967) 217–219; J.W. Holleran, *The Synoptic Gethsemane* (Rome: Gregorian University Press, 1973) 92–98.

2. This problem in the text has oddly been omitted in recent discussions of this passage; A. Feuillet, neither in his book *L'Agonie de Gethsémani* (Paris: Gabalda, 1977) nor in his article "Le récit lucanien de l'agonie de Gethsémani (Lc XXII.39–46)," *NTS* 22 (1975–76) 400, made mention of this redactional evidence; it went by unnoticed by J.W. Holleran, *The Synoptic Gethsemane* 82–87, 184–185.

3. Alfred Plummer, *A Critical and Exegetical Commentary on the Gospel According to St. Luke* (Edinburgh: T. & T. Clark, 1898) 508–511; W. Grundmann, *Das Evangelium nach Lukas* (Berlin: Evangelische Verlagsanstalt, 1971) 410–412; G.H.P. Thompson, *The Gospel According to Luke* (Oxford, Clarendon, 1972) 262–263; Erich Klostermann, *Das Lukasevangelium* (Tuebingen: Vandenhoeck and Ruprecht, 1975) 215–217; I.H. Marshall, *The Gospel of Luke* (Grand Rapids: Eerdmans, 1978) 828–833.

4. Two recent commentators have suggested that the background of "grief" might be worth investigation; Thompson (*The Gospel According to*

Luke, 262) alluded to the Stoic writings but did not pursue the lead further; Klostermann (*Das Lukasevangelium*, 216) suggested Plutarch *de fort. Rom.* 323C. The lack of interest in the background of this term may be due to the article of R. Bultmann ("Lypē/lypeō," *TDNT* IV.320) in which he categorically stated that the Stoic doctrine of the passions has no bearing on any use of "grief" in the New Testament.

5. Luke also did not retain citations from Ps 22 in the crucifixion scene, which citations suggest the same troubled state of soul as the allusions to Pss 41 and 42 in Mark 14:34. For Luke's view that "the Christ must suffer according to the Scriptures," see Lk 24:25–26. 44–46.

6. See Diogenes Laertius, VII. 110; E. Zeller, *Stoics, Epicureans and Sceptics* (London: Longmans, Green and Co., 1880) 249–254.

7. Cicero, *Tusc. Disp.* III. 7 & 10; see Bultmann, *art. cit.*, 315.

8. Plutarch, *Vit. Mor.* 449D.

9. Diogenes Laertius, VII. 110–112; Cicero, *Tusc. Disp.* III. 25; *SVF* III.394, 413–419.

10. Diogenes Laertius, VII.111; Cicero, *Tusc. Disp.* I.90; IV. 14, 66; *SVF* III. 386, 391–394.

11. Diogenes Laertius, VII. 111–112; Cicero, *Tusc. Disp.* IV. 16; *SVF* III. 414, 416.

12. Cicero, *Tusc. Disp.* III. 27.

13. Cicero, *Tusc. Disp.* III. 14.

14. The guilt of Cain—even before the murder of Abel—is heightened in the LXX; where the MT Gen 4:7 reads "sin is couching at the door," the LXX reads "you have sinned!" Philo (*Q. Gen.* I. 65–66) intensified the LXX reading, interpreting Gen 4:7 as "the beginning of every voluntary wrongdoing." *Tg. Yer.* I likewise presupposes Cain's guilt.

15. Diogenes Laertius, VII. 112.

16. While the formula for "kneeling" (*theis ta gonata*) is a favorite of Luke's, his preference for it may suggest a virtuous and dignified posture in the face of death, as was the case with Stephen in Acts 7:60; see also Acts 20:36 and 21:5.

17. See Acts 2:23 and 4:28.

18. Balancing the four cardinal passions are four primary virtues: wisdom, courage, justice, and temperance; see Diogenes Laertius, VII. 92, 102, 116.

19. Cicero, *Tusc. Disp.* III. 15.

20. Diogenes Laertius, VII. 125; *SVF* III. 266, 264, 274, 275; Plutarch, *de Stoicis Rep.* 1034D.

21. Cicero, *Tusc. Disp.* IV. 53: "parens summae legi . . . obtemperans summae legis."

22. Cicero, *Tusc. Disp.* IV. 12; Seneca, *Ep.* 116.1; Diogenes Laertius, VII. 116.

23. The volitional aspect of *andreia* is commonly stressed in philosophical literature; like Philo (*Leg. All.* i. 68), Diogenes Laertius defines *andreia* as "the knowledge of things to be chosen and things to beware of" (VII. 92). Together with Cicero, he stresses obedience (see *Tusc. Disp.* IV. 53); the virtue of *andreia* is thus a function of the will.

24. Bart Ehrman and Mark Plunkett, "The Angel and the Agony: The Textual Problem of Luke 22:43–44," *CBQ* 45 (1983) 401–416.

25. *Dial.* 103.8.

26. *Adv. Haer.* III. xxii. 2 and xxxv. 3.

27. "The Angel and the Agony," 404–405.

28. *Ibid.* 405–406.

29. *Ibid.* 407.

30. *Ibid.* 412.

31. "The Absence of Jesus' Emotions—The Lucan Redaction of Lk 22, 39–46," *Biblica* 61 (1980) 153–159.

32. In the history of the interpretation of *agonia,* it was taken to mean fear (Plummer, *The Gospel According to Luke,* 510; Grundmann, *Das Evangelium nach Lukas,* 412) or a gripping emotion (M.J. Lagrange, *Évangile selon Saint Luc* [Paris: Gabalda, 1948] 560); others see a suggestion of Jesus' martyrdom (Lescow, "Jesus in Gethsemane," 223; Holleran, *The Synoptic Gethsemane,* 97–99, 179, 219; and Feuillet, "Le récit lucanien," 413–416). For further examination of the difficulty of interpreting this term, see E. Stauffer, "agōn," *TDNT* I. 135–140 and V.C. Pfitzner, *Paul and the Agon Motif* (Leiden: Brill, 1967).

33. *LSJ,* 19.

34. See Philo, *Vir.* 24; *Praem.* 148; Diogenes Laertius, VII. 112–113; *SVF* III. 408, 409, 416.

35. G. Gamba, "Agonia di Gesù," *RivB* 16 (1968) 159–166; M. Galizzi, *Gesù nel Gethsemani* (Zuerich: Pas Verlag, 1972) 20–22, 202–203.

36. In Rom 15:30 and Col 4:12 there is a note about "struggling in prayer." O. Michel (*Der Brief an die Roemer* [Goettingen: Vandenhoeck und Ruprecht, 1957] 336) argued that these texts suggest a *Gebetskampf,* based on Jacob's wrestling with the angel (Gen 32:24ff); for a discussion of this, see V.C. Pfitzner, *Paul and the Agon Motif,* 121–124.

37. See H. Schuermann, "Luke 22, 42a, das aelteste Zeugnis fuer Luke 22, 20?" *MTZ* 3 (1952) 185–188; C.E.B. Cranfield, "The Cup Metaphor in Mark 14:36 and Parallels," *ExpT* 59 (1947–48) 137–138.

38. The suggestion, of course, is not recent; see R.S. Barbour, "Gethsemane in the Passion Tradition," *NTS* 16 (1969–70) 239–241; S. Brown, *Apostasy*

and Perseverance in the Theology of Luke (Rome: Biblical Institute Press, 1969)
8.

39. In his essay, "How from the thesis that we are akin to God may a man
proceed to the consequences" (*Diss.* I.ix.7), Epictetus argued that "to have God
as our maker, father, and guardian will suffice to deliver us from our griefs and
fears."

40. Gamba, "Agonia di Gesù," 162.

41. See L. Brun, "Engel und Blutschweiss," 276.

42. Cf. T. Dan: "For the angel of peace shall strengthen Israel, lest he fall
into an extremity of evils" (6:5).

43. Hartmut Aschermann ("Zum Agoniegebet Jesu, Luk 22, 43–44,"
Theologia Viatorum 5 [1953–54] 143–149) interpreted 4 Mac 7:8 in terms of
martyrdom. While granting the fact of Eleazar's death, one should not forget that
he also exemplified the triumph of reason over passion, especially *andreia,* the
virtue of courage which is the antithesis of grief; see 4 Mac 1:4, 6, 11, 18; 6:31–
7:1.

44. See L.E. Keck, "The Spirit and the Dove," *NTS* 17 (1970–71) 63.

45. Plummer, *The Gospel According to Luke,* 510–511; W.K. Hobart, *The
Medical Language of St. Luke* (Dublin: Hodges, Figgis and Co., 1881) 79–86;
Holleran, *The Synoptic Gethsemane,* 100, n. 100.

46. *BDF,* #210.

3. The Trials of Jesus in Luke-Acts

1. Previous discussions of Jesus' trial have tended to focus either on the
historicity of the event and reconstructions of the actual proceedings or on Luke's
sources. The standard studies are S.G.F. Brandon, *The Trial of Jesus* (London:
B.T. Batsford, 1968); Paul Winter, *On the Trial of Jesus* (2nd ed. revised by T.A.
Burkill; Berlin: Walter de Gruyter, 1974); and David R. Catchpole, "The Problem of the Historicity of the Sanhedrin Trial," *The Trial of Jesus* (SBT 13; Naperville: Alec Allenson, 1970) 47–65; A.N. Sherwin-White, *The Trial of Jesus.
Historicity and Chronology in the Gospels* (London: SPCK, 1965) 97–116. Even
if the history could be perfectly reconstructed and the nagging question of sources
resolved, one important area of scholarship would remain: Luke's interpretation
of the trial, his redaction of the sources, and the meaning of this trial in Luke-
Acts.

2. See E. Lohse, "Synedrion," *TDNT* VII. 868; Herbert Danby, "The
Bearing of the Rabbinical Criminal Code on the Jewish Trial Narratives in the
Gospel," *JTS* 21 (1920) 54–55; and Don Juel, *Messiah and Temple* (SBLDS 31;
Missoula: Scholars Press, 1977) 59–67.

3. Luke omits as well Jesus' scourging and crowning with thorns; compare Mk 15:15–20 and Lk 23:25–26.

4. Time does not permit an investigation of this mockery in terms of "honor and shame," a major anthropological perspective for assessing such events in the New Testament; but see Bruce Malina, *The New Testament World Insights from Cultural Anthropology* (Atlanta: John Knox, 1981) 25–50.

5. There has been a flood of literature on Lk 4:16–30 as programmatic of Luke's presentation of Jesus' ministry; see D. Hill, "The Rejection of Jesus of Nazareth (Luke IV 16–30)," *NT* 13 (1971) 161–180; H. Anderson, "The Rejection at Nazareth Pericope of Luke 4:16–30 in Light of Recent Critical Thought," *Int* 18 (1964) 259–275; J.B. Combrink, "The Structure And Significance of Luke 4:16–30," *Neotestamentica* 7 (1973) 27–47.

6. See D. Catchpole, "The Answer of Jesus to Caiaphas (Matt. xxvi. 64)," *NTS* 17 (1970–71) 213–226.

7. Compare H. Conzelmann, *The Theology of St. Luke* (New York: Harper and Brother, 1960) 77, and H.E. Toedt, *The Son of Man in the Synoptic Tradition* (Philadelphia: Westminister, 1965) 101–103.

8. A comparable density of Christological titles is found also in Luke's crucifixion scene, where Jesus is mocked as "the Christ of God, his chosen one" (23:35), "King of the Jews" (23:37), and "the Christ" (23:39). There is irony here in that the titles are true, and in mocking Jesus with them, the mockers are rejecting Jesus and so bringing judgment on themselves as they judge Jesus.

9. Whatever the history of the term "Son of Man" may be, its meaning as the vindication of the rejected one is well argued by C.F.D. Moule, "From Defendant to Judge—and Deliverer: An Enquiry into the Use and Limitations of the Theme of Vindication in the New Testament," *Bulletin of the Studiorum Novi Testamenti Societas* III (1952) 40–53; see also G. Vermes, *Jesus the Jew* (London: Fontana/Collins, 1973) 160–169.

10. The Lukan eschatological timetable has been the focus of several recent studies; see B.R. Gaventa, "The Eschatology of Luke-Acts Revisited," *Encounter* 43 (1982) 27–42; K. Giles, "Present and Future Eschatology in the Book of Acts," *RTR* 40 (1981) 65–71; S.G. Wilson, "Lukan Eschatology," *NTS* 16 (1969–70) 330–347; and Eric Franklin, *Christ the Lord* (Philadelphia: Westminister, 1975) 9–47.

11. These charges, then, are false accusations; see A.N. Sherwin-White, *Roman Society and Roman Law in the New Testament* (Oxford: Clarendon, 1963) 18, 21, 24, 113–115; and E.R. Goodenough, *Jurisprudence of the Jewish Courts in Egypt* (New Haven: Yale, 1929) 177. These false charges thematically will become charges against the accusers, as Jesus' trial becomes also the trial of Israel.

12. There is a serious lack of contemporary study of legal procedure in the

Roman provinces in the first century. The standard work is A.N. Sherwin-White, *Roman Society and Roman Law in the New Testament,* which replaced the older study by Henry J. Cadbury, "Roman Law and the Trial of Paul," *The Beginnings of Christianity* (London: Macmillan and Co., 1933) V.297–337. Valuable new insights may be gained from the less technical study by A.E. Harvey, *Jesus on Trial* (London: SPCK, 1976).

13. M. Dibelius, "Jesus und Herodes," *ZNW* 16 (1915) 113–126; A.W. Verrall, "Christ before Herod," *JTS* 10 (1908–09) 321–353; J.B. Tyson, "The Lukan Version of the Trial of Jesus," *NT* 3 (1959) 249–259.

14. A most persuasive case is made by Jack Finegan, *Die Ueberlieferung den Leidens und Auferstehungsgeschichte Jesu* (BZNW 15; Giessen: A. Toepelmann, 1934) 27–29.

15. Many past studies of the trial before Herod worked out of an historical bias or tried to depict Herod's psychology; see P.W. Walaskay, "The Trial and Death of Jesus in the Gospel of Luke," *JBL* 94 (1975) 87–90 and H.W. Hoebner, "Why Did Pilate Hand Jesus over to Antipas," *The Trial of Jesus* (ed. E. Bammel, STB 2nd series 13; Naperville: A. Allenson, 1970) 84–90.

16. Commentators on Luke-Acts now regularly call attention to the fact that Luke does things in twos: C.H. Talbert, *Literary Patterns, Theological Themes and the Genre of Luke-Acts* (SBLMS 20; Missoula: Scholars Press, 1974) 15–61; see also E. Haenchen, *Acts of the Apostles* (Philadelphia: Westminster, 1971) 226–229.

17. According to Luke, Herod's jurisdiction and influence was said to be effective in Tyre and Sidon (Acts 12:20–33), Galilee (Lk 13:31ff), as well as Jerusalem (Acts 12:1–5); see Plummer; and Josephus, *B.J.* III. 540–541.

18. For further discussion, see M.D. Goulder, *Type and History in Acts* (London: SPCK, 1964) 40–45; Volker Stolle, *Der Zeuge als Angeklagter* (BWANT 102; Stuttgart: W. Kohlhammer, 1973) 215–220.

19. Jerome Kodell, "Luke's Use of *LAOS,* 'People,' Especially in the Jerusalem Narrative (Lk 19, 28–24, 53)," *CBQ* 31 (1969) 331–332, 338–340.

20. See Sherwin-White, *Roman Society and Roman Law in the New Testament,* 24–27.

21. Although Lk 23:17 remarks on a "custom," this verse is generally discounted as inauthentic; see Bruce Metzger, *A Textual Commentary on the Green New Testament* (New York: United Bible Societies, 1971) 179–180.

22. In addition, Luke emphasizes the demanding character of the Jewish crowds: "They pressed hard with great cries . . . and their cries prevailed" (23:23).

23. The ironic character of Jesus' trial in other Gospels has been extensively noted; see Théo Preiss, *Life in Christ* (SBT 13; Chicago: A. Allenson, 1954) 14–22; I. de la Potterie, "Jesus King and Judge," *Scripture* 13 (1961) 97–111; W.A.

Meeks, *The Prophet-King* (Supplement to *Novum Testamentum* 14; Leiden: Brill, 1967) 61–81; Josef Blank, "Die Verhandlung vor Pilatus: John 18.28–19.16 in Lichte johannischer Theologie," *BZ* n.s. 3 (1959) 60–81; J.D.M. Derrett, "Law in the New Testament: The Parable of the Unjust Judge," *NTS* 18 (1971–72) 182–183.

24. See also A.A. Trites, "The Importance of Legal Scenes and Language in the Book of Acts," *NT* 16 (1974) 278–284.

25. See W. Nicol, "Tradition and Redaction in Luke 21," *Neotestamentica* 7 (1973) 61–71.

26. A.A. Trites, *The New Testament Concept of Witness* (New York: Cambridge U. Press, 1977) 128–153; see also Johannes Beutler, *Martyria* (Franfurter Theologische Studien 10; Frankfurt am Main: Josef Knecht, 1972) 43–72.

27. I am interpreting these verses in the light of Acts 4–5; 12:5–11; 16:35–40; 21–26 that escape and vindication are included, and not simply eternal life after death; yet see I.H. Marshall, *The Gospel of Luke* (Grand Rapids: Eerdmans, 1978) 770.

28. It is now axiomatic in studies of Luke-Acts to point out the parallels between the Gospel and Acts: see M.D. Goulder, *Type and History of Acts*, 40–45; C.H. Talbert, *Luke and the Gnostics* (Nashville: Abingdon, 1966) 33; A.J. Mattill, "The Purpose of Acts: Schneckenburger Reconsidered," in *Apostolic History and the Gospel* (ed. W.W. Gasque and R.P. Martin; Grand Rapids: Eerdmans, 1970) 120–121 and "The Jesus-Paul Parallels and the Purpose of Luke-Acts: H.H. Evans Reconsidered," *NT* 17 (1975) 15–46; W. Radl, *Paulus und Jesus im lukanischen Doppelwerk* (Frankfurt: Peter Land, 1975); V. Stolle, *Der Zeuge als Angeklagter*, 215–220, 232; R.F. O'Toole, *Acts 26. The Christological Climax of Paul's Defense (Ac 22:1–26:32)* (AB 78; Rome: Biblical Institute Press, 1978) 14–25.

29. Luke is very sensitive to the apologetic need for heavenly assistance in the trials of the apostles in Acts. Prophecy of this is only one aspect of this concern; in Acts, Jesus' actual assistance is noted: angels sent to release Peter (Acts 12:7–11); earthquakes which break Paul's chains (16:26); the theophanies to Stephen (7:55–56); visions warning witnesses (22:18–21; 26:17); and visions comforting those in prison (23:13; see 27:23–26). All of these events occur in *forensic contexts*.

30. See A.A. Trites, *The New Testament Concept of Witness*, 129; V. Stolle, *Der Zeuge als Angeklagter*, 233–234. *m. Sanh*. III.8 states that so long as the accused can bring forward evidence that may undo the decision, the trial must continue (see *t. Sanh*. VI. 4b).

31. On the forensic value of "proofs" (*tekmērion*, Acts 1:3–4), see J.H. Neyrey, "The Forensic Defense Speech and Paul's Trial Speeches in Acts 22–26: Form and Function" *Luke-Acts New Perspectives from the Society of Biblical*

Literature Seminar (ed. C.H. Talbert; New York: Crossroads, 1984) 216–218; see also W.S. Kurz, *The Function of Christological Proof from Prophecy for Luke and Justin* (unpublished Ph.D. dissertation; Yale, 1976) 108.

32. See G.F. Moore, "The *Am ha-ares* (the People of the Land) and the *Haberim* (Associates)," *The Beginnings of Christianity* (ed. F.J. Foakes-Jackson and Kirsopp Lake; London: Macmillan and Co., 1920) I.439–445; on what constitutes an acceptable witness, see A.E. Harvey, *Jesus on Trial,* 20–21, 46–48, and J.H. Neyrey, "The Forensic Defense Speech and Paul's Trial Speeches," 211–213.

33. On impartiality in Jewish judgment, see Jouette Bassler, *Divine Impartiality* (SBLDS 59; Chico: Scholars Press, 1982) 7–16.

34. This is confirmed in the Lukan parallel in Acts 13; when the Jews of Antioch of Pisidia reject Paul's eloquent testimony on Jesus' behalf (13:16–41), Paul tells them: "Since you *judge yourselves unworthy of eternal life,* we turn to the Gentiles" (13:46).

35. It is characteristic of Luke to point to dual witnessing on Jesus' behalf; see R. Morganthaler, *Die Lukanische Geschichtsschreibung als Zeugnis: Gestalt und Gehalt der Kunst des Lukas* (Zuerich: Zwingli, 1949) II. ch 1.; A. Wikenhauser, "Doppeltraeume," *Bib* 29 (1948) 100–111. V.E. McEachen, "Dual Witness and Sabbath Motif in Luke," *CJT* 12 (1966) 267–280.

36. A.A. Trites, *The New Testament Concept of Witness,* 121, 135.

37. For a fuller discussion of Moses and Jesus as leaders rejected by Israel, J. Dupont, *Études sur les Actes des Apôtres* (Paris: Cerf, 1967) 250; Richard J. Dillon, *From Eye-Witness to Ministers of the Word* (AB 82; Rome: Biblical Institute Press, 1978) 122; Johannes Bihler, *Die Stephanusgeschichte* (Muenchener Theologische Studien 16; Munich: Max Hueber, 1963) 51–61; and J. Via, "An Interpretation of Acts 7:35–37 from the Perspective of Major Themes in Luke-Acts," *PRS* 6 (1979) 190–207.

38. Nils Dahl, "The Story of Abraham in Luke-Acts," *Studies in Luke-Acts* (eds. J.L. Martyn and L.E. Keck; London: SPCK, 1966) 144–147.

39. Whether Stephen's speech answers all or any of the changes is hotly contested; for a convenient survey of the debate on this point, see John Kilgallen, *The Stephen Speech. A Literary and Redactional Study of Acts 7, 2–53* (AB 67; Rome: Biblical Institute Press, 1976) 6–10 and E. Richard, *Acts 6:1–8:4 The Author's Method of Composition* (SBLDS 41; Missoula: Scholars Press, 1978) 287–292, 315–317.

40. See Rudolf Pesch, *Die Vision des Stephanus Apg 7,55–56 im Rahmen der Apostelgeschichte* (Stuttgarter Bibelstudien 12; Stuttgart: Katholisches Bibelwerk, 1966).

41. I am accepting the arguments in favor of *estota* meaning that Jesus was "established" at God's right hand, just as Ps 110 indicates in Acts 2:34–36; see

C.K. Barrett, "Stephen and the Son of Man," *Apophoreta* (BZNTW 30; Berlin: Toepelmann, 1964) 32–34; and Earl Richard, *Acts 6:1–8:4 The Author's Method of Composition*, 294–298.

42. The function of this appearance of Jesus enjoys no consensus in scholarly discussions; for example, R. Pesch (*Die Vision des Stephanus*) sees it as the appearance of Jesus *the judge*, while Théo Preiss (*Life in Christ*, 50) describes it as the appearance of Jesus *the Paraclete*.

43. See W.C. van Unnik, *Tarsus or Jerusalem* (London: Epworth, 1962) 44–45, 52–58.

44. See J.H. Neyrey, "The Forensic Defense Speech and Paul's Trial Speeches," 211–213.

45. *Jesus on Trial*, 20.

46. G. Lohfink's studies of the apparition to Paul in Acts 9, 22 and 26 argue that this event is described by Luke in the form of an Old Testament revelatory and commissioning theophany: *The Conversion of St. Paul* (Chicago: Franciscan Herald Press, 1976) 62–66 and "Eine aelteste Darstellungsform fuer Gotteserscheinungen in den Damaskusberichten," *BZ* 9 (1965) 246–257.

47. On the forensic value of corroborating witnesses, see J.H. Neyrey, "The Forensic Defense Speech and Paul's Trial Speeches," 216–219.

48. For a fuller treatment of the thematic significance of Jesus' innocence, see the discussion of Jesus as the new Adam in Chapter Six; also, Joseph A. Fitzmyer, *The Gospel According to Luke I–IX* (Garden City: Doubleday, 1981) 34–35.

49. See G. Schrenk, "dikaios," *TDNT* II. 183–185.

50. For example, C.H. Dodd, *The Apostolic Preaching and Its Development* (London: Hodder and Stoughton, 1936); J. Dupont, "Less discours missionaires des Actes des Apôtres," *RB* 69 (1962) 37–60; Eduard Schweizer, "Concerning the Speeches in Acts," *Studies in Luke-Acts*, 208–216; U. Wilckens, *Die Missionsreden der Apostelgeschichte* (WMANT 5; 3rd.; Neukirchen-Vluyn: Neukirchener Verlag, 1974).

51. Bertil Gaertner, *The Areopagus Speech and Natural Revelation* (Lund: Gleerup, 1955).

52. Fred Veltmann, "The Defense Speeches of Paul in Acts," *Perspectives on Luke-Acts* (ed. C.H. Talbert; Danville: Association of Baptist Professors of Religion, 1978) 243–256.

53. See notes 28 and 35 above.

54. See J.H. Neyrey, "The Forensic Defense Speech and Paul's Trial Speeches," 213–216.

55. Quintilian (*Inst. Orat.* V.vii.15–21) calls testimony drawn from an involuntary witness the strongest possible.

4. Jesus' Address
to the Women of Jerusalem
(Lk 23:27–31)

1. Erich Klostermann, *Das Lukasevangelium* (HNT 5; 3rd ed.; Tuebingen: J.C.B. Mohr, 1975) 227; cf. Alfred Plummer, *A Critical and Exegetical Commentary on the Gospel According to Saint Luke* (Edinburgh: T. and T. Clark, 1922) 528; Norval Geldenhuys, *Commentary on the Gospel of Luke* (Grand Rapids: Eerdmans, 1951) 603; M.-J. LaGrange, *Évangile selon saint Luc* (Paris: Gabalda, 1948) 585.

2. Cf. *b. Sanh.* 43a.

3. W. Kaeser, "Exegetische und theologische Erwaegungen zur Seligpreisung der Kinderlosen Lc 23:29b," *ZNW* 54 (1963) 240–254.

4. Rudolf Bultmann, *History of the Synoptic Tradition* (New York: Harper and Row, 1963) 37, 115–116.

5. W. Kaeser, "Exegetische und theologische Erwaegungen," 241–244.

6. Vincent Taylor, *The Passion Narrative of St. Luke* (SNTS 19; Cambridge: University Press, 1972) 90; cf. F. Rehkopf, *Die lukanische Sonderquelle, Ihr Umfang und Sprachgebrauch* (Tuebingen: J.C.B. Mohr, 1959); J. Jeremias, "Perikopen-Umstellungen bei Lukas?" *NTS* 4 (1958) 115–119.

7. H.J. Holtzmann, *Die Synoptiker* (HCNT I.1; Tuebingen: J.C.B. Mohr, 1901) 482; W. Grundmann, *Das Evangelium nach Lukas* (THNT 3; Berlin: Evangelische Velagsanstalt, 1971) 249.

8. W. Kaeser, "Exegetische und theologische Erwaegungen," 247–253.

9. Erich Klostermann (*Das Lukasevangelium,* 227) calls it a "prophetische Drohwort."

10. Gustaf Dalman, *Jesus-Joshua* (New York: KTAV, 1971) 193.

11. W. Grundmann, *Das Evangelium nach Lukas,* 430; and F.W. Danker, *Jesus and the New Age* (St. Louis: Clayton Publishing House, 1972) 236–237.

12. Erich Klostermann, *Das Lukasevangelium,* 227; W. Grundmann, *Das Evangelium nach Lukas,* 429.

13. Most recently in Hans Conzelmann, *The Theology of St. Luke* (New York: Harper and Brothers, 1960) 134 and 199; but this is an old observation, found frequently in German commentaries; see W. Grundmann, *Das Evangelium nach Lukas,* 429.

14. Jerome Kodell, "Luke's Use of *LAOS,* 'People,' especially in the Jerusalem Narrative (Lk 19, 28–24, 53)," *CBQ* 31 (1969) 328.

15. The cogency of reading Lk 23:13 as a statement that "the people" joined their leaders in rejecting Jesus is weakened in the light of the suggestion of G. Rau ("Das Volk in der lukanischen Passionsberichte: eine Konjektur zu Lk

23:13," *ZNW* 56 [1965] 41–51) that "the leaders and the people" is a corruption of the original text, "the leaders of the people."

16. For discussion of the Lukan tendency in dealing with Israel and "the people" in Acts, see Jacob Jervell, *Luke and the People of God* (Minneapolis: Augsburg, 1972) 41–55; A. George, "Israel dans l'oeuvre de Luc," *RB* 75 (1968) 499–506; Jerome Crowe, "The LAOS at the Cross: Luke's Crucifixion Scene," *The Language of the Cross* (ed. A. Lacomara; Chicago: Franciscan Herald Press, 1977) 79–80, 88–90.

17. Luke T. Johnson, *The Literary Function of Possessions in Luke-Acts* (SBLDS 39; Missoula: Scholars Press, 1977) 115–121; Kodell, "Luke's Use of *LAOS*," 340.

18. See note 3 above. The linguistic basis for this, of course, is the common reference in the Old Testament to "daughters of Zion" (Pss 9:14; 72:28; 96:8; Ez 16:55; Mi 1:13; 4:8, 10; Zep 3:14; Zec 2:10; 9:9; Is 1:8; 10:32; 35:22; Jer 6:2, 23: 46:19). One finds similar expressions in regard to Babylon; see "daughters of Babylon" (Ps 136:8; Jer 50:52; Zec 2:7), "daughters of Egypt" (Jer 46:24), "daughters of Edom" (Lam 4:21–22), or "daughters of Moab" (Is 16:2; Jer 48:4).

19. See Is 1:8; 10:32; Mi 4:10; Jer 6:2, 23.

20. Judgment is repeatedly pronounced against Jerusalem, part of which material Luke accepts from the Q source (11:47–51; 13:33–35) and from Mark (20:16, 18; 21:6), but the bulk of this is unique to Luke (19:41–44; 21:20–24; 23:27–31 and Acts 7:51–53).

21. W. Grundmann, *Das Evangelium nach Lukas*, 417; F.W. Danker, *Jesus and the New Age*, 229.

22. It is not my contention that Luke simply created 23:28 on his own, for there is ample evidence that such expressions are commonplaces on the lips of persons going to death; see Dalman, *Jesus-Joshua*, 193; E. Klostermann, *Das Evangelium nach Lukas*, 227. But by citing Jer 9:17–22, I suggest a parallel nearer to what I consider Luke's intention, viz., to employ a prophetic judgment oracle against Jerusalem.

23. A. Plummer, *A Critical and Exegetical Commentary on the Gospel According to St. Luke*, 529–530; cf. G.H.P. Thompson, *The Gospel According to Luke* (Oxford: Clarendon, 1972) 270.

24. F.W. Danker, *Jesus and the New Age*, 237.

25. See *b. Moed Katan* 25b; *Seder Elijahu R.* 14; *b. Sanh.* 93a; see E. Klostermann, *Das Lukasevangelium*, 228.

26. The contrast between "in the green wood" and "in the dry" implies that the former situation is somehow explainable, which is just what Acts 3:17 says when it notes that they acted in ignorance when they rejected Jesus. But with the subsequent rejection of Peter's and Paul's testimony, the situation is inex-

plicable, seasoned, dead, and ripe for judgment. See Luke T. Johnson, *The Literary Function of Possessions in Luke-Acts,* 117.

27. *Str.B.* II 263–264.

28. The larger context of ch. 13 supports the observation that Luke's editorial hand is at work here; the chapter deals with guilt, repentance, and retribution: guilty inhabitants of Jerusalem are punished (13:4–5); the failure to accept Jesus (which is what "un-repentance" means here) brings judgment by fire (13:6–9); the urgency to repent (i.e., accept God's message in Jesus) runs all through the passage (13:3, 5, 8, 24–27). Hence Jerusalem's guilt in 13:33–34, its rejection of messengers of repentance (13:34), and its judgment are part of the larger perspective of Luke at this point.

29. *b. Sukka* 53a; see *Abot R. Nat.* 12; *Mek.* Tractate *Bahodesh* XI on Ex 20:24.

30. For more on this type of discourse, see Ernst Kaesemann, "Sentences of Holy Law in the New Testament," *New Testament Questions of Today* (London: SCM, 1969) 66–81.

31. See Is 3:26LXX; Ez 31:12; Nah 3:10. Every time *edaphizein* is used in the LXX, it signals the ruin of a city (Samaria or Jerusalem) as the object of divine judgment. The noun, *edaphos,* is used in Josephus to refer to the razing of a city to the ground (*Vita* 99; *Ant.* V.248; IX.41; X.126, 144; XII.383; XIII.215), but only once does he use it in the context of children dashed to the ground (*BJ* V. 433) and it is done by Jerusalem's own inhabitants during the terrible famine. The proper background, then, is the LXX, in regard to judgment against Jerusalem (see also Pss. Solomon 2:19 and 17:22). C.H. Dodd ("The Fall of Jerusalem and the 'Abomination of Desolation,' " *JRS* 37 [1947] 47–54) argued that *edaphizein* cannot come from Josephus' description of Jerusalem's fall, since he does not mention this horror although he seems to omit no other in his description of the ruin of the city.

32. See Aage Bentzen, *Introduction to the Old Testament* (2nd ed.; Copenhagen: Gad, 1952) 199–200; G. Gemser, "The *Rib* or Controversy Pattern in Hebrew Mentality," *Wisdom in Israel and the Ancient Near East* (VTSupp 3; ed. M. Noth; Leiden: Brill, 1960) 128–133; Herbert B. Huffmon, "The Covenant Lawsuit in the Prophets," *JBL* 78 (1959) 285–295; Julien Harvey, *Le Plaidoyer Prophetique Contre Israel Apres La Rupture l'Alliance* (Paris: Desclee de Brouwer, 1967); James Limburg, "The Root *RIB* and the Prophetic Lawsuit Speeches," *JBL* 90 (1971) 267–278.

33. See E. Klostermann, *Das Lukasevangelium,* 202–203.

34. Of course, Dt 32:35 could serve just as well, as would Jer 26:10; 27:31 (see Sir 5:7 and Ez 9:1); and that might be just the point here—that Luke alludes to a sure prophetic tradition of judgment.

35. No crime is cited in 21:20–24, but it is surely implied if the coming

days are truly "days of retribution" and "wrath on this people." At this point in the narrative, the audience has been repeatedly told of Jerusalem's crime of killing the prophets and rejecting God's visitation of salvation.

36. Kodell, "Luke's Use of *LAOS*," 330–332.

37. Raymond E. Brown, *The Birth of the Messiah* (Garden City: Doubleday, 1977) 460–462.

38. Jervell, *Luke and the People of God*, 47–48.

39. The phrase "I do not know you" is the formula used in the judgment against the antinomian charismatics in Mt 7:23 and against the foolish virgins in Mt 25:12. Paul also uses the same formula of judgment against disobedient prophets in 1 Cor 14:38.

40. This is identical with the formula of judgment in Rom 1:24, 26, 28.

41. See 2 Clement I.1; Polycarp II.1; Barnabas VII.2; Apocalypse of Peter 1; Epistola Apostolorum 16; see Jacques Dupont, *Études sur les Actes des Apôtres* (Paris: Cerf, 1967) 450–456.

5. THE CRUCIFIXION SCENE: THE SAVED SAVIOR

1. Most of the discussion of the crucifixion scene in Luke's Gospel has centered around questions of source and historicity; a few redactional studies have appeared, but in the main the assessment of Luke's redaction has been somewhat timid; see A. Buechele, *Der Tod Jesu im Lukasevangelium: Eine Redaktionsgeschichtliche Untersuchung zu Lk 23* (Frankfort: Knecht, 1978); and P.W. Walaskay, "The Trial and Death of Jesus in the Gospel of Luke," *JBL* 94 (1975) 81–93.

2. For many years now commentators have criticized Luke's version of the death of Jesus. Conzelmann (*The Theology of St. Luke* [New York: Harper, 1960] 201) went so far as to claim that there is no soteriological significance attached to the death of Jesus; others such as G. Voss (*Die Christologie der lukanischen Schriften in Grundzuegen* [Bruges: Desclee de Brouwer, 1965] 130) voiced dissatisfaction with Luke's perspective, because it lacks sacrificial or atonement significance. Still others charge that there is no *theologia crucis* (see E. Kaesemann, *Essays on New Testament Themes* [Philadelphia: Fortress, 1964] 92–93), or that the death is unexplained as to why and how (see U. Wilckens, *Die Missionsreden der Apostelgeschichte* [2nd ed.; Neukirchen: Vluyn, 1963] 216–217). The thrust of these criticisms of Luke maintain that Luke's view is not Paul's and that Luke's view represents a weakening or corruption of the ideal theology of the cross which Paul presents. Fortunately the negative thrust of such studies is being corrected in contemporary Lukan studies.

3. See Jerome Kodell, "Luke's Use of *LAOS*, 'People,' Especially in the Jerusalem Narrative (Lk 19, 28–24, 53)," *CBQ* 31 (1969) 328–331.

4. See J.F.A. Sawyer, "Why Is a Solar Eclipse Mentioned in the Passion Narrative (Luke xxiii, 44–5)?" *JTS* ns 23 (1972) 124–128.

5. It is a commonplace of Lukan style that he does things in twos; see C.H. Talbert, *Literary Patterns, Theological Themes and the Genre of Luke-Acts* (SBLMS 20; Missoula: Scholars Press, 1974).

6. On the Lukan motif of "division" see ch. 4; see also J. Kodell, "Luke's Use of *LAOS*, 'People,' " 331 and Jacob Jervell, *Luke and the People of God* (Minneapolis: Augsburg, 1972), 41–74.

7. There is a wealth of studies on "salvation" in Luke; see R. Zehnle, "The Salvific Character of Jesus' Death in Lukan Soteriology," *TS* 30 (1969) 420–444; B.H. Throckmorton, "Sozein, soteria in Luke-Acts," *Studia Evangelica* VI (T.U. 112; Berlin: Akademie Verlag, 1973) 515–526; and A. George, "Le sens de la mort de Jésus pour Luc," *RB* 80 (1973) 186–217.

8. See S.G. Wilson, "Lukan Eschatology," *NTS* 16 (1969–70) 330–347; Eric Franklin, *Christ the Lord* (Philadelphia: Westminster, 1975) 21–41; and Joseph A. Fitzmyer, *The Gospel According to Luke I-IX* (Garden City: Doubleday, 1981) 234–235.

9. For example, I.H. Marshall, *The Gospel According to St. Luke* (Grand Rapids: Eerdmans, 1978) 872.

10. See Joachim Jeremias, "paradeisos," *TDNT* V. 767–768.

11. K. Hanhart, *The Intermediate State in the New Testament* (Groningen: URB, 1966) 210–213; E.E. Ellis, "Present and Future Eschatology in Luke," *NTS* 12 (1965–66) 37 and *Eschatology in Luke* (Philadelphia: Fortress, 1972) 11–20.

12. Assessments of Luke's eschatology are quite controverted; but Jacques Dupont ("Die individuelle Eschatologie im Lukasevangelium und in der Apostelgeschichte," *Orientierung an Jesus* [ed. P. Hoffmann; Freiburg: Herder, 1973] 37–47) has offered a truly fresh insight which is redactionally grounded.

13. See C.K. Barrett, "Stephen and the Son of Man," *Apophoretha* (BZNW 30; Berlin: Toepelmann, 1964) 36–37.

14. Donald Senior, *The Passion Narrative according to Matthew* (BETL 39; Leuven: University Press, 1975) 312–313.

15. *The Passion Narrative according to Matthew*, 309–310, 321–322; see also Senior's "The Death of God's Son and the Beginning of the New Age," *The Language of the Cross* (ed. A. Lacomara; Chicago: Franciscan Herald Press, 1977) 29–53.

16. For an excellent example of the functional relationship of Christological title and social implications for the Church, see H.C. Kee, "Christology and

Ecclesiology: Titles of Christ and Models of Community," *SBL 1982 Seminar Papers* (Chico: Scholars Press, 1982) 227–242.

17. See William S. Kurz, *The Function of the Christological Proof from Prophecy for Luke and Justin* (unpublished dissertation, Yale, 1976) 57–96.

18. On Jesus as the Saved Savior, see Robert F. O'Toole, *Acts 26: The Christological Climax of Paul's Defense (Ac 22:1–26:22)* (Rome: Biblical Institute Press, 1978) 114–117.

19. See H. Gese, "Psalm 22 and the New Testament," *TD* 18 (1970) 237–243 and John Reumann, "Psalm 22 at the Cross: Lament and Thanksgiving for Jesus Christ," *Int* 28 (1974) 39–58.

20. See Donald Juel, "Social Dimensions of Exegesis: The Use of Psalm 16 in Acts 2," *CBQ* 43 (1981) 545–547.

21. See Raymond E. Brown, *Birth of the Messiah* (Garden City: Doubleday, 1977) 451–454.

22. "The Story of Abraham in Luke-Acts," *Jesus in the Memory of the Early Church* (Minneapolis: Augsburg, 1976) 74–78.

23. For a survey of the issues surrounding the "Binding of Isaac," see Robert J. Daly, "The Soteriological Significance of the Sacrifice of Isaac," *CBQ* 39 (1977) 45–75.

24. See my article on replacements in John, "Jacob Traditions and the Interpretation of John 4:10–26," *CBQ* 41 (1979) esp. 436–437.

25. It is distinctive of Luke that at key places in Jesus' career, he is presented praying: (a) at the baptism (3:21), (b) before the great discourse (6:12), (c) at the transfiguration (9:28–29), (d) in the orchard (22:41–42), and (e) on the cross (23:46). Luke even provides the substance of Jesus' prayer in 22:42, the Our Father. See Allison A. Trites, "The Prayer Motif in Luke-Acts," *Perspectives on Luke-Acts* (ed. C.H. Talbert; Danville: Association of Baptist Professors of Religion, 1978) 172–179, 184–186.

26. Compare Jesus' prayer "Father, into your hands I commit my spirit" with the prayer enjoined on all Christians in 1 Pet 4:19: "Let those who suffer according to God's will do right and entrust their souls to a faithful Creator." See 1 Clem 27:1.

27. For general expositions of the use of Ps 16 in Christian apology, see B. Lindars, *New Testament Apologetic* (London: SCM, 1961) 36–48; J.W. Doeve, *Jewish Hermeneutic in the Synoptic Gospels* (Assen: van Gorcum, 1954) 148–170; Jacques Dupont, "Messianic Interpretation of the Psalms," *The Salvation of the Gentiles* (New York: Paulist, 1979) 106–111; yet occasionally it is urged that Ps 16 suggests "Christ's hope in his personal resurrection"; see Robert O'Toole, *Acts 26*, 93.

28. See especially C.H. Talbert, "Promise and Fulfilment in Lukan Theology," *Luke-Acts* (New York: Crossroad, 1984) 91–103.

29. See my article, "The Forensic Defense Speech and Paul's Trial Speeches in Acts 22–26: Form and Function," *Luke-Acts* (ed. C.H. Talbert; New York: Crossroad, 1984) 213–216.

6. JESUS' FAITH: OUR SALVATION

1. See the beginning of Chapter 5 for survey of opinions on Lukan soteriology.

2. See A. George, "Le sens de la mort de Jésus pour Luc," *RB* 80 (1973) 186–217; Marie-Louise Gubler, *Die fruehesten Deutungen des Todes Jesu* (Goettingen: Vandenhoeck und Ruprecht, 1977); Hans-Ruedi Weber, *The Cross Tradition and Interpretation* (Grand Rapids: Eerdmans, 1975); for models of Jesus' death in the Pauline letters see Joseph A. Fitzmyer, *Pauline Theology* (Englewood Cliffs: Prentice-Hall, 1967) 43–53.

3. According to some scholars, there are two theologies of the death of Jesus: (a) *theologia gloriae*, which interprets the death of Jesus as the prerequisite for Jesus' entrance into glory (see Lk 24:26–27) and (b) *theologia crucis*, which sees Jesus' death as atonement or expiatory sacrifice for our sins (see Acts 20:28). For contrasting views on which *theologia* is found in Luke-Acts, see Ernst Kaesemann, *Essays on New Testament Themes* (Philadelphia: Fortress, 1964) 92–93 and C.K. Barrett, "Theologia Crucis—in Acts?" *Theologia Crucis-Signum Crucis* (ed. Carl Andresen; Tuebingen: J.C.B. Mohr, 1979) 73–84.

4. I.H. Marshall, *The Gospel of Luke* (Grand Rapids: Eerdmans, 1978) 174; Jerome Kodell, "Luke's Theology of the Death of Jesus," *Sin, Salvation and the Spirit* (Collegeville: Liturgical Press, 1979) 225.

5. In many circles the only acceptable soteriological category for interpreting Jesus' death is that of sacrifice, especially vicarious expiation for sins, as in the case of Is 53; for example, G. Voss (*Die Christologie der lukanischen Schriften in Grundzuegen* [Bruges: Desclee de Brouwer, 1965] 130) dismisses all soteriology in Luke's presentation of Jesus' death because he considers sacrifice the only worthwhile category: "In Luke the death of Jesus neither has the character of a sacrifice nor is it understood as an atoning work."

6. Eph 5:2 calls it "a fragrant offering" to God.

7. See Donald Juel, *Messiah and Temple* (SBLDS 31; Missoula: Scholars Press, 1977) 143–168; John R. Donahue, *Are You the Christ?* (SBLDS 10; Missoula: Scholars Press, 1973) 103–138.

8. Morna D. Hooker, "Interchange in Christ," *JTS* 22 (1971) 347–361; and E.P. Sanders, *Paul and Palestinian Judaism* (Philadelphia: Fortress, 1977) 463–472 and *Paul, the Law, and the Jewish People* (Philadelphia: Fortress, 1983) 3–15.

9. M. Black, "The Pauline Doctrine of the Second Adam," *SJT* 8 (1954)

170–179; Robin Scroggs, *The Last Adam: A Study in Pauline Anthropology* (Philadelphia: Fortress, 1966).

10. Hans Conzelmann, *The Theology of St. Luke* (New York: Harper, 1960); for recent discussion, see Joseph A. Fitzmyer, *The Gospel According to Luke I-IX* (Garden City: Doubleday, 1981) 171–187, 262. On Luke and historiography, see Jacques Dupont, "La question du plan des Actes des Apôtres à la lumière d'un texte de Lucien de Samosate," *NT* 21 (1979) 220–231.

11. Conzelmann, *The Theology of St. Luke*, 16, 22–27.

12. Although I have pointed to one stream of material in Luke-Acts, the periodization of history with its accompanying sense of discontinuity, Luke also stresses continuity in apology for the Church and for Jesus; see Nils Dahl, "Christ, Creation, and the Church," *Jesus in the Memory of the Early Church* (Minneapolis: Augsburg, 1976) 120–121. Dahl pointed out apropos of *urzeit/ endzeit* modeling that two factors are regularly stressed: *contrast* between the first and last times as well as *correlation* of the two.

13. In many of his writings, C.H. Talbert has argued that Luke presents Jesus as model, moral model or martyr; see "Martyrdom in Luke-Acts and the Lukan Social Ethic," *Political Issues in Luke-Acts* (ed. R.J. Cassidy; Maryknoll: Orbis, 1983) 99–110 and "The Way of the Lukan Jesus: Dimensions of Lukan Spirituality," *PRS* 8 (1982) 237–249.

14. William S. Kurz (*The Function of Christological Proof from Prophecy for Luke and Justin;* unpublished dissertation, Yale, 1976, 105–110) demonstrated how Luke uses traditional rhetorical proofs in the argumentation of Luke-Acts.

15. E. Jacquier, *Les Actes des Apôtres* (Paris: Gabalda, 1926) 106; yet see G. Delling, "archēgos," *TDNT* I.487–488 and P.G. Mueller, *Christos Archēgos* (Frankfurt: Peter Land, 1973).

16. See *Luke* (Philadelphia: Fortress, 1976) 6–17; *Benefactor* (St. Louis: Clayton Publishing House, 1982) 26–29, 417–435.

17. Jacques Dupont, *Études sur les Actes des Apôtres* (Paris: Cerf, 1967) 107.

18. E.K. Simpson, "The Vocabulary of the Epistle to the Hebrews I," *EQ* 18 (1946) 35–38; David Peterson, *Hebrews and Perfection* (Cambridge: University Press, 1982) 57–58.

19. G.D. Kilpatrick, "A Theme of the Lucan Passion Story and Luke 23:47," *JTS* 43 (1942) 34–36; see also Daryl Schmidt, "Luke's 'Innocent' Jesus: A Scriptural Apologetic," *Political Issues in Luke-Acts* 111–121.

20. Joachim Jeremias, "adam," *TDNT* I. 141–143.

21. M.D. Johnson, *The Purpose of the Biblical Genealogies* (SNTSMS 8; Cambridge: University Press, 1969) 233–234.

22. A Feuillet, "Le rècit lucanien de la tentation (Lc 4,1–13)," *Biblica* 40

(1959) 624–626; J. Thompson, "Called—Proved—Obedient: A Study in the Baptism and Temptation Narratives of Matthew and Luke," *JTS* 11 (1960) 7–8; Petr Pokorny, "The Temptation Stories and Their Intention," *NTS* 20 (1973–74) 120–122.

23. M.D. Johnson, *The Purpose of the Biblical Genealogies*, 233.

24. See R.E. Clements, *Abraham and David* (London: SCM, 1967); Moshe Weinfeld, "Covenants, Davidic," *IDBSupp* (Nashville: Abingdon, 1976) 188–192.

25. "Luke 3:23–38 and Greco-Roman and Biblical Genealogies," *Luke-Acts* (ed. C.H. Talbert; New York: Crossroad, 1984) 172, 177–179.

26. E. Schweizer, "huios," *TDNT* VIII. 347–353.

27. Oscar Cullmann, *The Christology of the New Testament* (Philadelphia: Westminster, 1959) 270; Geza Vermes, *Jesus the Jew* (Philadelphia: Fortress, 1973) 192–214; Joseph A. Fitzmyer, *The Gospel According to Luke*, 208.

28. M.D. Johnson, *The Purpose of the Biblical Genealogies*, 231.

29. Raymond E. Brown, *Birth of the Messiah* (Garden City: Doubleday, 1977) 64–65.

30. See H.W. Robinson, "The Hebrew Conception of Corporate Personality," *BZAW* 66 (1936) 49–62; P. Kaufmann, "The One and the Many: Corporate Personality," *Worship* 42 (1968) 546–558; H. Wansbrough, "Corporate Personality in the Bible. Adam and Christ—A Biblical Use of the Concept of Personality," *New Blackfriars* 50 (1969) 798–804; B.J. le Frois, "Semitic Totality Thinking," *CBQ* 18 (1955) 195–203, 315–323.

31. A. Feuillet, "Le récit lucanien de la tentation," 626–628; Petr Pokorney, "The Temptation Stories and Their Intention," 120–122.

32. Jerome Murphy-O'Connor, "Christological Anthropology in Phil., II,6–11," *RevBib* 83 (1976) 32–36.

33. Joseph A. Fitzmyer, *The Gospel According to Luke*, 507.

34. *Ibid.*, 165.

35. W. Grundmann, "dei," *TDNT* II. 21–25; E. Fascher, "Theologische Beobachtungen zu *dei*," *Neutestamentliche Studien fuer Rudolf Bultmann* (BZNW 21; Berlin: Toepelmann, 1954) 245–247.

36. H. Conzelmann, *The Theology of St. Luke*, 16, 28; there is considerable scholarly discussion of when and how Lk 4:13 is fulfilled. For example, S. Brown (*Apostasy and Perseverance in the Theology of Luke* [AnBib 36; Rome: Biblical Institute, 1969] 9–10) and, following him, Joseph Fitzmyer (*The Gospel According to Luke*, 518) admit that the devil returns in Lk 22:3, 31, 53. They consider this return as "the second diabolic onslaught to be made against the Father's plan of salvation-history in the passion and death of Jesus" (Fitzmyer, 518); yet they insist that this is not a "temptation" but only an "onslaught," an attempt "to destroy him," or a "renewed attack" (Brown, 16). Such a view of

"temptation" is overly subtle and not in keeping with the broad use of that term in post-biblical time; see Karl G. Kuhn, "New Light on Temptation, Sin, and Flesh in the New Testament," *The Scrolls and the New Testament* (ed. Krister Stendahl; New York: Harper, 1957) 94–113.

37. See Richard N. Longenecker, "The Obedience of Christ in the Theology of the Early Church," *Reconciliation and Hope* (ed. Robert Banks; Grand Rapids: Eerdmans, 1974) 142–152.

38. In an important argument, W. Kurz (*The Function of Christological Proof from Prophecy for Luke and Justin,* 64–83) demonstrated that "Christ" is more than a name or title for Jesus in Luke-Acts, but carries the meaning of "one anointed by the Spirit" (see Lk 4:18; Acts 10:38). This has a direct bearing on Lk 23:35, 37, 39 where "Christ" is not just a type of messianic ruler, but a holy figure, consecrated by God himself.

39. *Resurrection, Immortality and Eternal Life in Intertestamental Judaism* (HTS 26; Cambridge: Harvard U. Press, 1972) 180.

40. Joachim Jeremias, "paradeisos," *TDNT* V. 767–768; K. Hanhart, *The Intermediate State in the New Testament* (Groningen: URB, 1966) 27–29; see also R.H. Smith, "Paradise Today: Luke's Passion Narrative," *CurTM* 3 (1976) 323–336.

41. H. Gunkel, *Schoepfung und Chaos: Urzeit und Endzeit* (Goettingen: Vandenhoeck und Ruprecht, 1895) 367–371; Joachim Jeremias, "paradeisos," *TDNT* V. 767; D. Aune, *The Cultic Setting of Realized Eschatology* (NTSupp 28; Leiden: Brill, 1972) 37–44.

42. K. Hanhart, *The Intermediate State in the New Testament,* 29.

43. Perhaps less obvious, but still cogent are the parallels between T. Levi and Luke-Acts on two other points:

5. "He shall remove the threatening sword against Adam"—Angels do not separate Jesus from holy places or things, but associate with him and assist him: (a) his birth is announced by angels (Lk 1:26–38; 2:9–14; (b) angels announce Jesus' rescue from death (Lk 24:4–7, 23); (c) angels rescue Peter from prison (Acts 5:19–20) and from certain death (12:7–10); (d) angels direct the mission, assisting Philip (Acts 8:26) and announcing salvation to the pagan Cornelius (Acts 10:3–7, 22); (e) angels proclaim Paul's rescue from death at sea (Acts 27:23–26). The Psalm which Satan distorted (Lk 4:10–11/Ps 91:11–12) is ironically true. God's angels are now commanded to guard Jesus and his followers. Their threatening sword (Gen 3:24) is removed, they serve the new Adam and his descendants.

6. "He shall give them to eat from the tree of life"—Jesus instructs people "how to inherit eternal life" (Lk 10:25–28; 18:18–30; see Acts 13:46, 48). It may be that Luke would call the Eucharist the bread of life, as other Christians do (see Jn 6).

44. Rudolf Bultmann, "Adam and Christ According to Romans 5," *Current Issues in New Testament Interpretation* (eds. W. Klassen and G.F. Snyder; New York: Harper, 1962) 143–165; Robin Scroggs, *The Last Adam: A Study in Pauline Anthropology*, 75–114.

45. Wayne A. Meeks, "The Image of the Androgyne," *HR* 13 (1974) 180–189.

46. See Nils Dahl, "Christ, Creation, and the Church," 120–137.

47. *Studies in Paul* (Minneapolis: Augsburg, 1977) 89–90; "Two Notes on Romans 5," *ST* 5 (1951) 37–48.

48. D.W.B. Robinson, " 'Faith of Jesus Christ'—A New Testament Debate," *Reformed Theological Review* 29 (1970) 71–81; T.F. Torrance, "One Aspect of the Biblical Conception of Faith," *ExpT* 68 (1957) 111–114; George Howard, "Notes and Observations on the 'Faith of Christ,' " *HTR* 60 (1967) 459–465; Sam K. Williams, *Jesus' Death as Saving Event* (HDR 2; Missoula: Scholars Press, 1981) 19–58; Richard Hays, *The Faith of Jesus Christ* (SBLDS 56; Chico: Scholars Press, 1983) 157–176.

49. "The 'Faith of Christ,' " *ExpT* 85 (1973–74) 212–215.

50. "Romans 3:21–26 and the Faith of Jesus," *CBQ* 44 (1982) 77–90.

51. John Reumann, "The Gospel of the Righteousness of God," *Int* 20 (1966) 432–452.

52. Halvor Moxnes, *Theology in Conflict: Studies in Paul's Understanding of God in Romans* (NTSupp 53; Leiden: Brill, 1980) 216–223, 231–282.

53. See M. Barth, "The Faith of the Messiah," *HeyJ* 10 (1969) 365–366.

54. M. Barth, "The Faith of the Messiah," 366; Rudolph Bultmann, *Theology of the New Testament* (New York: Charles Scribner's Sons, 1951) 314–318.

INDEX OF PASSAGES

INDEX OF TOPICS